TELEVISION, POLITICS, AND THE TRANSITION TO DEMOCRACY IN LATIN AMERICA

TELEVISION, POLITICS, AND THE TRANSITION TO DEMOCRACY IN LATIN AMERICA

Edited by
Thomas E. Skidmore

The Woodrow Wilson Center Press
Washington, D.C.

The Johns Hopkins University Press
Baltimore and London

HE8700
.76
.L29
T45
1993

Editorial Offices:
The Woodrow Wilson Center Press
370 L'Enfant Promenade, S.W.
Suite 704
Washington, D.C. 20024 USA

Order from:
The Johns Hopkins University Press
2715 North Charles Street
Baltimore, Maryland 21218-4319
Telephone: 1-800-537-JHUP

Printed in the United States of America
⊗ Printed on acid-free paper

9 8 7 6 5 4 3 2 1

Library of Congress Cataloging-in-Publication Data

Television, politics, and the transition to democracy in Latin America
/ edited by Thomas E. Skidmore.
    p.   cm.
    "This volume . . . resulted from a conference held at Woodrow
Wilson Center, June 22–23, 1990"—Pref.
    Includes bibliographical references and index.
    ISBN 0-943875-44-7 (alk. paper) : $25.00
    1. Television in politics—Latin America—Congresses.
2. Presidents—Latin America—Election—Congresses.   3. Elections—
Latin America—Congresses.   4. Latin America—Politics and
government—1980—Congresses.   I. Skidmore, Thomas E.
HE8700.76.L29T45   1993   92-37345
324.7'3'098—dc20   CIP

The Center is the "living memorial" of the United States of America to the nation's twenty-eighth president, Woodrow Wilson. The U.S. Congress established the Woodrow Wilson Center in 1968 as an international institute for advanced study, "symbolizing and strengthening the fruitful relationship between the world of learning and the world of public affairs." The Center opened in 1970 under its own board of trustees.

In all its activities the Woodrow Wilson Center is a nonprofit, nonpartisan organization, supported financially by annual appropriations from the U.S. Congress, and by the contributions of foundations, corporations, and individuals.

WOODROW WILSON CENTER PRESS
The Woodrow Wilson Center Press publishes the best work emanating from the Center's conference programs and from Fellows and Guest Scholars, and assists in publication, in-house or outside, of research works produced at the Center and judged worthy of dissemination. Conclusions or opinions expressed in Center publications and programs are those of the authors and speakers and do not necessarily reflect the views of the Center staff, fellows, trustees, advisory groups, or any individuals or organizations that provide financial support to the Center.

CONTENTS

FIGURE AND TABLES

Figure

PREFACE

The importance of television in modern society is beyond dispute. The nature of the role that TV plays in one country or another is, however, very much a matter of debate. In the United States, we are constantly discussing whether or not there is too much violence on the small screen, whether our news is trivialized into sound bites, wondering if we mesmerized our children and made them functional illiterates. Similarly, how TV is used to convey images is a subject of considerable sensitivity. We cannot imagine conducting politics in the United States without the television, although not everyone is convinced that TV plays a positive role in our political life.

These debates, however divisive, take for granted that a free press and free media are vital to our democracy, but they are less certain about the relationship between TV and democracy.

The role of television in the conduct of democracy is even less clear in other countries, or, at least, has been studied less. In Latin America, the question of TV's interrelationship with democracy is particularly important because of the relatively recent transition to democracy from authoritarian regimes in most of the countries of the region. The considerable literature on the political transition says little about television, and its references to the media more generally echo the language used in the United States, assuming a direct correlation between political freedom and free use of the media.

The idea of conducting a conference to discuss the role of TV in contemporary democratic politics in Latin America began with a conversation Tom Skidmore and I had when I first came to the Wilson Center in 1990. I shared it with Philip Cook, who was at the time the director of the Media Studies Project at the Center and who shared my enthusiasm for it. Tom and I worked out the details of the Latin American cases and contacted potential participants. Phil took primary responsibility for contacting experts on TV in the U.S. as commentators and to give the discussion a broader, more comparative framework.

This volume, which is the first effort to look systematically at the relationship of television and electoral politics in Latin America, resulted from a conference held at the Woodrow Wilson Center June 22–23, 1990. Financial support was given by the Center's Media Studies Project and by the Tinker Foundation. I am particularly grateful to Martha Muse for her generosity and vision in allowing us to use the foundation's resources for such an innovative enterprise. Lucy Hetrick and Andrew Rudman of the Latin

American Program and Bruce Napper, formerly of the Media Studies Project, were instrumental in organizing the conference.

In order to put the conference papers into context, Tom Skidmore, who had helped organize the meeting, commissioned additional papers. His introductory chapter also incorporates a number of points made in the animated discussion participated in by the more than fifty scholars, journalists, and media consultants who attended the conference.

Tom Skidmore also saw the manuscript through to publication, with help from Aaron Vieira and Margaret McCrudden. The Latin American Program is pleased to bring this manuscript to the attention of a wider audience. It is a fascinating subject and one that warrants further study. We hope that this volume contributes to the ongoing debate and brings the discussion of the media in Latin America into a broader framework.

Joseph S. Tulchin
Director, Latin American Program
The Woodrow Wilson Center

1

Politics and the Media in a Democratizing Latin America

Thomas E. Skidmore

The 1970s saw most of Latin America suffer under repressive military rule. The targets of that repression invariably included the press, radio, and television. The generals knew how dangerous free access to the media—especially the broadcast media—could be. During the 1980s, however, democracy made a comeback, with civilian rule returning to such major countries as Argentina (1983), Brazil (1985), and Chile (1989), as well as to Paraguay, Uruguay, and Bolivia. Even Mexico, long ruled by a single party, may be heading toward a more pluralistic political system with a more competitive electoral process.

It is generally agreed that the mass media have played an important role in this transition to democracy.[1] Latin American broadcast media are for the most part privately controlled and commercially operated, like those in the United States—and unlike those in much of Western Europe, where state ownership (or at least some state regulation) has long been a constant. In Mexico and Brazil, huge media networks rival the U.S. "big three" in their viewership and wield far more influence than any one of their U.S. counterparts.[2] More than three-quarters of all Brazilian households have access to television, and the percentage in Mexico is probably well over half—remarkable for countries with large pockets of abject poverty. In the four countries that this book examines (Argentina, Brazil, Chile, and Mexico), TV is the primary medium for political information. It has also become the most powerful instrument of communication in political campaigns.

Shrewd use of TV programming in 1989 established the candidacy of Brazil's winning presidential candidate, Fernando Collor de Mello, and in 1988 played a crucial role in the national plebiscite that forced Chilean dictator Augusto Pinochet to call presidential elections and thus end his seventeen-year authoritarian rule.[3] It also enabled Argentina's maverick Peronist Carlos Menem to publicize his flamboyant style of opposition to the incumbent Radical government. In the case of

Mexico, which differs markedly from the three South American cases, the blatant manipulation of TV by the partisan progovernment monopoly network Televisa generated a popular backlash that played a role in generating the largest opposition vote in the fifty-year history of the reigning government party.

Thus TV is rapidly transforming the way in which political candidacies are constructed, marketed, and consolidated. It is also transforming the way politicians govern once they reach office, with Brazil, Latin America's largest country, leading the way. Yet the role of the mass media in Latin America's democratization has gone largely unstudied. While politicians and parties scramble to master the powerful medium, scholars have continued to fix their attention on the traditional aspects of electoral politics.

How is television being used in the new democracies? How do private ownership and public regulation mix? Is the U.S. model, the European model, or some other alternative prevailing? Can clever media consultants, importing the latest North American techniques, mold their clients into political winners through TV imagery?[4] Can audience-targeting skills produce winning electoral margins, rendering rallies and door-to-door campaigning obsolete? If free air time is granted, as in most of Latin America now, how will it be regulated? Who will pay the cost of producing the programming or buying the air time that is commercially available?

This book begins to fill the gap. Nine media analysts, U.S. and Latin American, furnish a wealth of data and analysis, offering an in-depth look at the power and the limitations of television in the new democratic era. The case studies all draw on new research data on public opinion, viewer surveys, and content analysis to help interpret a subject too often dominated by anecdotal or impressionistic evidence.

In order to structure the volume (and the Wilson Center conference, where most of the papers were first given), each author[5] of a country case study was asked to address a set of interrelated questions:

- Are the media controlled by private owners, by the state, or by some combination of the two?
- If the media are privately controlled, how do owners obtain their broadcasting rights? How are they held accountable to public authority?
- If the media are privately controlled, how do candidates and parties get air time? Is it purchased? How much free time, if any, is provided? What are the overall regulations regarding access to air time?

- If the media are state owned, how is access controlled?
- What role do professional consultants play in orchestrating speeches, debates, ads, and demonstrations?
- To what extent do politicians, media owners, and media consultants look abroad to learn about broadcast media techniques?
- How have the broadcast media evolved in the transition from military rule?

In interpreting the answers the authors give to these questions, it is important to keep in mind the whole process of democratization. Clearly the broadcast media were a conspicuous component in the process. But equally clearly, the process by which power was transferred from the generals to civilian politicians had many other dimensions. The next section of this chapter briefly discusses these dimensions as a prelude to considering how to examine the media's role. The chapter ends with summaries of each contribution.

THE DIMENSIONS OF DEMOCRATIZATION

How the rules of the democratic game are formulated is fundamental to the democratization process. Democracy is, after all, about compromise—an agreement to forgo the ultimate sanction of eliminating one's political enemy (all too often a Latin American solution) in favor of biding one's time to fight another day. In Argentina, for example, between 1930 and 1989, no popularly elected president even transferred power legally to another popularly elected president. In Brazil, between 1926 and 1990, such a transfer happened only twice. The Chilean tradition of democracy, Latin America's proudest in the twentieth century, was interrupted between 1973 and 1988 by one of the century's most brutal dictatorships. Mexico is again the variant. It maintained the necessary compromise, albeit one that effectively excluded any meaningful opposition.

In Argentina, Brazil, and Chile, the late 1980s have seen the establishment of new rules of political competition. New electoral laws, regulations, and conventions have been negotiated or imposed. New constitutions, amendments, court decisions, executive decrees have come forth to regulate the rebirth of pluralistic politics. We are still sorting out the contradictory reality created by this often ad hoc legal response to the new political reality. Politicians themselves are frequently uncertain of the rules under which they must compete.

The need to establish a new role for the military is a second important dimension of the electoral process. The generals may have relinquished formal power, but they remain a potent force. In neither Argentina, Brazil, nor Chile have the civilian politicians been able to impose *and maintain* punishment of the former torturers among the military, despite proof of guilt that would stand up in any criminal court. Even when discredited in public opinion, military officers have yet to be brought under effective civilian control as they have been in the industrial democracies of North America and Western Europe. Even if the men in uniform seem implausible instigators of new coups, few of their fellow citizens would discount their political role in the foreseeable future.

The need for the general public to resume political participation is equally important. In each of our three cases, the military took over with at least the tacit support of the upper and middle classes—exploiting these classes' self-interested apprehensions that offensives from the radical left would lead to a redistribution of wealth. In Brazil beginning in 1964 and in Argentina in 1976 (the crackdown was immediate in Argentina; in Brazil its full force was not felt until 1968), the military drove its opponents (and many innocent bystanders) into silence, exile, prison, or the grave. In Chile, the same alliance between the civilian right and an obsessively anticommunist military wreaked the same havoc with human rights. In retrospect we can now see that the "threat" from the left in Argentina and Brazil was much weaker than the public's perception of it. But, as often in history, the perception of the threat was the deciding factor. In Chile, the threat was very real.

In all three countries, as the generals had intended, the effect of the coup was to dismantle or emasculate the institutions on which democracy depends: free political parties, spontaneously organized social movements, and professional associations. Destroying or neutralizing these groups was essential to the task of suppressing (once and for all, argued the most radical of the authoritarian military *and* civilians) the threat to the established order and values. Liberation theologians, Marxist-Leninist intellectuals, trade union militants, university reformers, idealistic criminal lawyers, slum neighborhood activists—all were enemies in the eyes of the guardians of "national security" who seized control of every source of public authority. Every element of civil society that might challenge the established hierarchy—which had become synonymous with the military chain of command—had to be eliminated or anesthetized.

One product was the harvest of twisted and tortured human bodies, whose bones are now being exhumed by the human rights activists and volunteer medical forensic experts in Buenos Aires, São Paulo, and

Santiago. Another product was a censored and suppressed body politic. Just as the families of the "disappeared" watch the skeletons being reassembled, their fellow citizens must reinvent or resuscitate the political parties, interest groups, neighborhood associations, and professional bodies that allow civil society to resume its role of articulating and representing the interest of its members.

The socioeconomic context, most fundamentally economic growth, is a further dimension of democratization in the 1980s. Without a vigorous economy, any society will have difficulty expanding public participation, reconciling conflicting interests, and achieving greater social justice—all ostensible goals of democracy. Yet Latin America has experienced *negative* economic growth in the last decade. Since the foreign debt crisis struck in mid-1982, all the major countries, including Argentina, Brazil, and Mexico, have suffered a net decline in their per capita gross domestic product (GDP). Among the four countries studied in this book, Chile alone has shown a gain, and that came only at the very end of the 1980s. Can democracy find strong root in a hostile economic climate?

And even if growth is achieved, will it benefit those at the bottom— the rural masses of the Brazilian northeast, the slum dwellers of Mexico City, the downwardly mobile former factory workers of Buenos Aires? One shattering consequence of the economic decline has been the erosion of public services—education, health, housing, public transportation. These are the realities of government that the newly reenfranchised voters of South America find most immediate. Can these voters help but correlate the decline in their standard of living with the return of democracy? How can the elected politicians avoid being held accountable for the huge "social debt" their societies now owe partly because of the spending spree of their military predecessors?

As if these challenges were not enough, Latin America's elected governments face a more demanding world economy than did the military. Not only must they pay a crushing debt service on loans incurred by their military predecessors, not only have they faced a cutoff of further private lending, but they must also guide their inefficient industry through a painful adjustment to a world economy that has become more competitive since Latin America accelerated its import-substituting industrialization after 1945. Finally, all this must be accomplished while grappling with inflation rates that are profoundly destabilizing (over 1,500 percent in recent years in Argentina and Brazil).

Even worse, these economic pressures have all converged at a moment when the old paradigms of economic development appear discredited. Since 1945, and especially since 1950, Latin America has seen the predominance of populist, nationalistic economic formulae. Their architects focused on the domestic market, sought to restrict and control foreign investment, and distrusted the international economy as an instrument for attaining economic growth. This model, made famous by Juan Perón in Argentina, Getúlio Vargas in Brazil, and a long series of PRI (Partido Revolucionário Institucional) presidents in Mexico, and transformed into a far more radically nationalistic state socialism by Salvador Allende in Chile, has been overtaken by events both domestic and foreign.

The hard reality is that the old formulae, based on high tariffs, gigantic state sector enterprises, and noncompetitive corporatist capitalism will no longer work in the unforgiving world economy of the 1990s. A powerful lesson has been given by the "East Asian Tigers" of South Korea, Taiwan, Hong Kong, and Singapore, which in the 1970s rapidly passed Brazil and Mexico as the industrial success stories of the developing world. Although their record may have been distorted by their overly enthusiastic admirers, it is undeniable that their export promotion, emphasis on quality production, and investment in education and technical training have put Latin America in the shade.

A final dimension of the democratization process in Latin America is that it is taking place against the backdrop of the collapse of communism in Europe and of socialism in Africa. Economic nationalists in Latin America, who could depend on populist politicians to carry out their formulae, always harbored a strong sympathy for socialism, both in its democratic, Western European form and in its more state-centered Eastern European form. But with the bankruptcy of state socialism in Eastern Europe and the Soviet Union an important ideological reference point has been lost. With even the Communist party of Italy scrambling to purge the word "communist" from its name, the left in Latin America can no longer be sure of its own image. This development has intellectually disarmed many who have been the bravest opponents of the military dictators. In turn, it has strengthened those civilian allies of the military in Argentina and Brazil who had lacked the political power to apply their neoliberal ideas in the early transition to democracy.

In Chile, by contrast, neoliberals held power continuously during the Pinochet dictatorship and have only given way to a reformist government with the election of President Patricio Aylwin in 1989. In Mexico, the timing was very different. The neoliberal technocrats (pushing such measures as privatization, radical tariff reduction, easier regulation of foreign investment, and tough fiscal and monetary policy) did not gain sway until the late 1980s under cover of the PRI political machine, which endorsed a radical shift in economic policy.

ANALYZING THE ROLE OF THE MEDIA

In the four countries covered in this book, the media have had at least two essential functions in the democratization process: dissemination of information and political mobilization. The print media are more important to the former, the broadcast media to the latter. The quantity of information conveyed in one issue of a national newspaper or magazine normally exceeds the quantity available in several days of radio and TV newscasts. Print media are therefore highly important in informing the elite and the policymakers. In a country like Mexico, with its very low readership, that may be virtually their only function. But their highly limited circulation, even in a traditionally newspaper-oriented political culture such as Buenos Aires, makes it impossible for them to reach the millions of voters in mass democracies.

Dissemination of Information

Under the military, even the most elementary facts could be kept from reaching the public record. Whether it was bad economic news, criticisms from the Vatican, or financial scandals among the military high command, whatever aroused the ire of the censors was relegated to the realm of nonfact. With the return of open politics, the media, especially in Argentina and Brazil, resumed reporting the news, good and bad, at least within the limits of the capitalist ownership structure that had predated the military clampdown. In Chile, the media had to tread much more lightly immediately after the 1988 plebiscite since General Pinochet and the army retained most of the levers of power. Even after the election of the Aylwin government in 1989, Pinochet retained control of the army, and the latter retained a presence in politics much greater than that of its counterparts in Argentina and Brazil. Mexico's case was sui generis. Although never a military authoritarian regime, the civilian autocracy of the PRI political machine maintained its own grip on the principal organs of public opinion. Newspapers and magazines were routinely manipulated through bribery, intimidation, and control of newsprint, while television was in the hands of a highly progovernment private monopoly.

Political Mobilization

No citizen of a modern Western democracy can any longer doubt that television has assumed enormous importance in transmitting political messages to the voter.[6] Why have analysts paid so little attention to a medium that was, by common consent, of crucial importance in recent presidential elections in Argentina, Brazil, and Peru, as well as the 1988 plebiscite in Chile?

One reason is that many intellectuals, especially in Latin America with its traditionally European-oriented humanistic culture, instinctively distrust television as a cultural force and, by extension, as a factor in politics. In part they react negatively and understandably to the vulgarization television often assumes as it aims for a maximum audience, at the lowest common denominator. Latin America has frequently rerun the worst of U.S. television—endless cartoons (simply dubbed directly from the U.S. originals, although many are also from Japan), variety shows with clownish emcees who target audiences made up of rural in-migrants, or the infinite reruns of ancient U.S. police and action series. Latin American media critics tend to see the U.S.-style TV political spots and advertising agency packaging of candidates as simply another expression of the worst of the North American "teleinvasion."

One school of Latin American media critics sees this Hollywood-style appeal and its hold on the popular imagination not only as cultural vulgarization, not only as the glorification of violence and cynical greed in slick TV productions, but also as the arm of monopoly capitalism. Ariel Dorfman and Armand Mattelart's brilliant exposé of ideological bias in *How to Read Donald Duck* has been extended to all of U.S. media, especially television.[7] It has been part of the larger critique—predominantly Marxist in inspiration—of U.S. economic and political expansion in twentieth-century Latin America.[8]

Although this approach can be insightful in the hands of a Dorfman or Mattelart, it has often remained on the level of ritualistic and repetitive denunciation of U.S. cultural horrors. To write off the influence of TV as simply brainwashing or tranquilizing the potentially revolutionary slum dweller is ultimately unsatisfactory, although it may be part of the story. Two recent campaign experiences with television in Latin America provide convincing evidence that something more is going on.

One was the lavishly financed 1989 presidential campaign of the novelist Mario Vargas Llosa in Peru. One of Latin America's most glamorous cultural figures, with best-selling novels translated in Europe and North America, Vargas Llosa emerged as the darling of the neoliberal right in Peru when the disastrous presidency of Alan Garcia was drawing to a close. Vargas Llosa's well-heeled campaign hired a leading U.S. campaign consulting firm, which saturated Peruvian television with spots featuring the elegant Vargas Llosa as the country's political savior. But the campaign backfired. The novelist's huge lead in the polls began to melt away as the public saw an ultrawhite, handsomely attired figure who came across as the incarnation of an aristocratic elite that had long dominated a country inhabited largely by native Americans and persons of mixed ancestry *(mestizos)*.

The effect was so disastrous that Vargas Llosa, widely touted as a virtual shoo-in for the presidency, was forced to withdraw from the race. Seldom had Peruvian politics seen a candidacy so rapidly destroyed. And yet Vargas Llosa had been the candidate tailor-made to Washington's taste: committed to the neoliberal dogmas of privatization of state enterprises, extreme openness to foreign capital, embrace of free trade doctrines, and so forth. Furthermore, his rich supporters had brought in the finest U.S. media wizards. If the traditional leftist critique of mass media at the service of imperialism were to be believed, Vargas Llosa should have won. Instead, the unintended consequences of his use of that medium returned him to exile in London.[9]

The other example is the electoral success of Lula, the Workers' Party candidate in the 1989 Brazilian presidential race. Through the prism of radical leftist Latin American media criticism, Lula should have gone down to humiliating defeat. A former autoworker with only a grade school education, possessed of an uncertain control of grammar in a country used to rhetorical elegance from its politicians, the heavily bearded Lula was an unprecedented figure on the national political scene. Even the nationalists and populists who had frightened the generals and the middle class into the 1964 coup had been more traditional political products than Lula.

Yet Lula won more than 31 million votes and came close to upsetting the front-running Fernando Collor, who appeared to have locked up the election months before. How could an ill-educated factory worker (promising to double the minimum wage, suspend payment on the foreign debt, massively redistribute farm land, and so forth) have run so strongly against a candidate who was singing Washington's tune of privatization, free trade, and the free market gospel in the biggest media blitz Brazil had ever seen?

The answer was at least in significant part Lula's television strategy. An army of enthusiastic pop artists was recruited to produce TV programming that reached the mass voter via the free air time allotted liberally and equally to the two candidates in the runoff stage of the campaign. (No time could be bought for political purposes.) Most

Brazilians, even on the left, acknowledged that Lula's use of television had not only given the voters the most radical presidential alternative they had ever seen but also motivated many of them to work for his election.

The prejudice of some intellectuals may be an obvious reason for the failure to do empirical research on the role of television in Latin American politics, but it is not the only one. Another reason is that television has become a predominant medium much more recently in Latin America than in Europe and the United States. Only since the 1970s has mass viewership become possible, as the cost of TV sets has come down and the number of stations and geographical coverage have risen. Today Latin America stands out as one of the two third-world regions (along with the People's Republic of China) where television has most closely approximated its dominance in the industrial world, but its growth has been so swift as to have taken the print-oriented scholars by surprise.

Yet another factor contributing to the neglect is that the years since the rise of television were largely those of military dictatorship, when the media were used primarily for heavy-handed propaganda. Television was associated by analysts and viewers alike with lies, distortions, smears, and elaborate fantasies. Its emergence as a major factor on the cultural landscape coincided with an era of media manipulation that most Latin Americans would prefer to forget.

Finally, the field of media studies as an academic specialty is relatively new in Latin America. It has been dominated, on the one hand, by short-term commercial interests—audience surveys to guide advertisers —and, on the other hand, by a focus on media and culture in general, with the work on media and politics including little or no attention to television's effect on elections and the system of electoral democracy.[10] This neglect can in turn be partly attributed to the fact that electoral politics has returned only recently in most of Latin America, giving relatively little time for research. Equally, if not more important, is the difficulty in finding an adequate methodology to research the subject.

There are two common methodological approaches to examining the relationship between the media and politics, both of which are used in this book.

The first is to collect evidence from surveys, polls, and the like, to measure the characteristics of the media and the effects of media activity surrounding particular events. Authors taking this approach use the questions listed at the beginning of this chapter to try to measure the importance of the broadcast media, especially television, in three presidential elections (in Argentina, Brazil, and Mexico) and one plebiscite (in Chile). What impact did the use of television have on the voting? And what long-term effect did it have on the political institutions and the political culture of these democratizing polities? It should be noted that this first methodological approach is largely an application of behaviorist-style social science, which offers the opportunity to escape an impressionistic, journalistic, or anecdotal approach but often exhibits a statistical precision that in the end answers few of the important questions. Furthermore, by concentrating only on what is ostensibly measurable, behaviorist research can obscure the fundamental issue of how the increasing dominance of the electronic media may lead to a level of manipulation that throws into question our traditional commitment in the industrial democracies to the role of a "free press" as a vital agent in maintaining an informed electorate.

The second methodological approach might be called the interpretation of media in politics as cultural artifact. It is especially evident in this book's contributions by Venicio A. de Lima (chapter 6) on Brazil and Ilya Adler (chapter 9) on Mexico. Seen in this light, broadcast media perform a function far broader than informing or convincing, deeper than influencing elections. They are part of the larger drama of social interaction in the nation-state: a process of feedback between elite and mass, leader and led, but also within a complex emotive network where the symbols, actions, and words coming from television form an essential part of the ritual that mirrors and in turn shapes the relationship between state and society. Television becomes the preferred medium for the playing out of society's fears and hopes, independently of how the viewers may vote. The supposed line between entertainment and information blurs, as the interaction of the medium and the viewer substitutes for what was not so long ago the more intimate relations on the village or community level.

This is an inherently difficult realm to research and analyze, more congenial to the anthropologist than the political scientist.[11] Nonetheless, it may be important, because it can lead to a more profound understanding of how societies actually work, not only in choosing their political leaders but also in their choice of values and the style of their self-representation. What politician in the age of mass democracy does not want to discover the secrets of the deepest level of communication with the voter? The electoral appeal of a Dwight Eisenhower or a Ronald Reagan will never be understood through mere statistical findings. Nor will a Mario Vargas Llosa soon forget the lesson of the social dissonance that his TV presence provoked in the Peruvian psyche.

It is worth remembering that even in the United States and Western Europe, where social science research on the media is most developed, there is no clear consensus on how television influences elections. Indeed, controversy continues to rage about television's effect on culture and society in general. It is therefore appropriate that the authors of this book follow a variety of methodologies in seeking to show how the electronic media are shaping a new democratic era in Latin America.

THE REST OF THE BOOK

In chapter 2, Douglas Gomery and Lawrence Lichty, both experienced researchers and commentators on the U.S. media scene, provide useful background and context, reminding us how electronic technology has transformed the world of communications. First it was radio and film, in which the dynamic U.S. economy and Hollywood led the way. Then came television, with the powerful appeal of U.S. mass culture (and cheaply available U.S. reruns). Now two more innovations have opened another era: satellite transmission and videocassette recorders. The former has wiped out the technical barriers of distance (the first live trans-Atlantic telecast came only in 1962) while the latter has made possible relatively cheap storage and dissemination of all forms of programming. Television coverage of the Tiananmen Square massacre, the fall of the Berlin Wall, and the Gulf War provides only the latest examples of the instant global repercussions of key events. And as Gomery and Lichty argue, the proliferation of satellite dishes and VCRs make far more difficult the efforts of government to control their citizens' access to the news.

Are we therefore on the verge of a "new age" in world history, ushered in by the uncontrollable (and often unintended) consequences of this revolution in communication technology? The authors answer with caution. They suggest that access is not all that easy or cheap, especially in the poorer parts of the third world. Furthermore, "values and beliefs are shaped by more than TV news reports," as the appeal of the prime-time soap opera "Dallas" around the world (with the exception of Japan) has shown. No less important is the question of who owns the means of production of this technology and who can gain access. Will the U.S. capitalist model be uncritically adopted in developing countries, and will information flows be regulated? If so, how and to what ends?

Most important, "just because there are new sources of television news does not mean there will be an instantaneous effect." Many variables are yet to make themselves felt, and we must not be misled by the dazzling wave of "new" technology until we see "if any of it has radically changed the world."

In chapter 3, James Schwoch, author of an important study of the U.S. radio industry's activities in Latin America before 1939, gives a valuable historical overview of the relationship between broadcast media and politics. The story begins long before the arrival of television, going back to the introduction of radio transmission soon after 1900. From the beginning, the new technology was linked to politics in two key ways: It was rapidly adopted as a "successful disseminator of political propaganda," and it was established under a system of mixed public-private ownership, thus creating the tensions that still prevail in that unstable equilibrium.

The U.S. government quickly saw the political value in using radio and film to further its diplomatic and economic goals, as well as disseminating "democratic political values." That had begun in the First World War, but by the mid-1930s, the United States was engaged in a full-fledged "international propaganda war," in which Hollywood studios and famous personalities such as Orson Welles and Donald Duck were enlisted to counter the threat of Axis penetration in Latin America. Meanwhile, such Latin American leaders as Juan Perón and Getúlio Vargas had discovered the power of broadcasting and pioneered its use to strengthen their authoritarian regimes.

Schwoch traces the "transition from radio to television" that occurred after 1950, showing how in granting broadcasting concessions the "reciprocal relationship between broadcasters and politicians" exemplified (quoting John Sinclair) "the use of state power for public advantage," which has become highly typical of the Latin American broadcasting industry.

Schwoch argues that the transition to television in Latin America was shaped by two other power factors: "The massive activities of U.S. corporations and the tolerant behavior of authoritarian regimes." The former influence was felt through the heavy presence of U.S. multinational firms buying advertising time and through the advertising agencies themselves, which are overwhelmingly U.S. owned and controlled. The authoritarian tolerance was seen, not in any laxity of control over programming, which was tightly censored (especially for international programs, although less so for entertainment shows), but in the willingness to grant new broadcast concessions, perhaps in the belief that cheap entertainment (as well as the promotion of a variety of progovernment channels!) would be a stabilizing factor. In the end, the general presided over the strengthening of the industry's technical capacity and laid the base for a potentially more pluralistic system.

Schwoch, like Gomery and Lichty, sees no issue as more important than who controls the media. Both popular organizations and giant corporations have made their bid. The question, according to Schwoch, is whether the Latin American audience can "avoid the political apathy and lethargy that has become all too typical among the citizens of the United States" and thereby demonstrate that "politics and media can yield a more politically active and committed citizenship."

The next six chapters analyze the three presidential elections—in Argentina and Brazil in 1989; in Mexico in 1988—and the 1988 plebiscite in Chile. There is enough detail here to fascinate both analysts and politicians. A curious tension runs through the accounts of all the South American cases (Mexico is unique because of the television monopoly exercised by Televisa, as we shall see). All five authors struggle with the question of how decisive television was in the electoral outcome, and all waver in their estimate. They see it as highly important but draw back from saying that it made "the" difference. Indeed, all (except, perhaps, de Lima) seem so concerned not to overestimate television's electoral influence (perhaps reacting with a caution that parallels that of Gomery and Lichty) that they sometimes seem hesitant to entertain the hypothesis that the nature of television coverage (and its use by candidates) might have been decisive in some campaigns.

They can be forgiven for not wishing to fall into the trap of opting out of serious analysis—of saying that whoever has the cleverest or the most lavishly financed media campaign (as in the traditional image of California politics in the early U.S. TV age) will inevitably triumph at the polls. Furthermore, it is not clear how one would go about *proving* that the use of one medium was "decisive." The ingenuous might believe it could be shown by opinion polls correlated with specific TV programming. But can such research ever filter out all the other influences (discussed in detail in these papers) at work on the voter? And national electoral results in competitive democracies are normally too close (certainly in all three South American cases here) for any single-factor explanation to be plausible. Finally, the quality of the data available and the body of electoral and public opinion analysis already done are inadequate to attempt such measurement with any confidence. Searching for "the" decisive factor is probably quixotic in principle and certainly unrealizable in practice. But asking about the degree of importance is crucial, and each author answers in a different way.

In chapter 4 Enrique Zuleta-Puceiro, an Argentine expert on elections and polling, offers a rich portrait of the role of television in the 1989 Argentine presidential election. He contrasts the elections in Argentina and Brazil, pointing out key differences between the two cases.

He argues that Argentina's pluralistic media ownership, lack of national networks, and nonpartisan broadcasting tradition have made impossible the almost exclusively television-based campaign strategy recently seen in Brazil, where a more oligopolistic and more partisan broadcasting system is aimed at a less literate (therefore less susceptible to print media) public. According to Zuleta-Puceiro, a Fernando Collor de Mello "is, at present, unthinkable" in Argentina. Argentina is further distinguished from Chile, in his opinion, where heavy-handed control of television by the Pinochet dictatorship damaged its credibility and produced a backlash in the plebiscite and in the 1989 presidential election.

Zuleta-Puceiro stresses the complex and still ill-defined legal context in which the mixed public-private Argentine broadcasting system operates, describing how the private sector reacted defensively to the irregular privatization of broadcasting after the demise of the Peronist government in 1976. Argentine politicians, unlike Brazilian ones, do not control their own media, and broadcasters have succeeded in achieving notable balance and objectivity in their political coverage.

He sees the 1989 presidential campaign in Argentina as a contest between two party outsiders, running under the banners of the two traditionally strongest parties, the Radicals (UCR or Unión Civica Radical) and the Peronist (PJ or Partido Justicialista). Both the Peronist candidate, Carlos Menem, and the Radical candidate, Eduardo Angeloz, adjusted their campaigns to the fact that most voters no longer identified with traditional parties. This led each to make cautious use of television, although the Radical candidate resorted to a negative campaign that polling data show to have backfired.

If television was not the decisive factor in the Argentine presidential election, according to Zuleta-Puceiro, it played a powerful role by reminding voters of the most important issue in the campaign: the rapidly deteriorating economy. The atmosphere did not inspire voter enthusiasm, as the polls confirmed. Yet the candidates had little choice but to promise short-term solutions that not even their best rhetoric could convince most voters would work. He cautions politicians against uncritically adopting TV campaign tactics from elsewhere, especially the United States, warning that they can prove not only disastrous to the candidate but also destabilizing to a "democracy that is still weak and unsteady."

In chapter 5, María Eugenia Hirmas analyzes the role of television in the 1988 plebiscite in Chile. She explains how the structure of Chilean broadcasting evolved under the pre-1973 regimes when the state facilitated media access (via state-controlled broadcasting) to a range of political opinion. During the military dictatorship, after 1973, military officers maintained a veto over all programming. A transition began in 1988 when the Pinochet regime, under international pressure, established a free electoral program (Franja de Propaganda Electoral) of half an hour a day, scheduled at a maximally unattractive time slot, while the government continued its own unlimited propaganda blitz.

Hirmas argues that in spite of the unfavorable hour, television was "a key to mobilizing public opinion" but that it was not "the most important element" in the campaign. That element was the "social, economic, and political conditions," which voters had personally experienced and which no amount of government propaganda could obscure. All observers agree, especially the government apologists (a notable admission), that the "NO" campaign (those against the continuation of the Pinochet regime for another eight years and thus in favor of holding free elections within a year) produced superior TV programming. With a shrewd mixture of humor, music, and a low-key approach, the "NO" convinced viewers that it would be safe to vote against a government that continued to bombard them with propaganda. As the government became more desperate, having underestimated the political communication skills of the "NO" organizers (who tapped U.S. TV consultants on audience-targeting techniques), its TV spots became more intimidating, warning that civil disorder and economic chaos would ensue should military rule end.

Hirmas seems to have two arguments. On the one hand, she argues that the "NO" television programming played a "vital role" but in the end was less important than the influence of "community work, meetings, campaign trips, and personal contact with voters." In the short term, no amount of television skills can change the political predispositions established by long experience and deeply engrained political culture. But on the other hand, those predispositions might never have been translated into "NO" votes if the television campaign had not been "a key" to encouraging government opponents to express their views openly and, most important, to vote. Furthermore, it was youth and women, both targeted as undecided by the programming consultants, who became the focus of the media message. The "NO" won a close majority (54.7 percent), suggesting that this targeting might well have made the difference.

In chapter 6, Venicio A. de Lima, a specialist in communications research at the University of Brasília, gives us a rich theoretical contribution. He argues for extending our focus to concentrate as much on the reception of the media message as on its production. We need to see electoral media campaigns within the wider focus of the "beliefs, expectations, discussions, ceremonies, rituals, symbolism, gestures, memories, myths" that define a society. De Lima finds in the 1989 candidacy of Collor de Mello in Brazil a prime example of the worth of this analysis and comes closer than any other contributor to classifying the use of television as "the" decisive factor.

According to de Lima, one Brazilian TV network, TV Globo, which holds the lion's share of the prime-time audience, was the principal instrument Collor's supporters used to "construct" the political scenario that made his election possible. They were aided by the fact that Collor's father owned the TV Globo affiliate in his northeastern home state of Alagoas (although the son had grown up in Rio and Brasília, where his father was a senator) and the owner of the network, Roberto Marinho, was openly pro-Collor from an early stage. No less important, Marinho is known to exercise close personal control over the political orientation of his network's programming.

For two years before the election, TV Globo helped construct the scenario for the emergence of a "political savior" (read ideal candidate) in two ways. The first was to broadcast a series of highly popular *telenovelas* (nightly prime-time soap operas that have become a Brazilian passion) depicting a country languishing in corruption and despair, awaiting the dashing hero, a political "outsider" who would restore morality and banish the selfish politicians who had blighted the lives of an honest citizenry.

The second way was the favoritism shown to Collor in TV Globo's coverage. It began with the assignment of a special correspondent to cover him during his governorship of the minimally newsworthy state of Alagoas. It continued with the news emphasis given polls favoring Collor's candidacy—polls taken by a firm retained by both Collor and TV Globo. Interview data show that this heavy TV coverage of Collor's lead in the polls strongly influenced the least-educated voters (for the first time in a century, illiterates were the given the vote in 1988). De Lima also shows how Collor included in his appeal an endorsement of neoliberal economic doctrines—especially a proprivatization, pro–free market emphasis—thereby gaining the support of "establishment" sectors fearful of a possible revival of populism (or worse, as some thought).

Collor was not the only beneficiary of television, as mentioned earlier. Lula, the upstart in a political scene long dominated by the elite, amassed the startling total of almost 32 million votes, according to de Lima, having started from less than 5 percent support in the early polls, which would have produced less than four million votes. His supporters, buoyed by skillful TV programming in the daily free electoral hour, succeeded in constructing a "counterhegemonic" political scenario that was without precedent in Brazilian political history.

De Lima sees both danger and promise in this record. Danger in the degree to which a single network could set the political agenda and help construct a candidacy based more on "marketing" than substance. Danger also in the way in which the free radio and TV programs were manipulated through Collor's use of tiny political party fronts (minimal registration requirements made scores of splinter parties eligible for equal time in the campaign's first stage). Finally, danger in the failure of analysts to see that the consumption of media messages—and their intimate links to public mood and audience profile—must be studied in the same detail as the more conventional aspects of the campaign.

The other two chapters on Brazil downplay de Lima's message. In chapter 7, Joseph Straubhaar, Organ Olsen, and Maria Cavaliari Nunes argue, based primarily on survey data, that television, including TV Globo's campaign (although no reference is made to the *telenovelas*) certainly helped establish Collor's candidacy and lift his early rating in the polls but that the media were not "virtually omnipotent." Although they concede that TV Globo was the dominant broadcaster, especially in prime time, they point to increasing competition among Brazilian networks, of which there are now four. Most important, they found voters reporting (in a national survey taken at the height of the campaign) that among the top three sources of political information two were nonmedia: conversations with family and friends, and conversations with colleagues at work or school (all these conversations might, of course, have included comments on TV viewing). The third top source was the free political advertising time on radio and television. They also cite other research emphasizing the important role of families, along with church and neighborhood groups, in mediating the media messages.

They note that although Lula benefited from effective use of TV, his large vote owed perhaps even more to the unprecedented grass roots effort carried out by unions, progressive Catholic church activists, and neighborhood associations. Collor's overwhelming dependence on a media strategy also had its downside, according to this argument, as when its highly negative programming in the final weeks backfired with many viewers.

Although Straubhaar and colleagues contest the primacy of TV Globo's role, they acknowledge that the free political hour (carried by all media simultaneously) was widely watched and widely discussed. They see television as having helped "consolidate the democratic transition" by facilitating more direct communication between candidates and voters. They caution, however, that it has been much less effective on the state and local levels, where the need to present many candidates (and platforms) "fragments the informational space."

In chapter 8, Carlos Eduardo Lins da Silva, a Brazilian journalist and author of an important research monograph on how audiences perceive TV news in Brazil, presents an even fuller reply to those who see television, especially TV Globo, as the key to Collor's election. Although conceding that Collor's early television programs (in the first round, before the runoff against Lula) contributed "decisively" to his eventual victory, Lins da Silva offers evidence that the effectiveness of Collor's programming deteriorated in the later campaign stages. In the end, he argues, Collor won because he said "what most people wanted to hear," not because he was more "telegenic." Furthermore, Collor, with the advantage of presenting a new face, was more newsworthy and got the benefit of the doubt from an electorate that was alienated by the established politicians, who had already had time to break their previous campaign promises as they tried to run the country in the midst of the deepest economic crisis in a century.

Lins da Silva dismisses the "conspiracy theories" describing TV Globo's "incredibly Machiavellian" campaign to launch Collor's candidacy through such devices as soap opera plots with subliminal messages. He sees more traditional factors as crucial: ideology, class interests, influence of family and friends. By appearing "antipolitical," Collor fashioned an appeal wide enough (and shrewdly focused enough) to attract voters uninterested in politics. But he also attracted voters fearing the "red menace" by attacking Lula as a dangerous radical and voters yearning for Reaganism by preaching the virtues of the free market and privatization. Echoing most of the other contributing authors, Lins da Silva concludes that the media constitute only one field, "albeit the most important one," where candidates do battle. In the end, it is the candidate's ability to get voters to identify their most immediate interests with the candidate that counts.

In chapter 9, Ilya Adler, a specialist on Mexican media, analyzes the Mexican case, which is quite distinct from our other three cases. Since the 1930s, Mexico has been ruled by the PRI (Partido Revolucionario Institucional), a party that has enjoyed a stranglehold on politics at every level. Nominally an electoral democracy, Mexico had not seen a serious threat to the PRI's total dominance at the municipal, state, and federal levels in five decades. But 1988 brought a rude change. A dissident politician from within the PRI, Cauthémoc Cárdenas, challenged the official PRI candidate, Carlos Salinas de Gotari.

The context of the campaign was an economic crisis almost as serious as Brazil's. Capitalizing on the resulting discontent, Cárdenas tapped a profound popular anger against a political establishment that had grown overconfident of the public willingness to swallow its arrogant machine politics.

But the Mexican election campaign proceeded under different conditions from those in Argentina and Brazil. Whereas the latter two allowed presidential candidates equal free radio and television time, in Mexico both private and public broadcast media gave overwhelmingly disproportionate coverage to the government party candidate, with virtually no free time to the opposition. As Adler shows in his chapter, the same was only slightly less true of the Mexican print media.

There was another difference. Whereas Collor's victory in Brazil came in a reasonably honest election, Salinas's victory in Mexico was clouded by charges of large-scale vote fraud by the PRI. Suspicions in the Mexican case were reinforced when it took election officials more than a week to come up with a winning margin of just over 50 percent of the vote, the lowest percentage for an official party victor in the five-decade history of the party.

Despite their stranglehold on both the media and the ballot-counting process, the Mexican government and the PRI (virtually synonymous) expended enormous resources on media coverage and countrywide voter mobilization efforts. Why, if victory was so certain?

Adler finds the answer in the "dual" nature of both Mexican society and politics. Rhetorically and legally, Mexico is a democracy in which the individual voter is sovereign, all officials and political institutions are accountable, and civil liberties, the rule of law, and media freedom are guaranteed. In practice, however, it is an essentially hierarchial system in which higher authority (and links to it, often through personal and family influence) routinely prevail over formal rules. This duality is reflected in the behavior of the media, which ostensibly enjoy the freedoms of a democracy but in fact are highly authority oriented. This syndrome is encouraged through routine financial suborning by the government and party, with harassment and intimidation frequently meted out to critics who overstep the accepted limits. Truly independent journalism is rare in the mass media, as journalists seek to maintain their all-important sources of information in the government and in the PRI, without whose cooperation there is precious little "news."

The "information" function of the Mexican media is therefore fundamentally different from that in the more authentically pluralistic democracies of Argentina, Brazil, and Chile. The Mexican public widely distrusts its media, a discontent that surfaced when disgust over

Televisa's biased news coverage led to an organized boycott of its widely watched prime-time news program, "24 Hours." Yet voters *did* get enough information (or opinion) by other means to convince them to vote against the government candidate in unprecedented numbers. The Mexican case could therefore also be said to have demonstrated the limitations of media manipulation.

Adler also offers an extensive attempt to see the media's political function within the wider focus de Lima laid out for Brazil. The media role was not so much to convince the voter, as conventional analysis would suggest, but rather to share in the political rituals that surround the passing of ultimate power: in Mexico, the presidency.

The first stage is the "drama of uncertainty," as the official presidential candidate is chosen (through a highly secret process involving only a handful of high party and government leaders, usually dominated by the incumbent president) and then tours the country defining the major problems facing the society, promising to solve them and subtly hinting who will enjoy power in his upcoming administration. The second stage is the transformation of the candidate into a "national symbol with kinglike qualities." According to this logic, Mexican media therefore serve essentially as vehicles by which these political rituals are shared with the larger public.

Adler concludes that the fate of the media in Mexico is inextricably linked with the fate of Mexican democracy. A more authentic democracy will require more independent media, which in turn will require better salaries and more professional independence for journalists, and an end to the monopolistic structure of the TV industry. This is unlikely, according to Adler, unless the Mexican political system itself becomes more democratic (when opposition candidates, parties, and movements can operate free of harassment, intimidation, and systematic vote fraud). In short, if democratization faces a severe test in South America, it has barely begun in Mexico, the only major country of the four examined in this book to have escaped the scourge of military repression in recent decades.

NOTES

I am grateful to Douglas Gomery and Elizabeth Mahan for helpful comments on this chapter. Felicity Skidmore exercised her usual editorial skills. I also wish to thank Ilya Adler, Elizabeth Mahan, Emile McAnany, Joseph Straubhaar, and Joseph Tulchin for their help in organizing the conference from which this volume resulted.

1. See, for example, Elizabeth Fox, ed., *Media and Politics in Latin America: The Struggle for Democracy* (Beverly Hills: Sage, 1988), which is primarily a collection of country case studies.

2. The Brazilian case has attracted much recent attention. See, for example, Sergio Mattos, *Um Perfil da TV Brasileira: 40 Años de História, 1950–1990* (Salvador: A Tarde, 1990). See also the same author's *The Impact of the 1964 Revolution on Brazilian Television* (San Antonio: Klingensmith, 1982).

3. One of the first stories on the role of TV in Collor's rise was by James Brooke, "TV Making Obscure Brazilian the Candidate to Beat at 39," *New York Times,* 31 July 1989. Brooke was himself accused of highly biased reporting of the Brazilian presidential campaign in Richard Rivers and Richard McKerrow, "Brazil Tilt," *Lies of Our Times* (March 1991): 19–20. The crucial role of television in the Chilean plebiscite is documented by Hirmas in chapter 5 of this book.

4. This question has been amply debated in the U.S. case. See, for example, Robert M. Entman, *Democracy without Citizens: Media and the Decay of American Politics* (New York: Oxford University Press, 1989), and Sig Mickelson, *From Whistle Stop to Sound Bite: Four Decades of Politics and Television* (New York: Praeger, 1989). For examples from the frequent debates in the press, see James M. Perry, "New Breed of Political Consultants Threatens to Give Negative Campaigning a Bad Name," *Wall Street Journal,* 11 May 1990; Martin Schram, "The Making of Willie Horton," and Kiku Adatto, "The Incredible Shrinking Sound Bite," both in *The New Republic,* 28 May 1990; and Randall Rothemberg, "Political Consultants Agree Their Images Damage the Democratic Process," *New York Times,* 25 March 1991.

5. The exception is Venicio A. de Lima, whose paper was not presented at the conference.

6. Radio has been more important in Latin American political history than most analysts have realized, but research on its role is hampered by lack of physical records (tapes, transcripts, audience ratings, and so forth) and by the overshadowing influence of television since the 1960s. The papers in this volume for the most part do not consider radio, but that omission does not indicate that the authors themselves regard radio as peripheral to Latin American politics.

7. Ariel Dorfman and Armand Mattelart, *How to Read Donald Duck: Imperialist Ideology in the Disney Comic* (New York: International General, 1984).

8. Obviously the question of differing approaches to the study of media is a large one. Long-standing debate between the "Marxists" and the "liberal pluralists" is spelled out in the very useful survey edited by Michael Gurevitch, Tony Bennett, James Curran, and Janet Woollacott, *Culture, Society and the Media* (London: Routledge, 1982). For a very useful review of differing theoretical approaches, see the opening pages of the chapter by Straubhaar, Olsen, and Nunes in chapter 7 of this book.

9. See the analysis of the election campaign in David P. Werlich, "Fujimoro and the 'Disaster' in Peru," *Current History* (February 1991): 61–64; 81–83.

10. For an overview of recent contributions to the study of the relationship between media on the one hand and Latin American culture and society on the other, see the recent review articles by Elizabeth Mahan, "Communications, Culture and the State in Latin America," *Journal of Interamerican Studies and World Affairs* 32 (Spring 1990):146–54, and "Communication and Society in Latin America: Recent Studies," *Studies in Latin American Popular Culture* 9 (1990): 311–17, and the same author's "Broadcasting-State Relationships in Latin America: Are Generalizations Valid?" *Studies in Latin American Popular Culture* 6 (1987): 135–47.

11. For a book-length study of Brazilian television by a U.S. anthropologist, see Conrad Phillip Kottak, *Prime-Time Society: An Anthropological Analysis of Television and Culture* (Belmont, Calif.: Wadsworth, 1990). It should be noted that Kottak's treatment is based on a behaviorist paradigm that is no longer accepted by many communication scholars in the United States and Europe and finds even less acceptance among that community in Latin America.

2

Television: A New Role around the World?

Douglas Gomery and
Lawrence W. Lichty

Seventy years ago, Walter Lippmann said that the press "is no substitute for institutions. It is like the beam of a searchlight that moves restlessly about bringing one episode and then another out of the darkness into vision."[1] Never was his description more true than in the 1980s when what the light revealed was beamed into more and more homes. Our giant communications system begins and ends with a speck of light.

We saw a lone student defy the Communist Chinese government. We saw the Berlin Wall taken down, almost literally, brick by brick. We saw the Soviet Union turn into the CIS. The Gulf War of 1991 was reported live around the clock, seen "instantly" as it happened. But we should not be blinded by Lippmann's striking metaphor. His much deeper point was that while the press might reveal the ills of our world, it cannot cure them: People "cannot do the work of the world by this light alone. They cannot govern society by episodes, incidents, and eruptions."

While we lived through these and other dramatic changes in the world order, it seemed their images heralded a communications revolution. But this transformation has been going on for much, much longer. Indeed, we argue that it is better understood as an evolution that has been accelerating since the beginning of the twentieth century. "Instant global news" was first proclaimed a trend during World War I as newsreels proclaimed that they were the "eyes and ears of the world." A decade later, one radio news wire service boasted, "around the world, around the clock, the world's best coverage of the world's biggest news."

Yet we will argue that a radical technical change in instantaneous communication did occur during the 1980s. Satellite signals leapt conti- nents. Video recorders captured conflicts and conferences. Seemingly ubiquitous television outlets broadcast more and more information around the clock, around the planet. At the beginning of the last decade of the twentieth century, dramatic events seemed almost tailor-made for the technology now ready to relay their images to all parts of the globe.

Indeed, the international influence of the mass media had long been professed. Consider what Charles H. Sewall wrote for the December 29, 1900, issue of *Harper's Weekly*:

> The child born today in New York City, when in middle age, shall visit China, may see reproduced upon a screen, with all its movement and color, light and shade, a procession at that moment passing along his own Broadway. A telephone line will bring to his ear music and the tramp of marching men. While the American pageant passes in the full glare of the morning sun, its transmitted ray will scintillate upon the screen amid the darkness of an Asian night. Sign and sound will have unlimited reach through terrestrial space.

The revolution took longer than anticipated, but lest we forget, in 1972 Americans first saw the movement and color of China live—President Nixon's visit.

Nearly a century later, television has at times become a window on the world. We agree with Ted Koppel that under the right conditions "Television has fallen into the hands of the people . . . a form of television democracy is sweeping the world."[2] But how? And where? And under what conditions? Those questions are the subjects of this chapter. We intend to set up the study of the political effect of the coming of the television age in Latin America by first looking at the historical change in media communications.

In particular, the spillover media effects of the Gulf War of 1991 raise fundamental questions about the effect of the media on the ever-changing politics of third-world countries, in particular their possible, varied roads toward democracy. How has the coming of the new television means of mass communication altered the political process in the third world? Has it sped up or slowed down political reform? Can traditional societies retain the control they have long held over the means of public expression? Are we really approaching a new world information order?

In short, we shall argue that technological change is a necessary condition for the development of a new communications infrastructure. Only then can the profound effects of political and social change discussed in this book actually happen. Simply put, transmission and reception of television to mass audiences is a necessary condition.

Tipping our hand, we think the picture is neither as rosy nor smooth as some would have us believe. The appropriate technology must be in place before the public can even have access to the information the media provide. In addition, the means and time for use (by a stable, well-off middle class) must then be established. Only then can the new information order arise. It is our central point that such a transformation is far easier with "small," less-expensive media (for example, radio and the videocassette recorder) than with their "bigger," more expensive cousins (for example, the satellite dish and a major television network).

A vivid example of this transformation could be seen literally in the backyards of the rich in Saudi Arabia as thousands of illegally imported satellite dishes sprouted during the first months of 1991. The elite Saudi families, desperate for information and frustrated by their own tightly controlled state-run media, wanted simply to know what was going on. They were able not only to pick up news from CNN (Cable News Network) and Armed Forces Radio and Television Services, but also to receive soap operas from secular Egypt, political commentary from radical Syria, news from Israel, and, on rare nights, even soft-core pornography from Italy. One Saudi academic reported that a dozen stores had begun to sell microwave antenna boosters that allowed city residents to steal signals from their neighbors' receiving dishes: Even the effects of diffusion of media to the rich are not predictable.

Our conditional position is opposed to the strong views of many who have seen the simple introduction of the media as a threat to past ways of political and societal operations. Our world, for some, has been turned into an electronic playing field. Few are unaffected. This was vividly symbolized when Tariq Aziz, Iraqi foreign minister, argued before a largely foreign press corps (after meeting with the United States secretary of state, James Baker) that he was not ignorant of what the West thought of Iraq for he had "the great advantage of being able to watch CNN."

At first blush, this globalization of television seems to have had an almost radical influence in the third world—ushering in a new international era in communication. Consider how protests around the world are now commonly orchestrated. Demonstrators in Beijing and Baghdad regularly carry signs written in English, aimed at the common language of international television. When protestors did the same thing twenty years earlier in Cambodia, it was assumed their activities had been arranged by the CIA! Now, with CNN, demonstrators would hardly be up to par if they did not assume they would be seen in Washington, Moscow, London, Hong Kong, New Delhi, and Cairo. But first, we would point out, one must be able to see CNN.

That television is important, no one can doubt. This means today that television stations are fought over, prizes for the victors—as were radio stations earlier. In recent transformations of political power in Romania, it was the nation's television stations that were among the first places the opposition occupied. And in Lithuania's second city, Kaunas, in the early morning hours of January 13, 1991, word reached station director Raimondas Sestakauskas that Soviet troops had stormed the television tower in the capital, Vilnius. He therefore put his television station (normally on only a limited number of hours per day) on the air around the clock. Quickly it became a world-famous symbol of the resistance of an oppressed people. Controlling television and having its signals rebroadcast around the world became a valued symbol of the struggle for political power. But this can happen only once the technology is in place.

We must also remember that values and beliefs are shaped by more than TV news reports. Probably no image of the United States became more pervasive during the 1980s than the excesses and indulgences of the Ewing clan of "Dallas." While nighttime soap operas have long been a staple in Latin America and a leading export of the vast British tele-export system to Africa and Asia, they were not common on American prime time. But the coming of "Dallas" changed all that. By 1985, it could be seen in ninety countries. Stories of empty streets and surges in water pressure—when a nation flushed at the same time—became commonplace and repeated the experience of U.S. cities when television first arrived on the scene in the early 1950s. From Israel to Algeria, from Argentina to Mexico, millions of fans watched to see what happened at the South Fork Ranch this week and find out "who shot J. R.?"[3]

POLITICAL CHANGE—TV STYLE

The new television technologies have indeed begun to influence democratic process and change since the beginning of the 1980s. And world events now seem so much more dramatic. Climactic political change that we once read about days or weeks later has become the stuff of the nightly evening news, the CNN Special Report, instantaneously beamed to all parts of the world. When a television system is in place, as it was during the political upheavals in the late 1980s in Eastern Europe, then surely it becomes a ready, present influence in determining the course of events.

No better example can be found than what the East Germans heard and saw for themselves as the Berlin wall came down. One historian has called 1989 "the year of truth" for East Germany. Previously, the power of the state had combined strict censorship and party ownership of the mass media to control all sources of news and information. People did not necessarily believe what they saw and heard, but state control blocked the truth and numbed the citizenry.

It was in 1989 that these structures began to break down. The implicit direct link between the government and the state failed, and new voices suddenly appeared everywhere. Consider the cases of Czechoslovakia and Romania. In student demonstrations in Prague's Wenceslaus Square in November, the cameras of state television captured the images of the police brutalizing students. In a December rally in Bucharest, when Nicolae Ceauşescu was booed while addressing the crowd, his stunned look beamed across a nation on television suggested a vulnerability that would lead to his fall.

The process of change in nation after nation in Eastern Europe seemed to follow a predictable pattern. Invariably one of the first acts of the new government was the capture (they would say liberation) of the electronic media. This more than anything symbolized the break with the past. Small grassroots newspapers then seemed to spring up everywhere. The nature of the journalist changed, from an agent of the state to a person freely reporting and interpreting the events of the day.

People also gained renewed power from the spillover of Western media. Observers said that the East Germans learned the Berlin Wall was irrelevant from messages they saw on Western television—and heard from local West German radio stations. Many were tantalized by the riches they saw nightly in television advertisements (for luxury cars and extravagant vacations) and the seemingly ubiquitous "life-styles of the rich and famous" that were made commonplace on other American nighttime soaps such as "Falcon Crest" and "Knots Landing." And officials on both sides closely followed their ever-transforming images on CNN.[4]

But here was a case of traditional broadcast television that was available, that flowed easily across borders. What about the new technologies of satellite television distribution and videocassette recorders? They are the suggested causes of the political changes of the 1980s. But how, when, and where have these new technologies become available in various countries? We need to understand the answer to those questions *before* we can make broad claims about the universal applicability of the case of Eastern Europe to Latin America.

CHANGING TECHNOLOGIES I: SATELLITES

During the past two decades, the citizens of emerging countries of the third world have been able to see a new form of television. Twenty years ago, nations were more isolated, defined by national broadcasting. Today, images cannot be confined by national boundaries. From CNN in Atlanta to villages in Central America, from reporters telecasting live from Africa to students facing down tanks in Beijing's Tiananmen Square, from Bill Cosby to "I Love Lucy" seen throughout the entire planet, we seem to be entering a new age of international communication.

Behind this change in television communication lie two innovations. One is a simple relay system found more than twenty-two thousand miles above our heads—distribution of signals by space satellite. The other is the mass production of a simple-to-operate (especially for the young, if not their parents), inexpensive extension of the long-common audiotape recorder—the videocassette recorder (VCR), or as it also called, the home video recorder (HVR). The technology is new, but the principles—transmission and recording—have always formed the basis of mass communication.

Space satellites came first. There has long been international radio by which messages could circle the globe, literally skipping—like a stone across a pond—between the ground itself and the ionosphere. But such broadcasting was unreliable, subject to weather conditions, time of day, and even sunspots.[5]

Television could never match even this minimal radio service until the coming of orbiting relay stations, or "birds," to which signals are sent and then returned to earth. Thus video and audio signals can move from one part of the globe to another inexpensively and instantaneously. A press conference held in Geneva, Switzerland, can be beamed within seconds live to viewers in Iraq, Egypt, Israel, London, Paris, and Washington, D.C.

Just as important, distance is no longer *the* determinant of cost. There is very little difference between the charge for sending a signal from a close suburb to a television station in downtown Chicago and sending the same pictures across the entire United States or to Europe. Scud attacks on Israel during the Gulf War were seen "live" in Central and South America, Asia, Africa, and Australia, as well as Europe and the United States. And just a month after the Gulf War ended, an estimated billion people watched the Oscar awards live—some on tape delay—on television, including viewers, for the first time, in Albania. In July 1962, the first live trans-Atlantic television programs were exchanged between France and the United States. In November 1963, the funeral of President John F. Kennedy was seen live in twenty-three countries, carried across the Atlantic via satellite, then across Europe and the USSR on Eurovision, Intervision, and other networks.

While satellites could send messages around the globe, they were equally efficient in serving just one country or region. In the United States in the 1970s, television and radio networks moved their interconnection systems of land lines and microwave towers to satellite receiving dishes. More important, the ability of thousands of receiving stations— or downlinks—to snatch a signal from the orbiting space globes created a whole new industry providing pay cable and new advertiser-supported networks only seen on cable systems. And for nations without cable TV, the satellite dish made these new services available.

Developing countries—if they have the necessary substantial monies—began to use communication satellites to help their economies and societies in the 1980s. Educational programs could be beamed to the most remote villages in nations such as Cambodia, Indonesia, or Kenya. For example, the Arabsat system, launched in February 1985, was designed to provide varied services for twenty-two member countries in the Middle East and North Africa. Insat in India has been in operation since 1983. Brazil established Brasilsat in 1985. Other nations setting up satellite communication systems can be found from Colombia to Nigeria, from Pakistan to Thailand.

Often, however, the use of these systems has been limited by real-life political and economic constraints. For example, Indonesia is the fifth most populous country in the world, with nearly 190 million people dispersed over more than thirteen thousand islands. A satellite seemed to be an ideal technology for national broadcasting to this widely scattered population. Indonesia was thus the first developing country to get a domestic satellite system. Palapa-A was built by the Hughes Aircraft Corporation in the United States and launched by the United States' National Aeronautics and Space Administration (NASA) in 1976. Yet Palapa-A and its successors have had circumscribed impact. Few Indonesians can afford earth stations, all of which are under strict government control. Thus official use has been limited. The "average viewer" comes from a small class of richer citizens who have assembled backyard dishes from components smuggled in from Singapore just to watch, not educational television, but Malaysian commercial broadcasting also carried on the Palapa transponder.

One way the Indonesian government has dealt with this national telecommunications spillover is by blacking out all "foreign" advertisements while leaving on most programs. It considered advertisements more dangerous because they would allow poor citizens to see a culture they could never afford. In this way, the government seeks to keep expectations in check. The Indonesian government also keeps a sharp eye on critical programming. It tightly controls content to promote political stability and maintain power. Comedy and drama are acceptable only as long as they stay within noncritical boundaries. By keeping television in check, however, the Indonesian government defeats the "educational" purpose of the Palapa satellite system. "Teledemocracy" is not always that simple to fashion in worlds where having enough food and a simple home are far more pressing basic problems.

A similar experience arose in the attempt to use satellites to deliver television services to the villages and oases across the deserts of the Arab peninsula and North Africa. Arabsat links nations from Algeria and Egypt to Qatar and Syria. Two satellites were launched in 1985, but as in Indonesia, the vast promise has never been realized, in part because of economics—the sheer expense of earth stations. Thus, as we began the 1990s, only six countries—Saudi Arabia, Bahrain, Jordan, Oman, Tunisia, and Kuwait—of a possible twenty-two even had earth stations set up. Political instability in this region further limited the use of the technology that was in place. Simply put, no one could agree on joint tasks.

The most pressing example of this change is, of course, the spreading images of CNN, seen in 90 countries around the world. Many developed countries have CNN in every home, and although it is rarely seen in the homes of third-world citizens, it has a great influence in the third world. It is ubiquitous in government offices and hotels and thus serves as an important source of information for opinion leaders, offering them a chance to learn instantly what the world thinks of their latest actions.

CHANGING TECHNOLOGIES II: THE VCR

If satellite use was constantly constrained by expense and the difficulty of attaining common goals, this was not the case with portable video cameras and playback equipment. Throughout Eastern Europe, Africa, Asia, and the Americas, videocassette recorders and camcorders have found their way into any number of homes and viewing sites. Still, even though a VCR can cost as little as a few hundred dollars, only the rich and upper middle class in developing countries have such "disposable" assets.[6]

To make them affordable, videocassette recorders and cameras are smuggled into less-developed countries to avoid often-excessive excise taxes. This makes them virtually invisible to outsiders trying to judge their importance. We can only say in general that there are millions in use. Certainly, the official numbers underestimate the true acceptance and impact. Still, the numbers we have are staggering. Although VCRs are spreading more slowly in the third world than in, say, the United States or Japan, their presence in the less-developed nations is considerable. In Brazil, the number of VCRs had just nudged over 1 million; in Egypt, it is a half million; and in Uruguay, Zimbabwe, and Kenya—smaller, poorer nations—the best guess puts the number at several thousand. Taken together, these figures show us millions of working machines able to support a flourishing market in pirated, copied, and traded tapes.[7]

For a great many countries, we have only anecdotes about the varied uses of the videocassette recorder, but they seem to paint a consistent picture: the communal consumption of illegally copied tapes, mainly of Hollywood films. (This causes problems in fundamentalist countries because of the often-graphic depiction of sex and violence.) Other illegal uses are common as well. In Bangladesh, for example, videocassettes of Indian movies, which authorities do not allow into the country, as well as uncensored Hollywood films, have become freely available. In urban centers, video clubs rent or sell copies. In poorer areas, the vast majority watch in clandestine "video parlors." Thus, while less than 1 percent of households have their own videocassette recorder, this 1 percent represents a powerful medium. When the government of Indonesia banned the film *The Year of Living Dangerously*, which was critical of the government, copies circulated widely on the black market.

So far, the pattern of diffusion has some common characteristics. The rich in urban areas get machines first, then the members of the educated upper middle class. For the rest of society, the use of the videocassette recorder is best visualized as a communal, sporadic experience. In Mogadishu, Somalia, where the videocassette recorder is not the only new technology—television itself went on the air officially in October 1983—the growing number of televisions and videocassette recorders have been imported by Somalis working in Saudi Arabia, Kuwait, and the Arab Emirates as a way to repatriate their earnings to their families.

The ability of the VCR to circumvent traditional broadcasting systems has become an important political issue. For example, the rich in the

Arab world have, as one might expect, the highest VCR acquisition rates of any citizenry in the developing world. In Kuwait, prior to the war, more than 80 percent of households with a television set also had a videocassette recorder. By this means, they could watch unapproved Western programs in private, including Hollywood movies, frowned on by strict Muslims, and tapes critical of official positions. The down-to-earth videocassette recorder provided viewing alternatives through a multiplicity of tapes; programs coming from the space satellite could be monitored by the government and stopped.

It should surprise no one that videocassette recorders have become so widespread and influential in oil-rich Arab states that the governments have begun to regulate them. Because of its sensitivity to material inconsistent with conservative Islamic beliefs, Saudi Arabia enacted a video regulation law in 1980. It is typical of laws being passed throughout the developing world. To own a machine, one must be a citizen at least eighteen years of age with no criminal record. Rental or sales shops cannot be located near mosques or allow women to enter.[8]

The case of the Philippines provides a further example of videocassette regulation. Here the motivation was not so much the protection of religious purity but the desire to tax the rich who principally own the relatively high-priced machines. For a long time, the Philippines had relied on taxes of movie houses to supply needed revenues. The coming of home video sapped movie theater attendance. Before he was deposed, Ferdinand Marcos signed a bill that created the Videogram Regulatory Board, which strictly controlled who could rent or acquire tapes and levied a tax of 30 percent on rentals and sales.[9]

LEARNING FROM CONTEMPORARY HISTORY

The innovation and diffusion of the new television technology leads us to ask about economic and political control. Who can and does own the means of production? Who does and can have access? These questions have been settled in the United States by a market model, with control in the hands of a few large corporations. Outside the United States, ownership and control have usually rested with the central government. The model of state control is breaking down through technical pressures (it is too hard to monitor) and through a change in philosophy (governments now wish to privatize the media to boost the economy).

However framed, these are economic and political issues that have long determined the history of the mass media. Should there be some type of limits on the pure capitalist exploitation of the mass media in simple pursuit of profit? Should the state take control? And, in any case, how should access—the flow of information in a democracy—be handled?

The coming of space satellite technology and the videocassette recorder and camera may have transformed our world, yet the concerns they raise are hardly new. They have been a constant of media history since the turn of the century. In response to the rise of the mass media—from the cinema in the late nineteenth century to radio and television in more recent times—governments around the world have struggled to form policies of ownership and access.

For the third world, the core issue has been to weigh the interests of national development against the inroads of Western multinational media corporations. The common experience of media control goes back to precedents established by the American motion picture industry fifty years ago and by government responses to that Hollywood invasion. The motion picture technology was invented in the United States and Western Europe, then exported into the third world. Fans around the world clamored for Hollywood films while native film industries were never able to grow.[10]

By 1930, more than three-quarters of all films shown in most third-world nations were from Hollywood, including all the major money-makers. From Argentina to Ethiopia, from Korea to Mexico, the world embraced Hollywood stars and stories. Small native film industries could survive only through state subsidies and rigid censorship: Native filmmakers needed money to make films—which then had to be shown on screens reserved for their use. Governmental officials also worried about the images of their nations portrayed by Hollywood filmmakers. Only rarely did Hollywood make films without stereotypes; for example, the countries of Central and South America were able to pressure Hollywood to make positive images of Latin Americans only during the era of the "Good Neighbor Policy" of the late 1930s and early 1940s.[11]

Media domination by the West was not confined to film. By the 1920s, most radios were produced in the United States. Because only the wealthy could afford sets, governments in poorer nations were slow to develop stations. Thus radio broadcasting was confined to urban areas and to the well-off, as with the videocassette recorder half a century later. During the 1930s, Bolivia and Paraguay, for example, had only one station for a complete nation. Even massive Argentina had only twenty stations. And radio in Latin America must be considered a "success story." Africa and the Middle East never reached receiver penetration of even the poorest South American nation.

Television followed the pattern of the motion picture industry because many of the shows were indeed created on film, many produced and distributed by the major Hollywood companies. As with film, there was always a split in third-world nations. On the one hand, a foreign nation's television producers loathed Hollywood-made shows because they proved so popular; they left little time or demand for native products. However, station managers in third-world countries loved American products because they provided the bulk of their profits.[12]

PREDICTING THE FUTURE

Into this world of television production and distribution from Hollywood, the BBC, and the rest of the West came the satellite dish and the VCR. Yet even as this new technology was becoming available, vast stretches of the world were just getting TV sets. Even the well-off nations in the Middle East are still only today entering the television age. With the dominance of strict religious codes, the Arab countries moved slowly so as not to depend on imported material from the United States or the U.S.S.R. In poor areas of the world, such as most of Africa, television was still in its infancy as satellites and VCRs became available. Even by the mid-1980s, for example, of the forty-six broadcasting organizations in sub-Saharan Africa, fully one-half were in one nation—Nigeria—long assisted by Americans in the development of its system. Television sets in Africa are concentrated in urban areas because the cost of a receiver is beyond the means of most save the wealthy elite of the cities. In other words, not all nations enter each age of television on equal footing.

With the coming of space satellites and the inexpensive videocassette recorder, the world seems to have changed. But we argue that change has come only on the surface. Economic, political, social, religious, and historical constraints, some of which we have discussed here, have limited and will continue to limit the use of even the small number of television sets and production facilities in the third world. The rich nations will have a multiplicity of options; the poor will not.

But this picture of slow change based on real economic and political conditions should not be seen as a constant formula. There has always been and always will be an unpredictable variable in the matrix.

Consider technical change in mainland China. During the 1980s, vast numbers of Chinese acquired television sets so that by 1987 there were 130 million in the country or roughly one for every ten persons. For a largely rural population, this meant unprecedented access to the outside world. So the VCR has had an impact in rural China in a way few might have predicted. Indeed videocassettes through mail now serve as a "new medium" of international communication, particularly as sent in from Chinese living abroad. And perhaps more important, there is now a multiplicity of sources and channels.[13]

During the troubles in Tiananmen, the Chinese government prohibited television coverage, but in a wonderfully ironic twist it apparently forgot that there were several thousand satellite stations at schools, universities, and army facilities ordinarily used to receive educational programs. The American USIA's WorldNet television service provided radio (audio) coverage of events from the Voice of America and a written text "supered" on the TV screen. While the Chinese dialects are different in various parts of the country, all were able to read the text. It is not known how many might have seen these transmissions.[14]

There are many state solutions that seek to use television as an educational and instructional medium. In Ghana, for example, the government uses television to educate the people as well as entertain them. In Tamale, the poorest region of that impoverished nation, people come from miles around to watch videos of "local news." Videos of local native customs are played along with the latest Hollywood products. The governmental goal is to use the tools of the West without accepting the total ideological baggage. Fully three-quarters of Ghana broadcast television is locally produced because of the express philosophy of the Ghana Broadcasting Corporation. In 1986, with state funds and a grant from the Japanese, the government set up two new color television studios and sent out 200 television sets to schools, hospitals, and social centers around the nation. By 1988, there were more than a quarter of a million television sets in use, with broadcast television signals reaching 60 percent of the population of 13 million.

Hollywood's products have proven extremely tempting. Enterprising men and women in poor country after poor country have secured satellite dishes and videocassette recorders, pirated Hollywood movies, and then set up neighborhood movie shows. In isolated villages or shantytown neighborhoods (the rich can afford their own), one can see the sign: "Video Show Tonight." Scandals arise when it is discovered that children use their bus or meal money to skip school and attend daytime video shows.

Moreover, just because there are new sources of television news does not mean there will be an instantaneous effect. In the real world, we must remember that Israel is not marked on Saudi maps; there are no phone lines between the two countries, let alone mail service. Only for one historical moment, during the Gulf War, were Israel and Saudi Arabia closely linked. This real-time war, with its fleeting images of destruction sent across normally rigid boundaries, should not be confused with permanent change. Longer-term cultural and social transformation will need to be worked into the politics and economics of ordinary lives.

The power of the new television media is surely with us, but in the end we must remind ourselves that we have lived in wave after wave of "new" technologies in the twentieth century, yet we are still not sure if any of it has radically changed the world. There seem to be three possibilities.

First there is the "TV does not matter" school. Sadly, dictators and despots come and go despite the possibility of strengthening democracy through more media voices. This camp would stress that the media are just one part of a multifaceted world where powerful social, economic, and political forces still dictate what happens in the end.

Second, there is the "TV transforms the world" school. Think of the possibilities and power, these advocates tell us. Space satellites can leap boundaries; cheap videocassettes can make television productions accessible to all. Leaders who seek absolute control to dictate from the top will find their desires tested and challenged. Cheap "little" media technologies will help to play the defining role.

Third, there is the school of complexity, which holds that the media power does not simply flow in one direction (top down or bottom up) but interacts in a myriad of ways we are still working to understand. Certainly, the changing media play a role, but it is not a simple, straightforward one. Here is where we side.

We would also gently remind readers that the stage, or chronology, of TV adoption in a country may be a strong correlate of how the new media is perceived and used. The earliest American adopters were from households of a high socioeconomic level, not the "low-brow" stereotype many seem to now have of TV viewers. Similar results seem to have been discovered by Kottak and his colleagues in rural Brazil.[15] Thus, it is not surprising that they find viewing correlated with reading, information seeking, social contact, and "liberal" attitudes—the opposite of many American studies (in much later stages of TV adoption).

The case studies that follow start the process of understanding. The world of the new television—and its many effects—is a history that is just beginning to be written.

NOTES

1. Walter Lippmann, *Public Opinion* (New York: The Free Press, 1965; © 1922), 229.
2. Koppel Report, "Television Revolution in a Box," ABC-TV, 13 September 1989.
3. See Tamar Liebes and Elihu Katz, *The Export of Dallas* (New York: Oxford University Press, 1990).
4. For example, see these reports on the most recent changes in Eastern Europe: Everette E. Dennis and Jon Vanden Heuvel, *Emerging Voices: East European Media in Transition* (New York: Gannett Center for Media Studies [now Freedom Forum], 1990); Wilson Dizard, "Satellite Television: Eastern Europe's Window on the West," Via Satellite, February 1990, 41–45; "Eastern Europe: Please Stand By," Report of the Task Force on Telecommunications and Broadcasting in Eastern Europe, Advisory Committee on International Communications and Information Policy, U.S. Department of State, 1990; and *Broadcast Diversity in Eastern Europe: Challenges for the 1990's*, (Washington, D.C.: Center for Strategic and International Studies, 1990).
5. For more, see Heather Hudson, *Communication Satellites: Their Development and Impact* (New York: The Free Press, 1990).
6. See Christine Ogan, "The Worldwide Cultural and Economic Impact of Video," in *The VCR Age: Home Video and Mass Communication*, ed. Mark Levy (Newbury Park, Cal.: Sage Publications, 1989), 230–51.
7. See Gladys D. Ganley and Oswald H. Ganley, *Global Political Fallout: The First Decade of the VCR, 1976–1985* (Cambridge: Program on Information Resources Policy, Harvard University, 1987).
8. See Douglas Boyd, "The Regulation of Home Video Recorders in the Third World," Airlie House Telecommunications Conference, 2 October 1990.
9. For an interesting analysis of some examples, see Franklyn S. Haiman, "Citizen Access to the Media: A Cross-Cultural Analysis of Four Democratic Societies," Research Monograph of the Institute for Modern Communications (Chicago: Northwestern University, 1987); and Franklyn S. Haiman, "A Tale of Two Countries: Media and Messages of the French and American Presidential Campaigns of 1988," Research Monograph of the Institute for Modern Communications (Chicago: Northwestern University, 1988).
10. For more, see Jorge A. Schnitman, *Film Industries in Latin America* (Norwood, N.J.: Ablex, 1984).
11. See James Schwoch, *The American Radio Industry and Its Latin American Activities, 1900–1930* (Champaign: University of Illinois Press, 1990).
12. See Alan Welles, *Picture-Tube Imperialism? The Impact of U.S. Television on Latin America* (Maryknoll, N.Y.: Orbis Books, 1972), in particular chapter 7.
13. For a study of news dissemination in China in the past, see Stephen R. Mackinnon and Oris Friesen, *China Reporting* (Berkeley: University of California Press, 1987).
14. For a recent and comprehensive analysis of the origins of American propaganda broadcasting, see Holly Cowan Shulman, *The Voice of America: Propaganda and Democracy, 1941–45* (Madison: University of Wisconsin Press, 1991).
15. Conrad P. Kottak, "Television's Impact on Values and Local Life in Brazil," *Journal of Communication* 41 (Winter 1991): 70–87, and Conrad P. Kottak, *Prime-Time Society: An Anthropological Analysis of Television and Culture* (Belmont, Cal.: Wadsworth, 1991).

3

Broadcast Media and Latin American Politics: The Historical Context

James Schwoch

Several Latin American elections held during the 1980s have received the attention of scholars interested in media and politics. In part, this interest is sparked by the uses of television in these contests. Recent presidential campaigns in Brazil, Argentina, Nicaragua, and Mexico, as well as a plebiscite in Chile, all saw widespread use of television and radio by candidates and parties. Furthermore, these elections received extensive coverage from Latin American broadcast journalists as well as broadcast journalists from other nations.

While it is fair to say that broadcasting, particularly television, plays an increasingly influential role in the Latin American political process, it would be a mistake to assume that the 1980s marked the beginning of broadcasting's full integration into the Latin American political scene. The interplay between broadcasting and Latin American politics is evident throughout the twentieth century, even in the period before broadcasting when radio was used as a method of point-to-point communication (usually via Morse code) and was known as the "wireless." As the technologies of radio communications improved and the uses of those technologies expanded into governmental, commercial, and cultural spheres, the interplay between broadcasting and Latin American politics expanded and took on increasing complexity. Thus the historical underpinnings of Latin American broadcasting and politics are, in some ways, similar to experiences in the United States and Europe. In addition to some similarities, other conditions and practices are unique to the Latin American experiences of politics and broadcasting. This chapter places those similarities and specific features in a historical context, thus setting the stage for the analyses of contemporary Latin American politics and media in the rest of this collection.

1900–1920: THE WIRELESS ERA

The initial experiments in introducing radio technology in the early 1900s invariably drew Latin American governments into questions of the regulation and ownership of wireless communications: How should radio be regulated, and who should be granted ownership privileges? While the first question proved difficult if not impossible for many nations to resolve quickly, the second was often resolved through government ownership or the granting of government concessions.[1] In some cases, it remained unclear which politicians and representatives held the right to grant concessions. For example, in Brazil, the federal government and state governors battled for a decade over who held the right to grant wireless concessions.[2] Although few, if any, could precisely describe the importance of radio at this time, many politicians and government officials saw that it had great promise as a promoter of trade and commerce. Control of radio communications in the future could therefore also have important political implications.

By the onset of World War I, radio technology was in regular use in every Latin American nation. Questions of ownership were still unresolved, as U.S., European, and indigenous Latin American interests competed for contracts and concessions throughout the region. However, many nations were beginning to lean toward government ownership of radio communications, with Brazil, Peru, Uruguay, and Mexico all adopting policies encouraging government ownership by 1914.[3] Mexico's revolutionary government politicized the wireless far beyond the levels reached by any other Latin American nation during this period. In cooperation with Germany, Mexico helped finance the construction of stations for every Central American nation except Panama (where radio remained completely under the control of the U.S. Navy).[4] These stations allowed for communications between Mexico and Central America, and in addition supplied a prodigious amount of German propaganda. The Mexican government also gave receiving sets to individuals who were thought to have influence within their local community. German citizens living in Mexico during the war also occasionally spread pro-German information they had picked up on their own sets, and emigrant German populations throughout Latin America, such as in Brazil, were often relayed news of the war through German ships at harbor in those nations.[5]

The coming of the world war brought the first use of radio as a mechanism for propaganda to Latin American nations, spread via point-to-point communications similar to the telegraph. These experiences also suggested to U.S. public and private policymakers that government ownership and operations of radio facilities in Latin America raised a host of problems. This belief led the United States to adopt a postwar policy for Latin America that promoted private rather than government ownership of radio. During the years that followed, the United States was generally successful in implementing that policy. Nevertheless, the wireless era foreshadowed the establishment of radio technology as a disseminator of political propaganda and also introduced the notion of two types of coexisting owners: public and private. Thus the legacy of broadcast propaganda for Latin American audiences and of mixed systems of ownership (with inherent political implications) in Latin American nations goes back to the introduction of radio technology.

1920–1935: THE ESTABLISHMENT OF RADIO BROADCASTING

The initial growth of broadcasting for the general public—the widespread dissemination of voice, sound, and music to all who cared to listen—came not from governments or large corporations interested in radio but instead from small-scale inventors and radio amateurs.[6] When radio broadcasting first captured the imagination of the public around 1920, the broadcasting boom was not confined to the United States. Indeed, "listening in" became a simultaneous worldwide phenomenon, with Latin American listeners just as enthusiastic as any. When Latin American radio stations began regular broadcast schedules in the early 1920s, a common publicity event was the presentation of a high-quality receiving set to a nation's presidential palace. This helped to give a sort of imprimatur to the listening experience and suggested that political and social leaders were among the broadcast audience (a suggestion that indeed had some accuracy.)[7]

Latin American politicians sometimes transcended their role as listeners and became broadcasters. One of the first stations in Buenos Aires, Radio Cultura, was started in 1922 by a local politician who also had the backing of the provincial governor. As a part of its regular broadcast schedule, it occasionally broadcast debates and discussions held in the Argentine National Congress during the early 1920s.[8] Like many stations in the 1920s, Radio Cultura experienced boom-and-bust cycles. However, this station represented a growing interest in the political uses of radio by Latin American politicians, including issues of ownership and political journalism.

Radio stations also proved to be important in the revolutions and uprisings that seem to characterize Latin American politics. During the 1929–1930 rebellion in Brazil, radio stations became valuable targets for rebel capture and use, including the announcement of battlefield victories and other successes. The Brazilian government sent its navy to destroy some of these stations.[9] In 1931, the Brazilian government introduced strict censorship legislation that included "six to twelve months imprisonment for broadcasting false calls for aid, false news, or news intended to prejudice the public interest" and extended the same restrictions to the Brazilian public telephone system.[10] In Nicaragua, anti-Somoza forces operated several clandestine stations in the late 1930s. These stations operated irregular hours and were located mainly in northern Nicaragua.[11] The uses of such clandestine stations by anti-Nazi and resistance forces in Europe during World War II are well known by scholars of international communication. Interestingly, the genesis of radio broadcasting as a political component of war, revolution, and rebellion apparently had its roots in these early Latin American stations.[12]

Of perhaps greater importance than the broadcasting activities of Latin American politicians and revolutionaries (and supported by far more available evidence and documentation!) was the use by the United States of broadcasting and other forms of media culture to promote visions and values of democracy among the Latin American republics. Officials in the United States came to recognize that the language barrier coupled with relatively high levels of illiteracy could be a hindrance in using the printed word to promote political interests and ideals and therefore looked to the texts and artifacts of American popular culture as vehicles that might help disseminate democratic political values. Hollywood was seen as particularly important for this activity. Herbert Hoover, speaking to the Motion Picture Producers and Directors of America banquet for ambassadors, ministers, and representatives of Latin American republics in 1927, commented:

> Due to our separation from Latin America by the barrier of language, the penetration of intellectual ideas and social ideals between our nations [by the printed word] is a slow and tedious process. . . . The motion picture brings to this national interchange a new setting; it enlivens a new hope. . . . They speak a universal language. . . . Every picture of South American life shown to our people and every picture of North American life shown to the South American people should carry also those ideals which build for that respect and confidence which is the real guarantee of peace and progress.[13]

Hoover's florid prose exemplified the recognition that the texts and artifacts of popular culture and mass entertainment can and do carry images and messages reaffirming the values of democracy as practiced in the United States during the twentieth century—in this case, those values as perceived, portrayed, and disseminated by such institutions as the Hollywood film industry.

Throughout the latter half of the 1920s and into the 1930s, many Hollywood films and U.S. radio programs were disseminated to Latin American audiences with the implicit awareness that such programs could help foster the values of democracy as defined by the United States. The first reports of shortwave radio reception in Brazil from experimental broadcasts at KDKA Pittsburgh during 1925 led one Westinghouse engineer to remark that "the greatest propaganda agency the State Department could make use of is the Westinghouse Short Wave Relay System."[14] In addition, American advertising agencies began working extensively with stations in Latin America in the early 1930s, arguing that the dream of democracy was achieved through increasing access to goods and services and providing freedom of choice in the marketplace.[15] These campaigns often used Hollywood film stars and other entertainers popular in the United States.[16] Organizations such as the Pan American Union also provided training for Latin American journalists (including broadcast journalists) on newsgathering and newswriting techniques as practiced in the United States.[17]

In summary, the first fifteen years of radio broadcasting in Latin America saw many local politicians, revolutionaries, and governments experiment in the political uses of radio. Just as important, the complex and widespread U.S. influence in Latin American radio broadcasting was solidified, including the habits of spreading concepts of democracy through popular culture and mass entertainment. This vehicle for democratic ideals would take on increasing importance during the years surrounding World War II.

1935–1950: WAR—FROM GENESIS THROUGH AFTERMATH

By the mid-1930s, an international propaganda war was taking place over shortwave radio, with participants including the government-run broadcasting services of Germany, Great Britain, France, Italy, the USSR, Japan, and the privately run shortwave services of radio networks in the United States.[18] The Latin American audiences became a major target for all these broadcasters, with the total hours of Spanish and

Portuguese programming increasing each year before the war. The debates and issues centered on national political philosophies (and, by implication, their international expansion), including fascism, communism, and democracy, with persuasive powers exercised through a range of programming, from straightforward news reports and lectures through dramatic series and all-star spectaculars.

Researchers and scholars have provided excellent analyses of this era.[19] This chapter does not attempt to replicate the scale and scope of those studies; selected examples of the promotion of democracy by the United States to Latin America through shortwave radio are discussed in the next few paragraphs to help illustrate this facet of politics and broadcasting in the Latin American experience.

U.S. policymakers worked in conjunction with the commercial shortwave networks before the war in encouraging the growth of democracy in Latin America. This campaign included the regular broadcast of speeches delivered by Latin American political leaders and special programs that honored Independence Day celebrations in individual Latin American nations. "The Magic Key," a weekly NBC program broadcast both in the United States and over shortwave that pulled live remotes from across Latin America, regularly carried speeches from Latin American politicians and presidents. The commercial shortwave networks also allowed Latin American governments to use their facilities occasionally for their own broadcasting purposes.[20]

Another concern was countering Axis and antidemocratic propaganda from other nations. State Department representatives in Latin America regularly monitored shortwave broadcasts from other nations and paid special attention to cases in which those transmissions were rebroadcast over local Latin American stations.[21] Just as important, the U.S. government encouraged State and Commerce legations in Latin America to acquire airtime on local stations whenever possible for prodemocracy speeches and lectures by visiting Americans. A typical example was the visit of Edward Johnson, a Western Union executive, to the "Hora Do Brasil" (The Brazilian Hour) program on August 31, 1938. Johnson told listeners that Brazil and the United States needed to continue working together and to "dip our buckets in the fresh waters of Democracy and not be led into the brash, salt waters of the various European 'isms' by whatever name they may be called."[22]

The practice of pairing democracy with popular culture also continued unabated during this period. CBS executive F. A. Willis explained this philosophy at a 1938 U.S. Senate hearing when he argued that the CBS shortwave networks serving Latin America sought to

> portray American democracy to other peoples and nations [and]
> present a graphic cross section of all phases of our national life, a
> living pattern of democracy at work . . . [including] what we offer
> in the way of entertainment on the radio screen and stage . . . a
> general portrayal of American fashions, products, and produce; in
> short an unbiased, timely, and inviting tapestry of America today—
> a country which whatever its problems, still has room for Shirley
> Temple, Charlie McCarthy, and Snow White in the hearts of both
> young and old, rather than gas masks on the heads of both young
> and old.[23]

One of the most elaborate examples of this process centered on the
Latin American theatrical release of the Warner Brothers feature film
Juarez in 1939. U.S. shortwave stations serving Latin America gave extensive praise to this film, and local Latin American stations also broadcast programs in conjunction with its release and exhibition. Depicting
the story of Benito Juarez, a Mexican leader who fought against the
French invasion of Mexico in the 1860s, the democratic message was
clear to Latin American audiences. One Brazilian newspaper review argued that "the most impressive feature of this monumental production
is not the narrative of the Mexican epic . . . but the defense of democracy."[24] Paul Vanderwood rightly observes that the making of *Juarez* was
influenced by three factors: world tensions, presidential politics, and
Warner Brothers profits. The profit motive was essential, because the
implicit goals of instilling democratic virtues in Latin American republics were not only political stability but also economic progress and
increased consumption.[25]

The overall aims and goals of promoting democracy in Latin America and the Caribbean by American radio were supported by the U.S.
government during the war, and the fostering of democracy by radio
continued. Well-known U.S. citizens continued to speak on Latin American radio and extoll the virtues of democracy and hemispheric friend-
ship. Among the most prolific U.S. speakers was Orson Welles. Welles
spent much of 1942 in Brazil shooting *It's All True* (a film that was never
completed) and was a regular guest on several Brazilian radio programs, speaking in both English and Portuguese.[26] On occasion, however, certain democratic ideals were frowned upon. An interesting case
arose in 1944, when CBS was reprimanded by the Federal Bureau of Investigation for broadcasting over its shortwave networks a Puerto Rican
music group that sang songs lamenting the U.S. domination of Puerto
Rico and calling for independence. This reprimand occurred during a
period when CBS, like all networks, was under the wartime supervision

of the Coordinator of Inter-American Affairs. The FBI felt such broadcasts were inappropriate and also objected to the broadcast calling the attention of other Latin American nations to the possibility that some Puerto Ricans preferred independence to territorial status.[27] Although such incidents were unusual, they nevertheless suggested the limitations of democracy from the point of view of the United States.

Another important development in broadcasting and Latin American politics during this period was the increasing use of the microphone by Latin American political leaders as a direct conduit to their constituencies. Leaders like Juan Perón and Getúlio Vargas began to use radio to build a broadcast persona, emulating other world leaders such as Roosevelt, Churchill, Franco, Stalin, Mussolini, and Hitler. The microphone (and later the camera) became an important force for building and maintaining a base of power that partially depended upon a mediated persona. Programs such as "Hora do Brasil" became a regular part of Latin American broadcast schedules during the 1940s. When coups and rebellions such as the Argentine military revolution of 1955 toppled leaders from power, the basic mixed model of broadcast ownership and use tended to continue in many nations, despite occasional rhetoric calling either for complete government ownership or for total privatization. Latin American audiences were apparently satisfied with such a system; Perón's nationalization of television upon his return to power in the early 1970s actually undermined revenues and audience shares.[28] This mixed system seemingly continues to have a more-or-less permanent home in Latin America. Even in countries such as Chile, where television was originally established outside the government and under the control of universities, the emergence of the Pinochet dictatorship led to the development of a pattern of ownership more closely resembling the mixed system. Time will tell how this system evolves in the post-Pinochet years.[29] In a historical context, the mixed system emerges as a byproduct of politics and Latin American broadcasting that began with the dawn of radio broadcasting and had taken hold by the end of World War II.

1950–1970: THE TRANSITION FROM RADIO TO TELEVISION

The tendency for individual politicians to control the establishment of broadcast services—a tendency dating back to the days of wireless—continued with the introduction of television to Latin America after World War II. In Mexico, for example, television was established in

1947 by a presidential decree that authorized a commercial system, despite the recommendation of a government committee in favor of public broadcasting. This exemplifies what John Sinclair identifies as "the use of state power for public advantage," a phenomenon that has been (and continues to be) a trademark of Latin American broadcast development and regulation.[30] This reciprocal relationship between broadcasters and politicians has advantages for both parties and is yet another factor that contributes to the prevalence of mixed systems. For the politicians, such favors can buy access to airwaves and favorable news coverage. For the broadcasters, their cordial relationships with leading politicians help promote a sense of their own social legitimacy and value. Such relationships continue today; in 1988, the inauguration of subscription (scrambled-signal) television in Brazil came about by direct decree of President Sarney.[31]

The transition from radio to television in Latin America was marked by such reciprocal relationships and also by a whirlwind of activity from international capitalists of the broadcast and entertainment industry. To no one's surprise, the bulk of activity came from corporations centered in the United States. During a fifteen-year period (roughly 1955–1970), this range of activities included direct ownership of stations, investment in production companies, assistance in drafting legislation, massive exports of television programming, and extensive consulting services in the technical, administrative, regulatory, and programming spheres.[32] Among the consequences of this activity was the rapid growth of television stations in many Latin American major cities, thereby providing a semblance of programming choice for Latin American audiences.

Rather than restricting the activities of U.S. corporations in Latin American television, the right-wing and totalitarian regimes of the era generally seemed to tolerate, even encourage, a multitude of simultaneous activities, including competition among stations. While the tolerance of multiple stations may on the surface appear to run against the grain of the strict control associated with political totalitarianism, in practice, authoritarian regimes tended to control broadcast journalism strictly but simultaneously allow a wide range of entertainment programming (even if that programming had ambiguous tones of liberal-democratic social values and ideals). George Quester suggests that the benefits of providing cheap and plentiful entertainment to mass populations as well as the lucrative ownership of broadcast facilities outweighed the supposed risks of several loosely controlled television outlets rather than a single state system.[33]

Thus such factors as the special relationships between politicians and broadcasters, the massive activities of U.S. corporations, and the tolerant behavior of authoritarian regimes all shaped the transition from radio to television in Latin America. The Latin American audience continued to enjoy a wide range of choice among broadcast outlets and, in the form of certain American programming, occasionally received liberal-democratic political values that could be at odds with their own political experience. The continuing possibilities of political messages in entertainment programming also carried over from radio to television and held the potential for major impact on future political movements and elections.[34] The redemocratization movements of the 1980s have often carried mixed media messages, and perhaps the contradictions of media and politics that often characterize contemporary Latin American societies have their roots in this long tradition of obliquely instilling democratic values through entertainment programming.

FROM 1970: THE SOPHISTICATION OF MEDIA POLITICS

Although the direct investment of U.S. entertainment corporations retreated, and evidence suggests that total hours of U.S. programs aired declined (although those programs are still regularly aired at peak viewing hours), advertising on Latin American television into the 1980s tended to be dominated by U.S. and other transnational corporations rather than local or national advertisers.[35] This suggests that political advertising based on U.S. experiences, as well as the role of U.S. ad agencies and public relations firms as consultants, holds a large measure of potential influence over Latin American campaigns and elections during the redemocratization period. During the 1980s, the American public relations firm Sawyer Miller consulted on political campaigns and government public relations (including "image shaping") in Colombia, Ecuador, Panama, Bolivia, Peru, Argentina, and Chile. Their mixed success has not dimmed their enthusiasm for these clients.[36]

Venezuela was probably the first Latin American nation to show sophisticated use of broadcast media in the electoral process. The elections of 1973 and 1978 both saw extensive utilization of radio and television advertising.[37] Venezuela also experienced a failed coup early in 1992. The ability of the elected government to maintain access to television stations played a major role in the coup's failure; President Carlos Andres Perez serendipitously escaped an assassination attempt and, forewarned, secretly left the presidential offices to appear on Venezuelan television in a series of appeals to the people. As the coup collapsed, plotting officers destroyed copies of prerecorded videocassettes they planned to broadcast after seizing power.[38]

The attempted coup in Venezuela underscores the relative fragility of Latin American redemocratization. Yet, as the chapters in this book demonstrate, the process of redemocratization is discernible throughout the media systems of Latin America. Even in Chile, the establishment of Television Nacional in 1987 prior to the plebiscite began introducing a broader political spectrum into broadcast programming, and the inauguration of cable service in 1988 continued this process.[39] In October 1991, Chilean press and television gave extensive coverage to the local Polish emigrant community as they participated in the round of elections held in Poland.[40]

Evidence of broadcasting and redemocratization can be seen beyond the coverage of national presidential elections. Candidates for state and local offices in Argentina and Brazil have increasingly turned to broadcasting as a component of their political campaigns. In some cases, established politicians have discovered television; in other cases, television stars have discovered politics. Ramon "Palito" Ortega won election as an Argentine provincial governor by parlaying a singing career into a political career (and his singing career began when he worked as a janitor at a Buenos Aires television station in the 1960s). The Catholic church, long an influential institution in Latin American broadcasting, is using television to advocate the continuance of antiabortion legislation in several nations. Television talk show hosts and reporters have, on occasion, transformed into important conduits for the dissemination of opinions from political leaders and, in some instances, become public opinion leaders themselves. Even former and defeated leaders are on the airwaves; former Colombian president Alfonso Lopez Michelsen (1974–1978) now helps produce an evening television news program. The extensive uses of television and radio in Paraguay's 1991 local elections led one observer to remark enthusiastically that "television and radio reports are filled with mudslinging worthy of the most mature democracy."[41]

Entering the 1990s, the issues and questions regarding the relationship between broadcasting and redemocratization are complex, contradictory, and yet to be fully explored. Fortunately, the chapters in this book go far toward analyzing this process from a range of positions and viewpoints. Media culture and communications technology are currently being used in Latin American societies by different individuals and institutions with different aims and goals, resulting in a maelstrom of activity that, taken as a whole, usually cannot be fully encapsulated by the analysis of a single scholar. Many of the tensions and contradictions that emerge in analysis result from the extensive and simultaneous political uses of media and communications systems by reemerging popular organizations, trade unions, and grassroots movements concurrent with the media-based actions of large corporations. On the one hand, as Armand Mattelart has noted, Latin American popular organizations and movements in the 1970s and 1980s increasingly turned to political uses of media texts and artifacts in demanding changes in the traditional ways of making and conceiving politics.[42] These tendencies have some of their roots in the early use of radio broadcasting by rebel movements discussed earlier. A popular "community radio station" established by the Bahai church in Ecuador during the 1980s fostered local change in social, political, and cultural conditions.[43] The uses of radio broadcasting by Bolivian tin miners for local political change, dating back to the 1940s, serves as another historical precedent for this grassroots media politics.[44]

In addition to this realm of praxis exists the zone of media texts and artifacts created by and for the large corporations with major Latin American investments, pushing their political visions for Latin American societies. While the messages from popular organizations have tended, at least until recently, to be issue-specific, the large corporations have embarked upon the elaborate process of image construction and self-representation. As David Nye observed in his study of General Electric, corporate images, advertising, and public relations have historically bespoken not a single ideology but a group of ideologies, each suited to a specific audience and each therefore a part of the corporation's discourse, even if certain philosophies and messages are at times inconsistent with one another. Corporations cannot continually fulfill their self-professed multiple roles of research wizards, social benefactors, educators, and profit makers—yet they can and do consistently represent all these identities to their audiences. They provide both illusion and reality, and discerning the differences remains difficult.[45]

Thus the contemporary Latin American audience lives with dissonance in the political text of media culture, and while opposition elements are still often unheard or underrepresented, the audience nevertheless receives daily messages from an expanding matrix of speakers and presenters. Ultimately, this dissonance should not come as a surprise; indeed, it is as reliable an indicator as any of the unsteady, back-and-forth but nevertheless detectable process of redemocratization. Furthermore, this is a dialectic that emerges from the technologies of media globalization, because many of those same technologies utilized by transnational corporations also enable media minorities to find their own audiences in the media marketplace.[46] On occasion, the messages of popular organizations carry the day; at other moments, the corporations advance their agendas. In many cases, the outcome remains indeterminate.

If any lessons in media politics and redemocratization are to be learned from the rest of the world, perhaps the biggest issue at stake for the Latin American audience is the value of active, engaged viewers rather than passive receptors.[47] If the Latin American audience could avoid the political apathy and lethargy that has become all too typical among the citizens of the United States, they could demonstrate to the rest of the world that politics and media can yield a more politically active and committed citizenry. However Latin American models of media citizenship eventually develop, in their present forms they already have an impact and significance beyond their own borders. As one example, throughout the Gulf War, Iraqi diplomats stationed in South America appeared extensively on Brazilian television in attempts to sway viewers to the Iraqi perspective; the only counterpart for American views was Cable News Network.[48] The international significance of Latin American models of media citizenship also extends from times of crisis to times of peace and prosperity. For example, advertisers preparing to court the postapartheid South African consumer are abandoning a traditional "borrow-from-the-West" approach to a more distinctly "third-world" strategy. Agency consultants argue that the new South Africa's demographic, sociological, and economic models of consumers are not so much the citizens of the United States and Britain as they are of Brazil.[49] As always, the future remains indeterminate; yet this much seems certain: Throughout the range of Latin American politics and media, from producers through politicians to audiences, the issues surrounding broadcasting and redemocratization have a sense of urgency not only for the individual nations themselves but for all of modern global culture.

NOTES

1. James Schwoch, *The American Radio Industry and Its Latin American Activities, 1900–1939* (Champaign: University of Illinois Press, 1990), 11–55. Readers interested in newspaper accounts, manuscript collections, and unpublished government and corporate records regarding Latin American broadcasting prior to World War II should consult this volume. For the purposes of this chapter, I have confined my citation of such material primarily to instances where that material is not cited or otherwise discussed in my book.
2. Schwoch, *American Radio Industry*, 15–19; Victor Berthold, *The History of the Telephone and Telegraph in Brazil 1851–1921* (New York: American Telephone and Telegraph,

1922); Eugene W. Ridings, "Business Interest Groups and Communications: The Brazilian Experience in the Nineteenth Century," *Luso-Brazilian Review* 20 (Winter 1983): 241–57.

3. Schwoch, *American Radio Industry*, 35.
4. Schwoch, *American Radio Industry*, 43–46; Joseph Tulchin, *The Aftermath of War: World War I and U.S. Policy toward Latin America* (New York: New York University Press, 1971), 229–30; Susan Douglas, *Inventing American Broadcasting 1899–1922* (Baltimore: Johns Hopkins University Press, 1987), 269–76; Brady A. Hughes, "Owen D. Young and American Foreign Policy 1919–1929" (Ph.D. diss., University of Wisconsin, Madison, 1969), 72.
5. Schwoch, *American Radio Industry*, 43–46. Researchers will find discussion of German stations in Latin America scattered through State Department decimal files (Record Group 59) of this period on the internal affairs of El Salvador, Mexico, Costa Rica, Peru, Argentina, and Brazil.
6. One of the best chronicles of this development is Douglas, *Inventing American Broadcasting*.
7. For a discussion of the introduction of broadcasting in Brazil coincident with the 1922 Brazilian Centennial Exposition, see Schwoch, *American Radio Industry*, 97–99.
8. Schwoch, *American Radio Industry*, 138–40. Also see Raleigh Gibson, American Legation, Buenos Aires, to State Department, 27 June 1924, Record Group (RG) 59, Department of State, National Archives, Washington (hereafter DSNA); "Report Covering the History of Radio Sud America," 17 June 1924, file 11-14-10, Box 101, Papers of Owen D. Young, Van Hornesville, N.Y. (hereafter Young Papers.)
9. *New York Times*, 14 October 1930, 9; U.S. Ambassador to Brazil Edwin Morgan to State Department, 23 October 1930, RG 59, 832.74/86, DSNA.
10. Morgan to State Department, 30 June 1931, 832.741/3; Morgan to State Department, 13 February 1931, 832.751/1; both RG 59, DSNA.
11. Office of Naval Intelligence report, 25 January 1938, in RG 59, 817.76/7, DSNA.
12. I am unaware of any documented uses of radio broadcasting as a political component of war, revolution, and rebellion that predate the experiences in Brazil; Nicaragua is representative of the rise of global clandestine stations in the 1930s. On the origins of clandestine stations, see Lawrence C. Soley and John S. Nichols, *Clandestine Radio Broadcasting* (New York: Praeger, 1987), 303 especially. On the European experiences during World War II, see Holly Cowan Shulman, *The Voice of America: Propaganda and Democracy, 1941–1945* (Madison: University of Wisconsin Press, 1990); Derrick Sington and Arthur Weidenfeld, *The Goebbels Experiment: A Study in Nazi Propaganda* (London: John Murray, 1942). On the experiences of third-world postwar liberation movements, see Frantz Fanon, "This Is the Voice of Algeria," in Fanon, *A Study in Dying Colonialism*, (New York: Monthly Review Press, 1965).
13. Secretary of Commerce Herbert Hoover, Speech before the Motion Picture Producers and Directors of America, New York, 2 April 1927, Public Statements of Herbert Hoover #717, Herbert Hoover Presidential Library, West Branch, IA.
14. C. W. Horn, Westinghouse, to Commerce Department, 2 September 1925, forwarded to State Department, RG 59, 811.768.3, DSNA. For a discussion, see Schwoch, *American Radio Industry*, 102–3.
15. For a brilliant elaboration of these principles, see Roland Marchand, *Advertising the American Dream: Making Way for Modernity, 1920–1940* (Berkeley: University of California Press, 1985). On American agencies in Latin America during this period, see U.S. Department of Commerce, Trade Information Bulletin no. 771, "Broadcast Advertising in Latin America" (Washington: Government Printing Office, 1931); U.S. Department of Commerce, Trade Promotion Series no. 109, "Radio Markets of the World, 1930" (Washington: Government Printing Office, 1930).
16. Schwoch, *American Radio Industry*, 142–43.
17. See, for example, Pan American Union, *First Conference of Pan American Journalists* (Washington: Government Printing Office, 1926).
18. Shulman, *The Voice of America*; Roger Burlingame, *Don't Let Them Scare You: The Life*

and Times of Elmer Davis (Philadelphia: Lippincott, 1961); David Culbert, *News for Everyman: Radio and Foreign Affairs in Thirties America* (Westport: Greenwood, 1976); K.R.M. Short, ed., *Film and Radio Propaganda in World War II* (Knoxville: University of Tennessee Press, 1983); Fred Fejes, *Imperialism, Media and the Good Neighbor: New Deal Foreign Policy and U.S. Shortwave Broadcasting to Latin America* (Norwood, N.J.: Ablex, 1986); Donald R. Browne, *International Radio Broadcasting: The Limits of the Limitless Medium* (New York: Praeger, 1982); Charles Rolo, *Radio Goes to War* (New York: Putnam's, 1942); Julian Hale, *Radio Power: Propaganda and International Broadcasting* (London: Elek, 1975); Willy Boelcke, *The Secret Conferences of Dr. Goebbels: Nazi Propaganda 1939–43,* trans. Ewald Osers (London: Weidenfeld and Nicolson, 1970); Gerard Mansell, *Let Truth Be Told: Fifty Years of BBC External Broadcasts* (London: Weidenfeld and Nicolson, 1982); Lawrence Soley, *Radio Warfare: OSS and CIA Subversive Propaganda* (New York: Praeger, 1989); Daniel Headrick, *The Invisible Weapon: Telecommunications and International Politics 1851–1945* (New York: Oxford, 1991).

19. Shulman, *Voice of America;* and Headrick, *Invisible Weapon,* are recently completed studies of extraordinary quality and care. See also note 18 for several other good accounts.

20. For example, the Argentine 1938 Independence Day celebration, and a speech by Argentine president Roberto Ortiz, received extensive coverage on NBC shortwave networks. See Charles Carvejal to John Royal, NBC, 23 March 1938; B. F. McClancy to Frank Mason, NBC, 21 July 1938, both in Folder 58, Box 58, Central Office Files of the National Broadcasting Company, State Historical Society of Wisconsin, Madison (hereafter NBC Central Files). On *The Magic Key,* see Fay Gillis Wells, Oral History, Broadcast Pioneers Library, Washington. On the use of American shortwave networks by Latin American governments, see memo of Division of International Communications, State Department, 27 October 1938, RG 59, 811.76/262, DSNA; Secretary of Agriculture Henry Wallace to State Department, 6 February 1939, RG 59, 811.76/286, DSNA. Even such academic organizations as the American Historical Association, which had a Radio Committee in the 1930s, helped to prepare broadcasts, including a series called "The Bulletin of the Story behind the Headlines." See Evelyn Plummer Read, American Historical Association, to George Nessersmith, State Department, 18 May 1939, RG 59, 811.76/363, DSNA.

21. In Brazil, for example, German and Italian transmissions were rebroadcast with surprising frequency, given the fact that these nations also operated their own shortwave systems that could be received by many Latin American listeners. See R. M. Scotton to State Department, 24 January 1939, 832.76/32; William Burdett to State Department, 23 October 1939, 832.76/41; Burdett to State Department, 1 December 1939, 832.76/43; all RG 59, DSNA.

22. Text of radio address by Johnson in RG 59, 832.76/32, DSNA.

23. Memo of Division of International Communications, State Department, 27 October 1938, RG 59, 811.76/262, DSNA.

24. Burdett to State Department, 14 September 1939, RG 59, 811.4061 JUAREZ/37, DSNA.

25. Paul Vanderwood, "Introduction," in *Juarez,* ed. Paul Vanderwood, Wisconsin/Warner Brothers Screenplay Series (Madison: University of Wisconsin Press, 1983). Vanderwood's excellent analysis also makes extensive use of the State Department decimal files relevant to the exhibition of *Juarez* in Latin America.

26. These broadcasts were extremely popular with Brazilians. See Robert Stam, "Orson Welles, Brazil, and the Power of Blackness," *Persistence of Vision* 7 (1989): 93–112. After returning to the United States, Welles later campaigned for Roosevelt in 1944, even standing in for FDR in a debate with Thomas Dewey. See Michael Denning, "Towards a People's Theater: The Cultural Politics of Orson Welles," *Persistence of Vision* 7 (1989): 24–38.

27. Harry Reed, American Legation, Dominican Republic, to State Department, 16 September 1944, RG 59, 839.76/9–1644, DSNA.

28. Michael Morgan and James Shanahan, "Television and the Cultivation of Political At-

titudes in Argentina," *Journal of Communication* 41 (Winter 1991): 88–103. One of the first extensive studies of the Latin American broadcast audience is "Radio Survey in Brazil," conducted by Lloyd Free, American Social Services, 1941, in folder 22, Box 111, NBC Central Files. Also see Schwoch, *American Radio Industry,* 97–106.

29. Valerio Fuenzalida, "Television in Chile: A History of Experiment and Reform," *Journal of Communication* 38 (Spring 1988), 49–58.

30. John Sinclair, "Dependent Development and Broadcasting: The Mexican Formula," *Media Culture and Society* 8 (1986): 89. Also see Sinclair's "Neither West nor Third World: The Mexican Television Industry within the NWICO Debate," *Media Culture and Society* 12 (1990): 343–60.

31. "Brazil Prez Authorizes Subscription Television," *Variety,* 23 March 1988, 64.

32. Herbert Schiller, *Mass Communications and American Empire* (Boston: Beacon, 1969), 89–101; Rick Maxwell, "Early U.S. Investments in South American Television," presentation to University of Wisconsin Department of Communication Arts Graduate Colloquium, Madison, Fall 1989. For a contemporary summary of global activities by the American entertainment industry, see John Huey, "America's Hottest Export: Pop Culture," *Fortune,* 31 December 1990, 50–60.

33. George Quester, *The International Politics of Television* (Lexington: D. C. Heath, 1990), 51–52.

34. Venicio de Lima argues that the 1988 Brazilian presidential campaign and its "scenario of representation" cannot be fully understood without including an assessment of the Brazilian *telenovelas* of the period. De Lima, "Media and Democracy: The Construction of a Brazilian President," Paper presented to the International Communications Association, Chicago, April 1991.

35. Carlos Eduardo Lins da Silva, "Transnational Communication and Brazilian Culture," in *Communication and Latin American Society: Trends in Critical Research, 1960–1985,* ed. Rita Atwood and Emile McAnany (Madison: University of Wisconsin Press, 1986), 89–111.

36. Barry Siegel, "Spin Doctors to the World," *Los Angeles Times Magazine,* 24 November 1991, 18+.

37. John D. Martz and Enrique Baloyra, *Electoral Mobilization and Public Opinion: The Venezuelan Campaign of 1973* (Chapel Hill: University of North Carolina Press, 1976); Robert E. O'Connor, "The Media and the Campaign," in *Venezuela at the Polls: The National Elections of 1978,* ed. Howard R. Penniman (Washington: American Enterprise Institute, 1980), 171–90.

38. My discussion of television and the Venezuelan coup stems from the following reports: *Washington Post,* 11 February 1992, sec. A, 11; *New York Times,* 7 February 1992, sec. A, 3; *New York Times,* 9 February 1992, sec. 4, 3; *New York Times,* 6 February 1992, sec. A, 3; *New York Times,* 5 February 1992, sec. A, 10.

39. "As Chile Plebiscite Looms, Government Takes Cautious TV Stance," *Variety,* 23 March 1988, 45+.

40. "Turnout in Voting Centres abroad Higher than Expected," PAP Polish Press Agency News Wire, 28 October 1991.

41. Quoted from *The Economist,* 18 May 1991, 76 (U.K. edition.) This paragraph also draws upon the following: Julia Michaels, "Era of Political Responsibility Takes Hold in Latin America," *Christian Science Monitor,* 18 February 1992, world sec., 1; *The Economist,* 7 December 1991, 18; "Former Pop Singer Becomes Governor of Argentine Province," Reuters Wire Service, 29 October 1991, AM cycle; *The Economist,* 8 December 1990, 94 (U.K. edition); *Montreal Gazette,* 1 September 1991, sec. B, 5; *New York Times,* 16 November 1990, sec. A, 9; *Toronto Star,* 25 July 1991, sec. A, 17.

42. Armand Mattelart, *Transnationals and the Third World: The Struggle for Culture* (South Hadley: Bergin and Garvey, 1983), 151.

43. Kurt Hein, "Community Participation in Radio for Rural Development: Radio Bahai Otavalo" (Ph.D. diss., Northwestern University, 1985).

44. Alan O'Connor, "The Miners' Radio Stations in Bolivia: A Culture of Resistance," *Journal of Communication* 40 (Winter 1990): 102–10.

45. David Nye, *Image Worlds: Corporate Identities at General Electric* (Cambridge: Cambridge University Press, 1985), 148–56.
46. Anthony Smith, "Media Globalism in the Age of Consumer Sovereignty," *Gannett Center Journal* 4 (Fall 1990): 1–16.
47. For a discussion of active viewership and its political implications, see James Schwoch, Mimi White, and Susan Reilly, *Media Knowledge: Readings in Popular Culture, Pedagogy, and Critical Citizenship* (Albany: State University of New York Press, 1992); for an analysis centering on the problematic role of the news media, see Robert M. Entman, *Democracy without Citizens: Media and the Decay of American Politics* (New York: Oxford University Press, 1989).
48. *New York Times,* 4 February 1991, sec. A, 10.
49. Judith D. Schwartz, "South African Advertisers Sell the Future," *San Francisco Chronicle,* 10 November 1991, 10/Z1.

4

The Argentine Case: Television in the 1989 Presidential Campaign

Enrique Zuleta-Puceiro

The 1989 presidential election in Argentina was one of the most important events in Latin America's current redemocratization. It was the first transition in sixty years from one civilian president to another, based on a free and honest election, following the electoral rules stipulated in the 1853 Constitution. Moreover, it was the first transition between elected presidents belonging to opposing political parties since the advent of universal suffrage in Argentina.

This exceptional event had other important features. First, it represented a crucial test for the party system dominated by the Radical Civic Union (Unión Cívica Radical, or UCR) and the Justicialista Party (Partido Justicialista, or PJ), the two leading parties of modern-day Argentina. There was also a collection of provincial parties supporting the UCR presidential candidate—the Independent Federalist Confederation (CFI) and a liberal-conservative alliance influential in some areas—a coalition dominated by the Union of the Democratic Center (UCD). Although less important in voting strength, the United Left (IU) presented an electoral front made up largely of the Communist Party (PC) and the Trotskyist Movement toward Socialism (MAS). Between 1983 and 1989, all these political forces experienced a far-reaching generational, organizational, ideological, and strategic transformation. The 1989 elections therefore represented the first open competition among political parties that were undergoing a process of renewal while also preserving traditional features.

The UCR and PJ conducted a long, hard-fought electoral campaign. It began with the 1987 elections when the PJ obtained control of the Senate and most of the provincial governments and acquired veto power in the Chamber of Deputies. From the standpoint of the presidential campaign, those elections were the starting point for a bitter political struggle, waged in the midst of a grave economic and political crisis. The Peronistas' 1987 triumph made reconciliation impossible. It also thwarted any effective management of the economic emergency, stopped progress toward the structural reforms begun with the 1985 stabilization plan (the Plan Austral), and focused political attention on the upcoming election.

In the 1989 campaign, the three major parties made extensive use of the modern campaign techniques—strategic planning, public opinion polls, motivational research, mass media, direct and indirect advertising, and so forth. As in 1987, radio and television were used on a massive scale, with negative advertising playing an important role. Recent experience in the United States and Ecuador had offered the example of personalized attacks and rapid reply to mutual accusations. This cue was picked up in Argentina and gave the presidential campaign a tone of violence uncharacteristic of traditional Argentine politics. This type of campaign had been employed effectively by Antonio Cafiero (PJ) against Juan M. Casella (UCR) in the race for governor of the province of Buenos Aires in 1987, while in the presidential elections of 1989 it was the Radicals who first used violent personal attacks against the Peronist candidate.

Television was a central weapon in the campaign, mainly in defining the new terms of political confrontation. Although there are no systematic studies on the role of television in the shaping of Argentine political attitudes, its ability to influence opinion is undeniable. As in the rest of the world, no other medium enjoys the same presence in the daily life of the general public. Although television in Argentina is neither an exclusive concession nor dominated by one network (as in many countries of Latin America, especially Brazil and Mexico), it has assumed a privileged role in shaping the political spectacle—in what M. Edelman calls the "construction and uses" of major social problems, political issues, and even political leaders themselves.[1] Television functions above all as a large stage on which the friend-enemy relationship, so essential to the politics, is defined and styles of electoral competition are determined. In the case of Argentina, television enjoys less autonomy than in most democratic countries because it depends heavily on other media—radio and the press—for disseminating information. But its role as a creator of powerful myths, fictions, and hearsay can hardly be questioned.

The role of television in the 1989 presidential campaign differs from the role it has played in much of the rest of Latin America, especially Brazil. None of the basic campaign events depended on television as their exclusive medium, even though it was an indispensable tool for direct and repeated coverage of public ceremonies and parades.

In Argentina, none of the candidates turned television into their principal campaign tool. Television was used in a massive, planned, and technically sophisticated manner, but always to support, replicate, and consolidate styles and discourse defined in campaign settings more familiar to the candidates—grandiose public ceremonies and press coverage for Angeloz (UCR) and the marches around the perimeters of large cities for Menem (PJ). Only Alsogaray (UCD) could focus on the nonadvertising use of television, because his status as a specialist in economic affairs gave him permanent access to the major television news programs.

Let us now turn to an analysis of the campaign. Any such study as this faces major difficulties. First, no systematic studies are available for Argentina on the relationship between television, or even mass media, and political behavior. The information available is fragmentary or general, coming from public opinion surveys on general topics, personal orientation, consumption, and so on, or else from strictly political surveys. This type of research typically analyzes habits in the consumption of information—for example, reading newspapers, listening to the radio, and watching television—and uses the results, directly or indirectly, to prepare cross-tabulation indexes. Additionally, commercial public opinion studies based on research on levels of exposure to the media are produced and marketed for subscribers.[2] Another existing source of information is the body of studies measuring television audiences,[3] even though the two principal systems are limited to the identification of audiences and the development of indexes, with no reference to the impact of the media on the shaping of attitudes.[4]

There are other sources as well, to which access, however, is quite difficult. These are the basic strategic surveys for the election campaigns, usually prepared within the innermost confines of the campaign teams. They remain confidential during the campaigns and rarely become known beyond the inner campaign management and circle of media strategists. In the case of both the UCR and the PJ, such studies were few and began, in the case of the UCR, in the 1985 campaign and in the case of the PJ, in the 1987 campaign.[5] The reasons for this lack of base studies are many and varied. For one thing, they are costly and not considered a priority by the candidates, who are interested mainly in studies to determine the voting intentions of the public and to define the campaign themes and approach. In addition, media strategy is entrusted largely to advertising agencies, to whom general opinion polls are practically unknown. Their preference is for motivational research by means of focus groups, content analysis, or in-depth interviews. Even though media strategists from the political parties began to take the initiative during the 1989 campaign, the final decision almost always lay with the advertising agencies, for which developmental research plays a secondary role. This, in turn, helps explain the committing of gross strategic errors, which were otherwise inexplicable given the public opinion trends.

These gaps in our knowledge can be filled only by the kind of systematic and in-depth research we do not yet have—hence the importance of the Wilson Center conference. The conference participants were asked to analyze the structure and organization of the broadcast media, the access of the political parties to them, and their use for campaign purposes. This approach differs from an analysis of the impact of broadcast media on the shaping of attitudes, which requires the use of data to which access is difficult although not impossible. The viewpoint suggested for the conference, however, implies a previous step, which is to describe the generic relationships between the media and politics, a topic on which almost no comparative information is available. Once we have obtained such information, studies of the media's impact on electoral behavior will have a more solid and consistent foundation.

The difference between these approaches is important. We are dealing with different, although complementary, perspectives, which are frequently confused in the few available studies. It is one thing to study the structure, function, or political economy of the mass media in society, and its impact on politics, but it is quite another to research the concrete impact of radio and television messages on the electorate during a campaign. The objectives, methods, and sources of each type of investigation are different, and even though they may stem from the same types of concerns, they must be carried out separately.

This chapter is oriented toward the first of these approaches. Its purpose is, as requested for the conference, first to indicate some general characteristics of the structure and significance of the broadcast media in Argentina, especially television. A second purpose is to point out noteworthy examples of the use of media in the presidential campaign. Finally, it will suggest some hypotheses that might guide future research into the effects of mass media on electoral contests and, consequently, their role in the democratic transition.

MEDIA POLICY IN THE TRANSITION YEARS

The role of broadcast media is a central theme in any agenda for democratic transition. Even in the best-consolidated democracies, this role has no definitive models or exclusive alternatives. Political and cultural change, permanent technological innovation, and the transformation of society itself turn the debate on mass media into a pit of quicksand where neither government parties nor opposition parties can claim "the" correct position. In most countries, the legal regulations governing the broadcast media have been the subject of consensus policies intended to achieve solid support for public decisions. Where this has not been possible, instability appears to be the rule, and solutions are always partial and provisional. Proof of this can be found in the fact that countries such as Spain and Italy have long had a history of unstable regulation, with clear legal regulations not established until the mid-1980s, and with some important matters still unresolved. We are dealing, in short, with one of the most decisive factors in the consolidation of a modern democracy, and the solutions are not easy.[6]

Argentina is no exception to this rule. The broadcast media were among the most critical components in the legacy from the military era. Between 1981 and 1983, the military government privatized, in rapid and highly questionable fashion, many of the radio and television stations still under state control after the wave of nationalization by the Peronist government in 1973. This process was hindered by legal obstacles in the case of the four most important television channels, located in the federal district and greater Buenos Aires (which includes the nineteen municipalities surrounding the federal district). Despite criticism from the political parties, the government privatized twenty-four radio and television stations and granted nineteen new licenses to operate in areas that had not previously been assigned.[7] The serious irregularities in the licensing process led, in February 1984, to the establishment of a presidential commission to investigate that process and recommend eventual measures for reviewing or confirming each case.[8] After three months of work, the commission recommended the revocation of twelve licenses and confirmation of the rest.[9] Argentine legislation is extremely rigorous in its requirements for invalidating administrative acts, and the commission felt, even in the presence of irregularities, that it could only revoke a portion of the licenses.

This all occurred at a moment of vacillation in government policy. On the one hand, there was political pressure to revert to previous policy. On the other hand, it was necessary to create a climate of legal and economic security to facilitate investment and the urgently needed modernization of the mass media. In addition, a general revocation of licenses was seen as a dangerous governmental instrument that jeopardized the freedom of expression promised by the Alfonsín administration. These considerations, together with strong pressure from business and labor throughout the Radical government, led to an uneasy equilibrium. Only one of the contested licenses was revoked. When the rest were left without explicit confirmation, the previous decisions were, for all practical purposes, ratified.

During the democratic period, the government has continued to make use of the legislative legacy from the military era, centered on Law No. 22,285 of 1980 and its implementing regulations issued pursuant to Decree 286/81. This law has been primarily enforced in its functional aspects, while its organic portions, of a purely authoritarian nature, were in fact suspended. One provision, for example, still in force although no longer applied, created the Federal Broadcasting Committee (COMFER) to oversee the content of radio and television broadcasts. The committee is made up of representatives from the three military forces as well as from the private associations of radio and television broadcasting companies: a totally authoritarian and corporatist formula, impossible to apply in a democratic government. This situation led to only a partial enforcement of the law, with serious difficulties for the consolidation of a modern system of broadcast media.

The context surrounding government policy on radio and television was thus one of permanent conflict—of values, of alternative models of public policy, and of public and private interests, all compounded by the grave economic crisis battering communications enterprises. Consensus policies among the major political forces were impossible. Both Radicals and Peronistas assumed positions on the basis of contradictory interests and showed more interest in maintaining the status quo than in the reform and modernization of the system. The relative weakness of the parties vis-à-vis the interest groups led to a policy of détente, which seriously disturbed and blocked competition and innovation.

Deep down, the private sector distrusted the democratic government's handling of the issue every step of the way. They feared that new owners would be introduced—groups linked to the parties on the basis of open bids. Added to this distrust was pressure from government sectors interested, whether on the basis of principle or political opportunity, in keeping the broadcast media under state control. Finally, certain private television companies appeared to prefer the absence of competition stemming from the inefficient public management of government television channels.

This collection of interests largely explains the failure to reform and privatize. The lack of investment, the decline of the advertising market, and the general economic crisis led the radio and television sector into the most serious crisis in its history. Only after the Peronist victory, when conditions became more favorable, were those pressure groups most influential during the Radical era able to obtain rapid approval for licenses to operate the two principal government television channels in the area of the federal capital—channels 11 and 13. The deci- sion was criticized by those not benefiting from the action, but public opinion, overwhelmed by the inadequacies of the government- controlled mass media and longing for swift privatization, accepted it.

This final stage of privatization, pursuant to military legislation still in force, occurred on the basis of a summary proceeding that lacked any legal or institutional guarantees. During this process, the Peronist ad- ministration responded to a strong public demand for privatization and looked to the support of the groups that benefited: the largest newspa- per of Argentina, firms controlled by some of the largest TV station owners from the country's interior, one of the largest newspaper pub- lishers, and the country's first private university. All these sectors had, during Alfonsín's government, preferred to obstruct privatization pro- moted by a government they did not trust because of the distance it kept from corporate interests. With the advent of the new administra- tion, they felt the time had come for immediate privatization of the two most important television channels, before the new government adopted any procedures that might jeopardize privatization.

Unlike their counterparts in Brazil, Argentine politicians lack their own media or close ties to media or print publishers. This situation pre- vails, not because they prefer it, but because business, accustomed to perennial political instability, prefers to be close to the seat of power and to the various competing economic sectors, avoiding permanent commitments and waiting for more favorable times. In fact, the broad- cast media are more powerful than the political parties, and the virtual absence of legislation governing communications and public enforce- ment agencies is a clear sign of that power. In a hyperregulated coun- try, the mass media are virtually unregulated. Indeed, no norms are specifically designed to protect freedom of expression or the right to information. Nor do Argentines enjoy the right of protest or the most elementary norms for the protection of privacy. Government regulation of the media is almost nonexistent and is limited to a very superficial formal oversight of the economic functioning of individual enterprises (based exclusively on revenue concerns, given that COMFER's sole source of income is a tax levied on broadcasting stations and calculated on the basis of advertising billings). For the private sector, the best law is no law at all. The political parties and democratic institutions are too weak to alter this state of affairs, and only a few measures enacted by ju- dicial authorities have created the kind of institutions that enjoy legiti- macy in other democratic countries.

Although there have been few positive achievements, the debate has been profound and many solutions have been attempted. From 1983 to

1989, no less than fourteen draft radio and television laws were submitted to Congress. Four were drafted within the executive branch and the rest by lawmakers from political parties, principally the Radicals and Peronists. In addition, at least three draft laws have been prepared by private associations, and a number of provisional drafts have been prepared by experts or commissions established to promote dialogue between the two principal political parties.[10]

The principal differences among the proposals lie in areas such as the law enforcement environment (Argentina is a federal country, and it is arguable whether legislative competency is federal- or state-based), the type of services to be regulated by law, the control mechanisms, the possible existence of national networks (nonexistent in Argentina, unlike Brazil or the United States), the issuing of multiple licenses to a single individual or multiple ownership of different types of media, and the ultimate configuration of the government radio and television system. Even so, the similarities have been more important than the differences, and the failure to reach legislative resolutions is due solely to the existence of political and economic sectorial pressures. One symptom of the immaturity of Argentina's nascent democracy is the lack of definitive public policy on the broadcast media. This is perhaps not surprising. Spain, for example, enacted its first law in this field ten years after it began its dramatic transition. Italy has yet to enact uniform legislation in this area, and the resulting institutional chaos is even greater than in Argentina.

THE STRUCTURE OF THE TELEVISION INDUSTRY

Argentina's electronic media have traditionally been organized as a mixed system, composed of private stations coexisting with a government sector whose role has varied in importance with each political era. During the first era of Peronist government (1945–1955), government control was virtually absolute; there was one government network and three private radio networks operating under strict government supervision. In 1958, seventeen radio stations were privatized, eight were licensed to universities, and thirty-three remained under government control. In that same year, the first private television channels were licensed in Buenos Aires—channels 9, 11, and 13. It was then that the mixed system began, and subsequently the mix has been subjected to constant modification. In 1967, for example, the military government created a structure that, though never applied, was later to constitute the basis for the current law of 1980. It consisted of an official network coexisting with a private network made up of the rest of the commercial radio stations. The decision was also made to privatize the remaining state-controlled commercial radio stations—together with a network of noncommercial radio stations in the provinces—known as the Servicio Oficial de Radiodifusión (SOR), or Official Broadcasting Service.

As for television, the Buenos Aires channels began to come under private-sector management in 1958, with a hiatus occurring in 1973 as a result of the government intervention decreed by the Peronist administration. The process of issuing private operating licenses in the major provincial cities of the interior began in 1963.

Thus, by the time of the 1989 presidential campaign, Argentina had a television system based on a government channel with national coverage (channel 7 ATC—Argentina Televisora Color); three government channels in the federal capital area in the process of being privatized (channels 9, 11, and 2), the first two of which had already been privatized by the new government administration; and one private channel (channel 9) licensed by the Radical government. There were also thirty-four channels broadcasting in the interior of the country, two of which were still operating under government intervention—La Plata and Formosa—with the rest under private administration. These channels account for the twenty-seven areas of geographic coverage (fig. 4.1), reaching a highly varying percentage of homes (table 4.1).

The system of over-the-air television is complemented by the existence of cable TV stations. The fact that licenses for cable TV operations are not granted on the basis of public bid procedures but rather by direct decision of the executive branch has spawned considerable growth in the cable industry. Stations of this type exist in all the major and intermediate cities of the country, broadcasting simultaneously over different channels. At the time of the presidential elections, there were two cable TV stations in the federal capital area, each broadcasting over more than four channels. In the rest of the provincial capitals and major cities, the situation was basically the same.

There is practically no concentration in the ownership of these media. Current Argentine legislation does not allow the existence of national networks, and the issuance of multiple licenses is possible only in very limited cases, normally in the interim, where financially troubled stations can be acquired by other licensees. Attempts by national businesses to expand into the interior have met with the previously mentioned legal difficulties.

This situation has, however, produced high concentration in program production. The channels operating in the capital city are also

TELEVISION

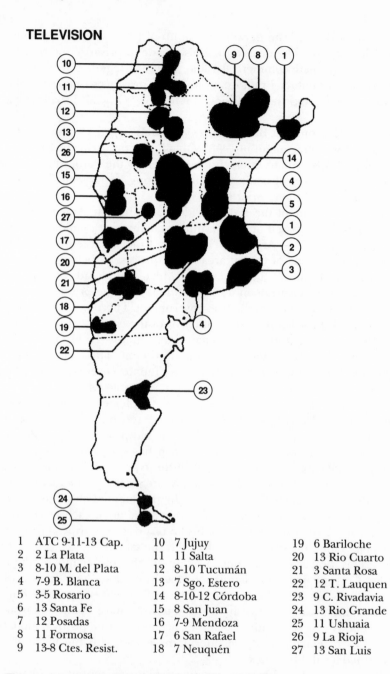

1	ATC 9-11-13 Cap.	10	7 Jujuy	19	6 Bariloche
2	2 La Plata	11	11 Salta	20	13 Rio Cuarto
3	8-10 M. del Plata	12	8-10 Tucumán	21	3 Santa Rosa
4	7-9 B. Blanca	13	7 Sgo. Estero	22	12 T. Lauquen
5	3-5 Rosario	14	8-10-12 Córdoba	23	9 C. Rivadavia
6	13 Santa Fe	15	8 San Juan	24	13 Rio Grande
7	12 Posadas	16	7-9 Mendoza	25	11 Ushuaia
8	11 Formosa	17	6 San Rafael	26	9 La Rioja
9	13-8 Ctes. Resist.	18	7 Neuquén	27	13 San Luis

Figure 4.1 Coverage of TV Channels in Argentina
SOURCE: J. Noguer, *Radiodifusion en la Argentina* (Buenos Aires: Ed. Bien Comun, 1985), p. 481.

Table 4.1
TV AREA COVERAGE

Area of Transmission	Number of Homes Reached	% of the National Total
Capital y G.B.A.	3112.1	43.8%
Mar del Plata	240.5	3.4
Bahía Blanca	150.6	2.1
Junin	16.0	0.2
Trenque Lauquen	33.0	0.5
Rosario	444.4	6.3
Santa Fe/Paraná	223.6	3.1
Córdoba	499.3	7.0
Río IV	51.9	0.7
Mendoza	221.4	3.1
San Juan	82.9	1.2
San Rafael	29.5	0.4
Tucumán	155.3	2.2
Salta	119.8	1.7
Stgo. del Estero	60.5	0.9
Jujuy	59.4	0.8
La Rioja	34.6	0.5
Ctes./Resistencia	166.1	2.3
Posadas	112.7	1.6
Formosa	33.1	0.5
Neuquén	68.3	1.0
Comodoro Rivadavia	29.2	0.4
Santa Rosa	41.0	0.6
	5985.2	84.3

Distribution Percentage	
Capital and Greater Buenos Aires	52%
Interior	48

SOURCE: H. Lauzan, et al., *La Estrategia de Medios* (Buenos Aires: n.p., 1989), p. 221.

the major producers, while those located in the interior do minimal programming and generally depend on material purchased from national production corporations or the channels in the federal capital area. With regard to channels that were until recently under government administration (channels 11 and 13) and the government channel (channel 7 ATC), the frequent coproduction with private producers only increases the existing concentration in production and programming, although this process does not have any specific political consequences.

As for government-controlled media, both the official channel and channels 11, 13, and 2 are on the same footing as the private channels, since they sell advertising in competition with private channels. They are therefore also subject to market requirements, depend on audience surveys, and suffer from the same economic crisis affecting the entire television industry. Official financial support has traditionally been substantial and hence creates conditions for political pressure. Indeed, although one now sees much evidence of a government line of interpretation, once channels 11 and 13 are privatized, no major changes are foreseen in television. As in most countries, governments have the advantage of defining much of the agenda on matters of public interest. The data provided in this chapter demonstrate that partisanship during the campaign was minimal, with no significant imbalances observed. This is not surprising; we are dealing with large firms with hundreds of workers and active labor committees, where the ability to manipulate decisions is limited.

From the institutional perspective, the television system reflects relative political neutrality. This is explicable, given that most of the laws in Argentina—and especially Law No. 22,285 currently in force—have been enacted by military governments. Article 21 provides that "the official radio broadcasting stations may not broadcast politically partisan programs or messages." In fact, this norm has been followed even by private radio stations, which are generally interested in remaining politically neutral, especially in preelection periods. In practice, this norm has implied, at least through 1989, the absence of political advertising prior to a period beginning sixty days before the elections. This period is approximately the same as that defined by the electoral laws granting free television time, financed by the Ministry of the Interior. During the preelection periods, political topics are dealt with on news programs or political opinion programs. During the campaign periods, the parties are provided with free time granted by the Permanent Party Fund (Fondo Partidario Permanente) administered by the Ministry of the Interior,[11] or they contract for political advertising through normal commercial means on public or private channels.

With the consolidation of democracy, politics has begun to lose the drama it assumed in the 1985 election. In the 1989 presidential campaign, the originally rigid legal criteria were becoming more flexible, a process begun in the 1987 elections when access to government media became more equal and private broadcasting adapted more evenhanded policies. Private broadcasters provided significant free advertising to the parties, covered major events and rallies, broadcast special programs on the candidates, and provided broad campaign coverage. Channel 9 in Buenos Aires even began an editorial commentary on the major candidates during peak viewing times. This practice has continued after the elections.

Here Argentina differs significantly from Mexico, Brazil, and Chile, where the basic rule favors a high concentration of ownership or decision-making power in broadcasting. In Argentina, the mixed system, combined with a tradition of nonpartisan press and radio, has precluded all partisan broadcasting in television. Although the campaign committees generally establish agreements with private media, these agreements do not favor one party but concern the coordination of operational aspects or the achievement of significant economic advantages. These agreements have rarely created situations of inequality among competing parties or candidates.

Arbitrariness does occur, but only in monopolistic or quasi-monopolistic situations in cities of the interior, where there are only relay stations controlled by the provincial governments. Even so, this manipulation rarely reaches the news management, because these stations depend on programs purchased in Buenos Aires. The major news programs in the capital are generally balanced. Manipulation is therefore to be found only in the provincial programs, in the inequitable coverage of political events, in the breaking of the conventional rules on coverage of public debates, and in the blocking of information or even advertising from adversaries. In general, these abuses have worked against those who practice them and have rendered their influence insignificant, at least in the 1989 presidential election.

It is, at present, unthinkable that an Argentine candidate could be "created" primarily by television exposure. Television plays a central, but limited, role in Argentine daily life. Experience proves that politicians who attempt to use television beyond very narrow limitations find it working against them. The principal objective has become, not how to attain greater access to television, but rather how to defend oneself against its effects and how to achieve a calculated and limited use of the medium. Cafiero (PJ) in 1987 and Menem (PJ) in 1989 triumphed over candidates who based their strategies on television. Much of their opponents' defeat must be attributed to a mistaken use of this medium, influenced by U.S. campaign practices, which cannot be easily applied in Argentina or in the rest of Latin America. That lesson was demonstrated in the case of Sánchez de Losada in Bolivia and that of Mario Vargas Llosa, who was defeated in Peru in 1989, both of whom had employed similar advertising campaigns by the same external consultants.

As this experience shows, using television to manipulate images and candidates depends more on the existence of monopolies or oligopolies in television ownership and management than on the influence of the medium itself in the daily life of the public. In Argentina, the pluralism resulting from the fragmented media ownership and management, the lack of national networks, and the absence of partisan commitments have given television an important, though not a decisive, role in elections. It has had a greater effect on the organization of the parties and the campaigns and on the identity and discourse of the candidates themselves than on the behavior of the electorate.

THE PRESIDENTIAL CAMPAIGN OF 1989

The 1989 presidential campaign paired off two candidates who were unusual in the patterns of their political emergence. Both Menem (PJ) and Angeloz (UCR) had prevailed over their respective party apparatuses. In July 1988, Menem unexpectedly defeated Antonio Cafiero, the leading figure of the Peronist renovation and principal architect of the 1987 electoral comeback and the campaign progress achieved in 1988. Both traditional Peronism—with its provincial and labor bases—and renovational Peronism—with its political base in the large urban areas—were hostile to him. Angeloz, on the other hand, represented a very different political position from that of then-president Raúl Alfonsín, himself a renovator of Radicalism and chief architect of the electoral defeat of Peronism in the 1983 congressional elections and his own triumphant election as president in 1985.

Both candidates started in disadvantageous situations, and both lacked not only party support but also access to funding, to their parties' more experienced campaign advisors, and to the mass media, especially television. Both were provincial governors, and both received most of their support from personal and family networks and small, isolated party circles in the provinces. In a second circle were located, for both men, individuals who had either been excluded from active party life or negatively affected by the politics or ideological style of Cafiero or Alfonsín.

The candidacies of both Menem and Angeloz sprang more from society than from their respective political parties. Both candidates were governors, although the level of socioeconomic development, resources, and possibilities for success of their provinces were diametrically opposed. They represented different styles of administration, leadership, and political projection, which in turn implied completely different strategies for using television.

Menem and Angeloz both had campaign advisory teams consisting largely of nonparty or independent individuals assisted by external consultants. Neither felt indebted to his party or even to any particular sector. Both based their campaigns on strategic and practical considerations, paying almost no attention to party, ideological, or doctrinal issues. In this respect, the 1989 Argentine campaign resembled U.S.

campaigns, more in the powerful skills and abilities of the candidates than in ideological debates or political styles prevailing in the country.

The General Context

The 1989 election campaign was not carried out in a vacuum. The context included the serious economic situation, and, going back as far as the 1987 elections, the political crisis, the stagnation of parliamentary activity, and the confrontation between the political parties. All these factors made the electoral struggle a "crucial election."

The sense of drama was further heightened by Argentine society's perception of the crisis. Data available at the time pointed to a high and constantly rising level of concern and anguish, of rejection of government economic policy, and of increased pessimism about the possibility of an immediate solution. The general awareness of the crisis transcended party lines. Opinion surveys at the time showed that no party or candidate was able to win an advantage. No candidate was able to capture the elusive quality of hope. No matter who came out on top in the elections, the voter saw no way out. An opportunity was thus created for a communication strategy aimed at presenting promises without proposals, for making rhetorical gestures and projecting personal images. It was a context that gave television a privileged place among the mass media.

Another key contextual factor was the general pessimism about the capacity to manage the economic crisis. Sixty-two percent of the national population thought two months before the election that current economic policy had made things worse. A smaller proportion, 43.5 percent, felt that policy had no other objective than to create a favorable climate for Angeloz, the incumbent government party's candidate, and that it would be successful (although it was not).

Negative attitudes toward government economic policy were based largely on the economic team's lack of credibility. Lending support to this skepticism was the fact that the latest economic stabilization program (Plan Primavera), similar to the 1985 Austral Plan, was technically ill-conceived and that the government had failed to take action on the substantial reforms the country demanded. In general, the public rejected noneconomic explanations for Argentina's economic plight, such as the energy crisis, the military crisis, the recurrence of political violence, or the lack of support from abroad. Instead, critics fixed on government economic policy, with 62 percent feeling the solution lay in a complete change of administration and program.

The areas reflecting this mass rejection of economic policy were those related to peoples' daily economic experience: prices, the dollar exchange rate, unemployment, inflation, social unrest. These were the cornerstones of public concern and were driven home daily through the mass media, with television playing a key role, particularly among the lower-income sectors. Thus, within the political campaigns and their television strategies, daily economic news itself assumed a central role shaping political attitudes. Even if Menem had suspended his campaign—as, in fact, he did in response to Angeloz's violently negative campaign (in order to neutralize the negative effect of the weakness of his own platform)—or if Angeloz had tried even harder to distance himself from the government, or if he had stepped up his attacks on Menem, the depressing images of the crisis would have continued with their own impact. Pessimism overtook even partisan loyalties, as firm party supporters on both sides proved unable to convince their constituencies that they had the ability to overcome the crisis.

The Crisis of Party Identification

Party identification was thus weakened and the resulting dominance of the candidates' personal image was increased, giving television the opportunity to play a major role. Two months before the election, 53.2 percent of the national electorate declared itself politically independent, and it was even higher in the capital (55.2 percent), Mendoza (59.5 percent), and Santa Fe (72.1 percent). Córdoba and the province of Buenos Aires showed average levels of independence, while in the rest of the country party identification increased: 46.7 percent considered themselves to be independent and 47.6 percent as affiliated with some political party as opposed to 44.4 percent nationally (table 4.2).

This situation reinforced a long-term trend in Argentine society, in which the expansion of the communications media, especially television, had played a major role. Nor was it new for political independence to be affirmed among women (50.4 percent), youth (56.4 percent), the middle income (54.3 percent) and high income (59.9 percent) sectors, and the inhabitants of the major cities (57.1 percent) (table 4.2). Even more important was a predominance of those who declared a "rational" independence, an intention to vote for the best candidate. Accordingly, there was reduced independence based on the lack of interest in politics (21.9 percent), a feeling of having been deceived by the political parties (21.8 percent), the inability to distinguish between the political parties (6.6 percent), or the feeling of not being represented by any party (7.9 percent). It is important to note that the last-mentioned sentiment increased among youth, middle-income sectors, and residents of the metropolitan areas (table 4.3).

This electoral context meant that the transmission of information

Table 4.2
POLITICAL IDENTIFICATION AND POLITICAL INDEPENDENCE

Total		Simpatizant	Independent	Don't Know/ No Reply
Sex	Male	44.4	53.2	2.4
	Female	47.5	50.4	2.1
Age	17–29	41.1	55.9	2.7
	30–49	41.1	56.4	2.4
	50–64	43.2	49.9	1.9
	65 and older	50.9	46.5	2.6
Socioeconomic	Low	45.8	51.3	2.9
Level	Medium	43.8	54.3	1.9
	High	39.1	59.9	1.0
Vote Intention	UCR	52.7	45.2	2.2
	PJ	64.8	34.0	1.1
	Alianza de Centro	39.9	59.4	0.7
	Others	33.8	62.9	3.3
	Undecided	9.6	86.8	3.6

SOURCE: E. Zuleta and Equas Cons, *Estudio Preelectoral en el Area de Capital Federal y GBA* (March 1989).

Table 4.3
GENERAL TYPOLOGY OF INDEPENDENTS

		Sex		Age				Socioeconomic Level		
	Total	Male	Female	17–29	30–49	50–64	65+	High	Medium	Low
Rational	39.3	44.0	35.3	38.3	43.1	40.1	27.2	32.3	41.1	67.6
Disenchanted	36.3	38.0	34.9	35.3	36.9	35.0	39.8	34.8	42.3	23.1
Apolitical	21.9	15.6	27.4	25.0	17.9	21.9	26.7	30.4	13.9	7.6
No/No	2.5	2.5	2.4	1.4	2.0	3.1	6.2	2.5	2.6	1.7

Table 4.4
POLITICAL SELF-IDENTIFICATION BY PARTY PREFERENCE

			Vote Preference				
		Total	UCR	P.J.	A. Cent	Others	Undecided
Close or Very Close	UCR	32.1	84.3	6.4	19.3	9.0	22.0
	PJ	38.5	8.2	85.9	9.0	16.6	19.9
	UCD	14.7	12.6	4.8	78.1	7.5	12.2
Far or Very Far	UCR	48.8	7.0	81.1	62.1	70.8	36.9
	PJ	43.9	78.4	7.2	75.3	67.6	40.6
	UCD	60.4	62.7	77.6	8.4	77.1	46.3

SOURCE: E. Zuleta and Equas Cons, *Estudio Preelectoral en el Area de Capital Federal y GBA* (March 1990).

Table 4.5

COMPARATIVE ASSESSMENT OF PERSONAL ATTRIBUTES

	Angeloz	Menem	Alsogaray	None of the Three	Don't Know/ No Reply
Credible	32.6	33.2	8.6	18.9	6.8
Sensitive to social demands	23.6	47.3	4.2	14.3	10.5
Capable	33.7	28.9	12.7	11.1	13.5
Coherent	33.2	26.5	14.6	11.4	14.4
Democratic	38.0	31.3	6.9	9.6	14.2
Good administrator	30.1	25.2	14.1	10.2	20.4
Has better collaborators	21.7	24.6	9.1	10.0	34.6

SOURCE: E. Zuleta and Equas Cons, *Estudio Preelectoral en el Area de Capital Federal and GBA* (March 1990).

took on great importance. It should be noted that in this analysis of the public's ability to make its own choice, the definitions of closeness to and distance from political parties seemed sufficiently vague as to embody expressions of loyalty, a phenomenon distinguishable both on the basis of political affiliation and on the basis of voting intentions. Table 4.4 confirms the slight though significant advantage of the PJ over the UCR, not very different from the advantage existing in the 1983 election when, with very similar indicators of affinity, the electoral outcome was precisely the opposite.

The priorities typical of an economic emergency—control of inflation, compensation for sectors most affected by adjustment policies— must be considered in light of the fact that the PJ already led the UCR in voting preference. This was not the case between the candidates, where Angeloz reflected a more favorable overall profile than Menem (table 4.5). Menem's advantage in (1) his perceived proximity to the neediest sectors and (2) his effective capacity for developing strategies of social justice was eventually decisive. These attributes were clearly preferred by a society battered by the crisis and not trusting the efficiency-oriented proposals of Angeloz, who promised larger and more consistent doses of the post-1985 stabilization policy.

THE ROLE OF TELEVISION

As already indicated, information on the role of television in shaping political attitudes and, more concretely, in shaping electoral behavior in the 1989 campaign is fragmentary and not easily available. It would nonetheless be useful to mention several points of reference that suggest possible areas for future research.

Table 4.6
TV EXPOSURE

		High	Low
Political Interest	High	48.4%	48.7%
	Low	51.5	51.3

SOURCE: E. Zuleta and Equas Cons, *Estudio Preelectoral en el Area de Capital Federal y GBA* (March 1990).

Table 4.7
RADIO EXPOSURE

		High	Low
Political Interest	High	47.5%	48.7%
	Low	52.5	51.2

SOURCE: E. Zuleta and Equas Cons, *Estudio Preelectoral en el Area de Capital Federal y GBA* (March 1990).

Table 4.8
NEWSPAPER EXPOSURE

		High	Low
Political Interest	High	69.1%	36.5%
	Low	30.9	63.5

SOURCE: E. Zuleta and Equas Cons, *Estudio Preelectoral en el Area de Capital Federal y GBA* (March 1990).

Political Attitudes and Exposure to the Media

Most important is the relationship between media exposure and inter-est in politics. What attitude toward politics predominates among those who are exposed to television more than to other media? Tables 4.6, 4.7, and 4.8 illustrate a few provisional hypotheses, formulated on the basis of data gathered in February 1989 for the federal capital.

These data show, for example, that the greater the exposure to televi-sion, the less the interest in politics (table 4.6). This negative correla-tion is somewhat greater in the case of radio (table 4.7) and changes radically in the case of exposure to the written press, where high levels of exposure to newspapers correlate strongly with high levels of interest in politics (table 4.8).

These trends are not new and are no doubt common in most societies. What is important, however, is the magnitude of the phenom-enon. In the case of the federal capital, 79 percent of the population read newspapers, 66.4 percent listen to radio news, and 81.1 percent watch television news. This is, therefore, a population with a high and widely diversified exposure to communications media, unlike the citizens of most Latin American countries and even of the more developed countries.

The television news audience is greater in the lower socioeconomic sectors, where newspaper reading also decreases, even though holding steady at a strong 70.2 percent. The lower socioeconomic sectors also reflect a high degree of general exposure to television. It can also be seen how the television news audience is noticeably greater among the right-wing and Peronist sectors of the electorate than among Radical voters.

Another factor reinforces the relative balance among the media. In Argentina, radio and television newscasts depend for their information largely on newspapers and wire services. Many of the more influential programs are built around news commentary based on published news reports, reflecting the absence of specialized editorial staffs. But there is one contrary trend. *Clarín*, read by 74.7 percent of the inhabitants of Buenos Aires controls Radio Mitre (the leading radio station in news audience, accounting for 35.2 percent of the total news audience) and since 1989 has controlled TV channel 13 (second in terms of news audience, accounting for 41.4 percent). The trend toward the oligopolization of the Argentine media market has recently been strengthened by the governmental tolerance of the hostile takeover of TV channel 2 by the Eurnekian Group—owner of the TV cable network Cablevision, the newspapers *El Cronista Comercial* and *Extra*, and Radio America. At the same time, another strong editorial group—*Vigil*—allied to a group of provincial broadcasters took control of TV channel 11.

The Use of Television

The use of television in the campaigns was strongly conditioned by the campaigns themselves. The candidates used teams exhibiting more specialization and professionalism than in earlier elections. The absence of normal political constraints and the distance from the regular party campaign organizations allowed them to contract independent consultants, use almost unlimited funding, and prepare arguments based on the candidates' strategic interests and not ideological or party demands.

Another distinguishing characteristic of the 1989 campaign was its relative uniformity, explained by the fact that this was a national election. In 1987, there had been an election of twenty-two governors, municipal officials, and one-third of the Congress. In 1989, the presidential campaign overshadowed the interest in congressional elections. That, added to the absence of party structures, allowed greater concentration on the presidential election.

The greater degree of freedom for campaign professionals was also reflected in more refined strategic planning and campaign management. Although the true campaign managers were once again the candidates, there were now more individuals given broad decision-making authority. The greater specialization was in turn reflected in the greater and better use of data on public opinion. Both Peronists and Radicals commissioned surveys during the campaign, and the information gathered played a key role in decision making. Even though neither Menem nor Angeloz—unlike Alfonsín and Cafiero—were highly poll-oriented politicians, they made intelligent and sensible use of the data.

On the basis of the sparse information available, it can be inferred that both the UCR and the PJ improved their use of television advertising. During the final two weeks of the campaign, the PJ accounted for 37.6 percent of political advertising time, and the UCR accounted for 29 percent. The difference lay in a more intelligent planning of resources. The UCR experienced serious financial problems, largely as a result of poor campaign budget planning. With far less funding, concentrated exclusively in the final phase of the campaign, the UCD managed to buy 17.2 percent of the total time, which included the 0.1 percent related to the free time granted by the Permanent Party Fund (table 4.9).

The strategy of both parties was directed at the best utilization of each medium. The UCR preferred channels 13—middle- and higher-income audience—and 9—lower-income audience—whereas the Peronistas made greater use of channels 11—lower-middle-class audience—and 7—national coverage through the use of relay stations. Each party attempted to reinforce its weakest flank. The UCR simultaneously fought the PJ and the UCD—which drew off votes from the right, indispensable in the latter's battle against the PJ. The PJ, in turn, faced with the risk that Menem's candidacy might produce losses among voters fearing renovational Peronism, fought to avoid losing its own electorate. The UCD opted mainly for channel 13, attempting to convince its own voters not to cast a "useful vote" for the UCR and instead to cast a "vote of conviction." The subsequent alliance between the PJ and the UCD revealed a complex and difficult UCR strategy that was on target for its objective.

Table 4.9
SHARE OF POLITICAL ADVERTISING SPOTS

Party	Channels					
	13	11	9	7	2	Total
PJ	54	69	59	68	21	271
	(19.92%)	(25.46%)	(21.77%)	(25.09%)	(7.75%)	(37.6%)
UCR	68	32	61	24	27	212
	(32.07%)	(15.09%)	(28.67%)	(11.32%)	(12.7%)	(29%)
Alianza de	32	21	40	8	23	124
Centro	(25.8%)	(16.9%)	(32.3%)	(6.5%)	(18.5%)	(17.2%)
Confed. Fed.	16	11	9	1	16	53
Independ.	(30.2%)	(10.8%)	(16.9%)	(1.9%)	(30.2%)	(7.5%)
Unidad	6	1	1	7	1	16
Socialista	(37.5%)	(6.3%)	(6.3%)	(43.8%)	(6.3%)	(2.2%)
Frente Hum.	0	1	1	2	2	6
Verde		(17.42%)	(16.7%)	(33.3%)	(33.3%)	(0.8%)
Partido	0	0	5	1	6	12
Obrero			(41.7%)	(8.3%)	(50%)	(1.6%)
P. Blanco	0	1	0	1	0	2
Jubilados(*)		(50%)		(50%)		(0.3%)
Alianza(*)	0	0	0	1	1	2
Ac. Popular				(50%)	(50%)	(0.3%)
Izquierda	9	0	8	0	4	21
Unida	(42.9%)		(38.1%)		(19%)	(2.9%)
Partido(*)	0	0	0	0	0	(0.1)%
Liberación					(100%)	
Fuerza(*)	0	0	0	1	0	(0.1%)
Republicana				(100%)		
TOTAL	185	136	184	113	102	721

SOURCE: *Centro de Estudios Unión para la Nueva Mayoría.*
(*) Gained publicity only in time granted by the Ministry of the Interior.

The Electoral Competition

We need also to discuss the type of electoral competition between Peronism and Radicalism in 1989. Generally speaking, the norm since 1983 has been that of a competition "above" the ideological center of the electorate. The UCR and the PJ are two "catchall" parties—multiclass, increasingly deideologized, and open to the incorporation of new voters. They thus respond to a society in which voter independence is increasingly common. The areas of difference or friction are minimal, and the distance between the political platforms is virtually nonexistent. The most substantive differences occur in political and management styles, alliances with interest groups, and institutional priorities. The debate over whether democratic institutions are substantive or in-

Table 4.9 continued
SHARE OF POLITICAL ADVERTISING SPOTS

Party	Channels					Total
	13	11	9	7	2	
PJ	1645	1985	2019	2150	1816	9615
	(17.1%)	(20.6%)	(21%)	(22.30%)	(19%)	(26.1%)
UCR	2937	865	1681	833	2258	8574
	(34%)	(10%)	(20%)	(10%)	(26%)	(23.3%)
Alianza de	1703	541	1918	234	839	5235
Centro	(32.5%)	(10%)	(37%)	(4.5%)	(16%)	(14.2%)
Conf. Fed.	546	895	868	50	472	2831
Independ.	(19%)	(31%)	(31%)	(2%)	(17%)	(7.7%)
Unidad	98	945	630	94	106	1873
Socialista	(5.2%)	(50%)	(34%)	(5%)	(5.8%)	(5.1%)
Frente Hum.	0	900	14	914	39	1867
Verde		(48.2%)	(0.8%)	(49%)	(2%)	(5.1%)
Partido	0	0	93	879	699	1671
Obrero			(5%)	(53%)	(42%)	(4.5%)
P. Blanco	0	600	0	885	0	1485
Jubilados		(40%)		(60%)		(4.0%)
Alianza	0	0	0	900	583	1483
Ac. Popular				(61%)	(39%)	(4.0%)
Izquierda	240	0	1050	0	93	1383
Unida	(17%)		(76%)		(7%)	(3.8%)
Partido	0	0	0	0	600	600
Liberación					(100%)	(1.6%)
Fuerza	0	0	0	240	0	240
Republicana				(100%)		(0.7%)
TOTAL	7169	6731	8273	7179	7505	36,857
	(20.5%)	(18%)	(22%)	(19.5%)	(20%)	(100%)

SOURCE: *Centro de Estudios Unión para la Nueva Mayoría.*

strumental defines perhaps one of the only important differences—if not in theory, at least in practice—between the two leading political parties.

As in the United States, one difficulty of this kind of party system lies in the methods used to differentiate between candidates at election time. The first method has traditionally been the enhancement of the image and ideas of the candidates through political marketing techniques. The second method, much more recent, has been that of confrontation, by means of the kind of negative advertising widely found in advertising campaigns for other products such as food or pharmaceuticals. In 1987, the PJ tested this technique with some success in the election campaign waged in the province of Buenos Aires. In 1989, it was the UCR that used it, placing more emphasis on the personal

Table 4.10
GENERAL ASSESSMENT OF ADVERTISING CAMPAIGNS

	UCR	FREJUPO	Alianza de Centro
Like	23%	31%	26%
Indifferent	31	31	34
Don't Like	43	35	35
Don't Know/No Reply	3	3	5

SOURCE: H. Haime, and J. Aurelio, cited in R. Fraga, *Claves de la Campana Electoral 1989* (Buenos Aires, Ed. Centro de Estudios Unión para la Nueva Mayoría, 1989), p. 47.

strengths of its candidate, Angeloz, than the ideology or policies of his party. This strategy—strongly criticized both in political sectors and by the government—imitated, with little success, the most recent American presidential campaign. It not only diminished Angeloz's strength and drawing power but also mitigated some controversial aspects of Menem's personality by accentuating the contrast with the latter's message of national unity and harmony. The promise of increased economic hardship, as well as the candidate's combative and even violent image (in his attacks on the Alfonsín government, the Peronistas, and the right), reduced Angeloz's chances for victory.

The public generally rejected this aggressive television campaign. Data available for the capital area for the two weeks preceding the elections show that the Radical campaign displeased 43 percent of the population, pleased 23 percent, and left 31 percent indifferent. The less violent PJ campaign pleased 31 percent, left 31 percent indifferent, and displeased only 35 percent (Table 4.10).

The Radical party's defeat resulted almost as much from the misdirected nature of its television campaign as from the effect of the economic crisis. Its campaign emphasized the fear of Menem and uncertainty about the future of democracy. It also promised greater austerity, making it virtually indistinguishable from the rightist campaign. The consumer price index (CPI) rose 8.9 percent in January, 33.4 percent in April, and 78.5 percent in May, with an inflationary carryover from May to June that has been estimated at more than 30 percent. The value of the dollar increased 177 percent between the beginning of February and the end of May. During the election month, tax receipts totalled only 23 percent of the amount collected in February. Argentines, fearing a Menem triumph or a victorious Angeloz of the kind portrayed in the Radical campaign, fled the national currency and sought to protect themselves. The campaign thus created a climate of uncertainty and rhetorical confrontation typical of hyperinflationary situations. The PJ campaign saw its efforts rewarded, and by simply following these trends, it managed to overcome Menem's weakness as a presidential candidate. Almost a year later, in Peru, Mario Vargas Llosa would repeat these errors of political nearsightedness created by identical campaign techniques.

CONCLUSIONS

Certain general conclusions can be reached in comparing Argentina in 1989 with other campaigns in Latin America. First, we must note the differences between the situation in Argentina and that in other countries being considered. In Chile, the strong government presence converted television into an important protagonist but also a double-edged sword. The regime's lack of legitimacy and the public's distrust of it were transferred to television, and the government's massive use of the latter generated adverse reaction, totally unexpected by the military regime. In Brazil, the oligopolization of the system, together with high illiteracy and underexposure to other media, has turned television into a decisive political instrument. The existence of large national networks, the tradition of political commitment to those networks, and the existence of powerful electronic tools for measuring audience levels make television even more important for campaign purposes. The frustrated presidential candidacy of TV host and impresario Silvio Santos—who in only five days of campaigning in 1989 reached the same level as Collor de Mello—or the phenomenon of Collor himself, who emerged almost exclusively on a television-based strategy, illustrates television's influence over the second-largest electorate in the democratic world, 73 percent of which have no access to any other media.

Argentina presents a very different set of conditions. A mixed system strengthened over time, the spread of ownership, the lack of national networks, the expansion of urban cable TV, the nonpartisan industry, and the relative underdevelopment of audience surveys explain television's relatively limited power in shaping electoral attitudes, even though its importance in other aspects cannot be underestimated.

The use of television on a mass scale has harmed the candidates who have tried it in Argentina. As in other countries, however, television has revealed itself to be an important instrument in the initial campaign phase, in portraying the candidate as a credible presidential candidate endowed with the necessary personal and political attributes.

The difficulties for political parties arise in the later campaign phases when negative advertising has proven largely fruitless and even counterproductive. The lesson is clear: A negative campaign does not produce positive results. It assumes a confrontation with the present, and the present is, from the voter's viewpoint, already part of a past that must be overcome. In the 1989 elections, victory went to the candidate best able to demonstrate an ability to overcome that "present-past" the great majority so strongly repudiated. An abstract message is not enough; nor are detailed platforms or programs. The goal is to develop a personality, support teams, and an image of independence sufficient to convince the voting public that change is possible. As in most democracies, people vote for *change* and the most credible candidate for bringing about that change. In some cases—Argentina and Brazil in 1989 or Peru in 1990—the best platform may paradoxically consist of no platform at all—at least not in the traditional sense—but rather the promise of radical change vis-á-vis the other candidates' platforms.

The PJ achieved a victory by means similar to its opponent's victory in previous elections. In the 1983 elections, the UCR made up for its inferiority by assembling a coalition that overcame its initial disadvantage. The 1983 election offers the example of an almost ideal polarization, in which the PJ, with a less intensive effort than that of 1989, also suffered a generalized defeat. In 1985, the UCR began to lose votes from its initial coalition to both right and left, although without any significant gain for the PJ. In 1987, that gain occurred, especially in the larger districts, starting an erosion of the 1983 coalition, which accelerated in the PJ victories in 1987 and 1989.

Thus society establishes strict conditions on the candidates' margin to build prestige, support, and enthusiasm. A society that is well informed but disillusioned and skeptical about politics and politicians demands candidates who project unity, an ability to attract nonaligned voters, an absence of major conflicts, lack of partisanship, patience, the ability to establish dialogue with their opponents, and a talent for providing immediate solutions to problems that have no apparent solutions. This is a society willing to reward both perseverance and, above all, independence in a candidate.

Consequently, the voters reject any image of technocratic indifference or social insensitivity. The "red pencil" used by Angeloz (for budget cuts) or the "blank check" (for stronger executive powers) claimed by Vargas Llosa project an image that terrifies much of the population, who long for change but are not willing to suffer, or even understand, the costs of such change. They seek above all a guarantee of *security*, construed not as predictability, but rather as protection against uncertainty, indigence, and the lack of opportunity. In the face of these trends, imposed by severe and prolonged crisis, little can be achieved by manipulation through mass media. Those who follow the path of assumed success in other countries and attempt to experiment in uncertain situations not only risk the chances of those who entrust their campaigns to them but also contribute to the destabilization of a democracy that is still weak and unsteady, although not for that reason any less a cause for hope.

NOTES

1. See M. Edelman, *Constructing the Political Spectacle* (Chicago: University of Chicago Press, 1988).
2. Among the better-known systematic and periodic public opinion surveys, we can consider SOCMERC, Gallup, Demoskopia, and Equas Consultores.
3. The two systems of audience measurement are IPSA and Mercados & Tendencias. IPSA is based on a traditional notebook methodology, and Mercados & Tendencias has developed its own electronic peoplemeter. Both systems are strongly criticized by the market.
4. Mercados & Tendencias has published the only media-planning handbook related to the Argentine specific situation. See E. H. Lauzan, J. Alisio, F. J. Alfonso, and H. Rival, *La Estrategia de Medios* (Buenos Aires: n.p., 1989).
5. See H. Haime, *Votando Imagenes* (Buenos Aires: Ed. Tesis, 1988).
6. For a general overview, see J. E. Noguer, *Radiodifusión en la Argentina* (Buenos Aires: Ed. Bien Comun, 1985), chap. 5; Consejo para la Consolidación de la Democracia, *Radiodifusión. Proyecto y dictamen* (Buenos Aires: EUDEBA, 1988), chap. 4.
7. Noguer, *Radiodifusión*, 86–114.
8. The Presidential Commission was chaired by Enrique Zuleta-Puceiro and included Antonio Gil, Reynaldo Pizarro, and Raul Pereyra.
9. The scope of the Presidential Commission was strictly limited to reviewing the legitimacy and legality of administrative procedures. The questions of political judgment were beyond the original jurisdiction of the commission.
10. For a summary of the different legislative initiatives, see Consejo para la Consolidación de la Democracia, *Radiodifusión*.
11. The Political Parties Statute provides for a system of free TV time during political campaigns. There is also a specific and detailed set of regulations for each election.

5

The Chilean Case:
Television in the 1988 Plebiscite

María Eugenia Hirmas

On October 5, 1988, after fifteen years of dictatorship, the Chilean people voted in a plebiscite to decide on General Pinochet's future in government. Those voting "YES" endorsed his remaining president for another eight years. A "NO" vote meant free elections within one year.

The political opposition to Pinochet, most of which joined in a historic agreement in the Concertación de Partidos por la Democracia (hereafter referred to as the concertación) won, with 54.7 percent voting "NO."

The victory was unprecedented. A popular vote brought the beginning of the end of the military regime that had seized power in a coup d'état on September 11, 1973. Since his rise to power, General Pinochet had ruled Chile with an iron hand. As he said, "Not a leaf will move that I do not know about." And that is how it had been until October.

Televised political advertising, available for the first time to an organized political opposition under the Franja de Propaganda Electoral, was pivotal to the results. Some analysts claimed it was the most important factor in producing the victory.

This chapter will analyze the role of television in the plebiscite. I believe it was a key to mobilizing public opinion and to developing a political climate that allowed supporters of the "NO" vote to express themselves openly without fear. But I do not think it was the most important element in the campaign.

What most influenced the public were social, economic, and political conditions rather than television messages. But television was important in reminding viewers of those conditions. During the dictatorship, the government-controlled mass media, especially TV, had presented none of the issues raised by the democratic opposition, such as human rights violations and the difficult economic plight of the majority. Now the opposition's television campaign was effective in raising those issues (even if sometimes indirectly), in breaking down the public's reluctance to get involved, and in stimulating them to participate and vote. It also helped socialize the feelings that many had never expressed publicly.

The *franja* had been set up by the government as a way of giving the plebiscite legitimacy in the eyes of the international community. The Pinochet regime then erred, however, by assigning its television campaign secondary importance within its overall strategy, believing the opposition to be totally incompetent. That proved a costly miscalculation.

TELEVISION DURING THE DICTATORSHIP

When created in the early 1960s, Chilean television was owned and operated either by universities or by the government. Channel 11 was run by the University of Chile; channel 13 by the Catholic University of Santiago; channel 5 by the Catholic University of Valparaíso; and channel 7, known as the National Channel, by the government. The university-based stations gradually became more independent, while the National Channel remained under close government control.

With the military coup of 1973, all television came under government control. University presidents, appointed by the government, acted as overseers totally controlling the university channels.

Television changed during these years. From 1962 to 1973, television had had a limited audience, since few people owned sets and all programming was in black and white. Its impact was negligible. Today, more than 90 percent of Chilean homes have a television set. Programming is generally of high quality and is a more common source of information than radio. The result of these changes was that television became the military government's preferred medium for disseminating its values, ideology, and propaganda and for molding public opinion. TV was the only national mass medium.

Television News

Under the military government, television newscasts determined which events and people were "legitimate" news. This list conformed strictly to official government policy. Television therefore presented a highly one-sided and limited view of reality. Reports about Chilean society were restricted to only a few sectors, not including the poor. Dissidents were also excluded. Members of the political opposition were mentioned only in a judicial context, where they were presented as if they were criminals.

The media's lack of impartiality and objectivity was more

pronounced at the National Channel than at the university-based channels. Occasionally, channel 13 made attempts to provide a more balanced presentation, but with little success.[1]

An analysis of national news broadcasts from April to August 1988 on channel 7 and channel 13 showed that broadcasts virtually ignored the existence of the opposition leadership.[2] Only 1 percent of the national news presented on channel 7 reported on it. Conversely, between 82 and 86 percent of the news was about the government or progovernment groups. For channel 13, the numbers were slightly different. Between 45 and 53 percent of the news referred to the government or its supporters, while that dedicated to the political opposition totaled only 4 to 6 percent. Only in the month before the referendum did coverage of the opposition rise to 10 percent of the news reported on channel 13.

This unbalanced presentation did not go unnoticed by the public. Surveys demonstrated a low level of confidence in television news, especially in comparison to news from radio and newspapers. Nonetheless, the surveys demonstrated that television was also the preferred medium for getting the news.[3]

Political Opinion Programs

From the military coup of 1973 until 1988, there was no political debate on television. From its beginning, the Pinochet regime worked to diminish the prestige of politics and of politicians, presenting them as working only in their self-interest. This image was meant to contrast with those in power, who were presented as working strictly for the nation's welfare.[4] In 1988, all channels began to broadcast political discussions and debates, thus providing air time to government supporters as well as members of the opposition. The only exception was the National Channel.

At first, the opposition had to overcome the harassment of the progovernment program directors, who tried to obstruct the use of cameras and audio equipment.[5] Nonetheless, for the first time, the heads of the democratic parties had the opportunity to speak on television and make their political opinions known to the television-viewing public.

Government Use of Television

In 1973, the government began a systematic propaganda campaign on television, reinforced through other media. Although objectives varied, the goal did not, and the same message was relentlessly presented.

Three themes were reiterated, according to the situation: (1) General Pinochet, (2) the military government, and (3) the future of the military regime and Chile. On commemorative days, especially those with patriotic overtones such as Independence Day and the anniversary of the coup, memories of Unidad Popular (UP) rule (1970–1973) were evoked by scenes of people lining up to buy food or shots of street disturbances. These were always crowned by scenes of the bombardment of La Moneda (the presidential palace) during the military coup. The objective was to maintain a vivid public memory of the problems that had rocked the previous government, thus justifying continued military rule.

In 1987, government propaganda changed and intensified. The purpose was to prepare the public for the upcoming plebiscite on which the regime's future depended. Two months before the plebiscite, the content changed from praise of government successes to attempts to frighten the public about the possible consequences of political change. This negative advertising pointed to the "horrors" of the Allende period and predicted they would return if the majority voted for the NO. The government's final campaign message ended: "YES. You decide. We continue moving ahead or we return to the UP."[6]

The campaign was intense. From January to August of 1988, a total of 7,302 spots were telecast. They averaged 912 per month, totaling 109 hours of broadcast time. As there was no access to television, the opposition could not broadcast any message of its own.

The government had declared repeatedly that both sides would have equal access to television. This was said to quiet national and international concerns about the fairness of the plebiscite. Opposition access was seen as a minimum to guarantee that the plebiscite would be honest, thus creating adequate conditions for a peaceful transition to democracy.

But this equality of access was limited to the thirty minutes set aside for the officially sanctioned televised political campaign, the Franja de Propaganda Electoral. It did not extend to the rest of the broadcast day, which also included the news, the progovernment political opinion programs, and the government propoganda.

THE FRANJA DE PROPAGANDA ELECTORAL

The National Television Council named by the Pinochet government had established the regulations governing electoral advertising for the plebiscite. They provided that air time would be given without charge on all the TV channels and would total thirty minutes daily—fifteen for the "YES" and fifteen for the "NO." The broadcasts were scheduled for late in the day, from 10:45 P.M. to 11:15 P.M. on weekdays and from 12:00 noon to 12:30 P.M. on weekends.

The schedule was designed to reduce the audience to a minimum, especially important to the government since it was the opposition's only opportunity to present its message to the entire nation. There were four aspects to this government strategy:

1. The television campaign was concentrated in a daily half-hour broadcast. Political consultants agree that this is not the way to sway undecided or uninterested voters, who usually decide an election. Experts recommend spots of not more than one minute, to be shown between other commercials, and during programs with the highest ratings. In this way, the largest audience may be reached, including those who do not normally watch the news.
2. The time slot for the broadcast was late in the weekday, which automatically left out many of those who go to work early. The small potential audience had been verified by an earlier study.[7] Likewise, at 12:00 noon on the weekends, the audience is at its lowest.
3. Since the total time slot was thirty minutes, it was considered to be a television program. As such, it was forced to compete against other programming and thus be entertaining.
4. It was labeled as "political propaganda," after the government had spent fifteen years denigrating everything to do with politics and politicians. The intention was to reduce public interest.

Despite these precautions, the government failed to accomplish its objective. From the outset the *franja* had one of Chile's largest TV audiences. It became the most-discussed program on television and "the" subject of conversation for the month it was broadcast. The fact that so large an audience immediately and consistently adjusted its daily actions to watch the *franja* indicated the public's enormous desire for change.

A CROSSROADS FOR THE OPPOSITION

The major part of the *concertación* campaign was completed before the *franja*, which was broadcast only during the start of the last month of the campaign. This earlier effort consisted of house-to-house visits, small meetings, and public assemblies throughout the country.

The opposition transferred the responsibility for the *franja* campaign to a team of producers, advertising executives, reporters, and political scientists, supervised by two politicians. The group operated completely separately from the political parties.

Before the television campaign began, research was done through a series of focus groups to determine the most appropriate strategy. It had two goals. The first was to define voters' problems, aspirations, expectations, and fears so as to decide how to respond. The second, highly important goal was to draw a profile of the typical undecided voter and then target him or her.[8] The results of this research were crucial in deciding the kind of advertising to use. It was discovered that the majority of the undecided consisted of women and the young. The opposition campaign therefore concentrated on these two categories.

In the research stage of the campaign, the *concertación* had a brief consultation by a U.S. firm that specialized in the relevant techniques. It was the only stage at which foreign experts were used.

During the dictatorship, television producers had gained much experience in commercial advertising, the only kind of work possible then. Their experience was reflected in the high quality of the messages broadcast in support of the "NO."

These campaign strategists faced a set of difficult challenges. The most important was the need to persuade the public to vote against a ruling dictatorship without being able to guarantee them there would be no reprisals. And even if the "NO" were to win, the effects would not be immediate. Part of the campaign had to be spent explaining that even with a victory for the "NO," Pinochet would remain in power, although within a year there would be a presidential election.

Moreover, it was an election without a candidate, a party, or a program. All the essential features of a political campaign were lacking. This was overcome partly by using the rainbow as a symbol representing the diversity of the political parties in the opposition alliance. Even more important was the campaign's emphasis on certain values: democracy, justice, respect for human rights, truth, reconciliation, and concern for the poor. Highlighting these themes established a major difference between the two sides.[9]

Finally, the opposition campaign concentrated on projecting credibility by showing that the *concertación* was a viable option, that it was sincere, responsible, and prepared for the task that lay ahead. This was essential for destroying the negative image Pinochet had created of an inefficient, incapable, and violent opposition.

THE STRATEGY OF THE "YES" SUPPORTERS

The campaign for the "YES" also concentrated on the undecided vote. Its results were mixed.

A great part of the *franja* of the "YES" supporters simply continued government campaigns dating back to 1987. It borrowed themes, music, logo, and even some scenes from previous programs. These were based on two different messages. The first painted a rosy economic future for the country if the "YES" won. The second instilled fear of the consequences that a victory for the "NO" would allegedly bring.

The "YES" programs consisted of nonsequential two-to-three-minute spots on a variety of issues. The slogan was, "Chile, a winning country." Spots portrayed Chile as "a nation of champions," which had surpassed the rest of Latin America economically.

They included testimony by government representatives or progovernment political parties praising General Pinochet. The "evils" of the Unidad Popular years were invoked, and the risks posed by a victory for the "NO" were constantly reiterated.

Pinochet had his own spots. In "The President in Action," he was shown inaugurating public works or making other public appearances. Often these were clips that had already been aired on daily news broadcasts. After the first week, they were replaced by another spot called "To This We Are Committed." Here the general was shown seated at his desk, addressing the nation in a conciliatory tone. These programs, taped two weeks earlier, were his only appearances in government TV propaganda during the campaign. The intention was to counter his prevailing image of harsh intransigence. But the attempt was contradicted by his appearance in the daily newscasts where he came across as cold and threatening.

For the first fifteen days of the *franja*, the political parties supporting the "YES" also participated in a broadcast called "Democracy, Yes." Later they withdrew, citing economic and technical problems.

There was a more negative side to the government campaign—an attempt to intimidate the public. The purpose was to crystallize fears the public might have harbored about the consequences of an opposition victory. There was the constant charge that a victory for the NO would bring back the past, and, with it, Unidad Popular. In a section entitled "1973," scenes from the Unidad Popular period were shown: food lines, riots, street barricades, destruction, disorder, chaos, and fires (a continuous motif in the campaign). The effect was dramatized by strident music, with scenes shown in sepia or black and white, and a deep voice recalling the "horrors." The same approach was used in another spot called "You Decide," which contrasted the conditions of 1973 with the "progress" of the military period.[10]

Personal attacks were also employed. These aimed at ridiculing the opposition's political leadership and damaging its credibility. They played on differences within the leadership, hoping to provoke internal conflict. They ran contradictory statements made by the opposition leaders at different times; for example, Patricio Aylwin was quoted immediately after the military coup in 1973 and as opposition leader fourteen years later. The words of political leaders returning from exile were distorted and their comments taken out of context.

The government's advertising agency was not prepared for the scope of the campaign or for the quality of the opposition broadcasts. Once the advertisers saw how they had been outdone, they started to adjust their programming by adding sections, eliminating others, and working to counter opposition messages. After the second or third week, they were merely reacting, offering nothing new or original. A new host and two new producers were brought in to imitate the opposition's strategy and to develop continuity in the spots being aired. For the first three days, they tried to present a positive image, but on the fourth they reverted to a negative campaign. For example, they took clips from the opposition programs, editing them to look ridiculous and giving them a violent tone. By now, their entire strategy was negative.

All this shows that the government had not at first considered the television campaign to be important. Its faulty estimate was also reflected in the low quality of its broadcasts, their lack of original material, and their need to fall back on improvisation. When the government strategists realized the importance of the campaign, they tried to change direction but ended with a disorganized attack.

THE OPPOSITION STRATEGY

The *franja* was the first opportunity in a decade and a half to show the "other Chile," the Chile never seen on television during the dictatorship. It was the moment when the political opposition, as well as artists, professionals, and representatives of social organizations could show their faces and express themselves.

The main problem in getting out the "NO" vote was the public's fear of political participation. It came from insecurity in the face of repression, a feeling of isolation, and the lack of opportunity to participate in groups beyond the family. There was an understandable and widespread fear of possible retaliation. Many felt that losing their jobs, being expelled from subsidized housing, or just getting caught up in violence was always possible. People feared the unknown, harboring doubts about moving toward anything new. All this worked to inhibit political participation. So a fundamental opposition objective was to reduce the fear of the unknown.

Survey results indicated that most people believed the "NO" would win. At the same time, however, they did not think that the government would allow such a result to stand. The public's perception of Pinochet's personality was a key here. Accordingly, many answered surveys by saying they planned to vote "NO" but that the "YES" would win.

The opposition decided that the campaign's main goal had to be to destroy the myth of Pinochet's omnipotence. This involved a number of steps. The first was to show the opposition reality, not the distortion that the government constantly imposed. They also wanted to end their treatment as second-class citizens under the dictatorship.

In addition, voters needed to see that their personal circumstances often resulted from social problems the government had left unsolved, and not, as they were often told, from their personal deficiencies. A feeling of security had to be fostered, to assure the people that their rights would be protected during the balloting and that the vote count would be honest. The image of the government as representing progress and development and the opposition as representing a backward and underdeveloped past also had to be countered. Finally, it was urgent to break the image fostered by the government of a close connection between opposition to the regime (and therefore support for the "NO") and violence.

The opposition campaign successfully met all these challenges.[11] The campaign slogan was, "Joy is coming" (*La Alegría ya viene*). The logo was a rainbow, representing the sun's arrival after the dictatorship, as well as the combined party effort behind the NO campaign.

The opposition strategy consisted of a combination of numerous spots and short programs introduced by a single host to provide continuity. The host was a well-known, respected figure who projected warmth, had a sense of humor, and could inspire confidence. Each day, a different subject was addressed: poverty, health, youth, delinquency, housing, exile, repression, torture, the *allegados* (squatters), and so on. Differing approaches were used. There were musicals, humorous sketches, quick reports, personal accounts by artists or politicians, and even "NO-news" ("*NO-ticias*").

Consultants had discussed at length the best broadcast techniques. They decided to avoid images of suffering and tragedy. What they wanted was a positive stimulus to move people to vote. A decision was made to use humor and satire to disarm the public's fears.

By making Pinochet the primary target of this humor, they sought to dispel his air of omnipotence. By playing on his physical image and a few of his phrases, the opposition put together a strong critique, concentrating on the idea that although Pinochet presented himself as a democrat, he was still a dictator. They succeeded in making people laugh without feeling afraid.

Painful and unavoidable subjects, such as the violations of human rights by the military regime, were also raised. Such was the case with the "disappeared." This was approached symbolically, with caution and dignity, with the intention of teaching about the past to avoid repeating it. It was also a way of acknowledging a common experience that had been downplayed during the military regime. The living conditions for many were also addressed but a way out was always suggested.

Also emphasized was the impossibility of fraud or reprisals in the voting. This was repeated, with an explanation of the precautions that had been taken, a demonstration of how to vote, and a demonstration that it would be impossible for any vote to be traced to the person who cast it. The host of the opposition TV programs described the role of the poll watchers and foreign observers during the upcoming voting, noting that there would be a member from the opposition at every polling place.

By using the motto "We are more," the campaign sought to instill confidence in the public. People were made to feel that they were part of a broad-based movement acting in the common interest.

The past was presented as part of a successful process leading to the current economic development. This worked to end the idea that the past was synonymous with the Unidad Popular and therefore with backwardness. Economists and social scientists appeared, refuting the military regime's claims that progress was the government's work alone. By presenting a positive message emphasizing an upbeat and conciliatory attitude, the opposition countered the charge that a victory for the "NO" would produce violence. Between each broadcast segment, while a ballot was shown being marked "NO," a speaker would intone: "Without hate, without violence, and without fear, vote 'no.' "

Presentations made by opposition politicians followed in the style of the other broadcasts. Their messages were short, clear, well documented, and addressed specific issues. They differed greatly from traditional political speeches. This worked to counter the government's negative campaign, which presented politicians as egotists who worked only in their own interest.

The "NO-news" (NO-ticias) presented information about the political oppositions never broadcast in regular newscasts. The clip with which the opposition broadcast began and ended was highly successful—well produced, with skillfully edited images—and soon everyone was humming its attractive theme song.

Joy and optimism were the main feelings projected in these broadcasts, and they succeeded in encouraging the public to vote.

THE IMPACT OF THE BROADCASTS

The effect of the broadcasts was great, especially among those supporting the "NO." Ten days after the start of the campaign, "NO" sympa-
thizers began to appear wearing a distinctive button. It was the first
time government opponents had dared to identify themselves without
fearing repression.

The quality of the broadcasts was up-to-date and entertaining. The
public did not associate the *franja* solely with political discussion. It was
interesting to see how difficult issues could be aired and how substantial criticism could be made, all in an entertaining manner. The fifteen
minutes passed quickly, without, as many had feared, becoming boring.

Meanwhile, the regime's supporters kept a low profile in reacting to
the enthusiasm generated by the opposition campaign. After the
plebiscite, it was discovered that many who had described themselves as
undecided voted "YES," but had not wanted to voice their opinion.

The television campaign soon became news in its own right and was
in turn covered by all the media. Besides commenting on the
campaign, the Santiago opposition press answered charges and downplayed accusations leveled by the "YES" *franja.* The team producing the
opposition broadcasts had earlier debated whether to respond on TV
to charges made in government broadcasts. They decided against it for
two reasons. First, it would use part of their already very limited time.
Second, they reasoned that "a leader does not react to accusations."
The opposition print media therefore complemented the television
messages.

Meanwhile, the broadcasts did not go unnoticed as the government
had hoped. On the contrary, they reached every sector of society.[12]

AN EVALUATION

What effect did television have on the final vote?

As noted earlier, the undecided vote, composed mostly of women
and the young, was the principal target in the campaign. But the two
sides used very different approaches in going after this vote. While supporters of the "YES" used fear, the opposition used hope to break
through voter apathy and passivity. While the government depicted the
economic gains that a victory for the "YES" would bring, the opposition
concentrated on winning over young people by responding to their aspirations and apprehensions.

The campaign for the "YES," on the other hand, failed to win over the younger vote. Neither the issues on which their publicity focused nor their accompanying music moved this constituency: It simply did not address their questions and aspirations. Because they had often felt the brunt of the government's economic policies, they were not enamoured of Chile's economic growth record. They were also unmoved by references to a troubled past in which they had no role, and they were unresponsive to the appeal of fear. The first of two studies conducted during and immediately after the campaign concluded that between 63 percent and 80 percent of the young did not believe that a victory for the "NO" would bring chaos, lines, and shortages, that communism would be strengthened, or that Unidad Popular would return.[13] They also remained unconvinced that Pinochet would begin acting democratically. The young people surveyed showed strong preference for the television spots supporting the "NO" vote.

The fear tactic seems to have been more effective among women, who, at least in Chile, are generally more sensitive to threats to the security of their families. Talk of violence, insecurity, shortages, lines, and unemployment all found a receptive audience among women. Twenty percent of those surveyed said that they were fearful about the future.[14]

The two surveys confirmed that the TV campaign was seen, at one time or another, by more than 90 percent of the population. They also showed that most people agreed that the opposition's TV spots were more entertaining, more optimistic, more honest, more conciliatory, more helpful in tone, and better received.

The public remembered some spots better than others. The opposition ones were recalled more often. The best remembered were two on the violation of human rights (police repression and torture) and one on poverty. Of the government broadcasts, those most often mentioned were several considered threatening and one on terrorism.[15] Violence was the motif most often used in the "YES" programming.

The values emphasized in the "YES" campaign were development and order, while democracy and reconciliation were those most often stressed in the "NO" campaign. Although this reflected the effectiveness of the campaign conducted by each side, it was also the result of a discourse between government and opposition that had been going on for two years before the plebiscite.

CONCLUSIONS

There is still disagreement about the relative importance of television's role in the plebiscite. Party representatives and analysts who supported continued military rule argued that the vote was decided by the high quality of the opposition's television campaign, in contrast to the government's poor TV effort.[16]

I believe the television campaign played a vital role but not a decisive one. Even allowing for the deficiencies of the government effort, to attribute such influence to television is to ignore its function in politics and its negligible effect on public opinion in the short term. Experts agree that such a campaign can convince the undecided or those without definite opinions, but that it is very unlikely to change previously held views.

The opposition television campaign was undoubtedly very important. It accomplished the purpose of covering events and people ignored by the media in the past fifteen years. But to attribute the victory to television fails to recognize most people's living conditions and the level of discontent with the Pinochet regime. It also ignores such factors as the groundwork laid by political parties before the vote, the influence of social organizations, and the political maturity that Chilean people had acquired over the years.

Because Chile has a strong political culture, as well as political parties and social organizations with great influence in certain social sectors, the public cannot be manipulated or molded in the short term merely by a well-produced television campaign. Political advertisements did not displace the influence of community work, meetings, campaign trips, and personal contact with voters. The televised campaign may have reinforced positions but did not change them.

The "NO" won the day, but not with as wide a margin as many had predicted. This is especially significant, given the fact that the regime had been in power for fifteen years and that it could have been expected to lose some support in that time. Furthermore, a great majority of the public had expressed some dissatisfaction with the government.

The strong vote in favor of the government reflected the influence of two factors: fear, not easy to dispel in the short run, and the cumulative effect of fifteen years of concentrated government programming. After hearing the same message for years, with no alternative voice, any television audience internalizes the message, even given initial resistance. Persistence reinforced by threats can finally prove persuasive. This was demonstrated by the vote.

The television campaign also demonstrated that serious ethical and political themes can be presented in an esthetically pleasing manner. In addition, it was discovered that undecided and indifferent voters can be influenced by television spots longer than a minute.

The usefulness of opinion surveys in guiding a political campaign was also firmly established. The kind of political intuition that had directed campaigns before 1970 was no longer sufficient. That marked a fundamental break with the past.

Another important change was the reduced ideological content in political advertising. Unfortunately, negative advertising was also used by the progovernment campaign. This was an error and provoked an unfavorable public reaction.[17]

Chile has finally modernized its electoral system after fifteen years of military dictatorship. Its negative side can be seen in the indiscriminate use of political attacks. But it also has positive aspects: the use of new technologies and audience surveys, more skillful use of television time, and the enlisting of specialists for campaign planning.

Television in Chile should continue to be used in politics, but only as a campaign instrument. It cannot replace the work of political or social organizations in their task of informing and shaping a political following, nor can it create the conditions needed for voter participation and the consolidation of a democracy.

NOTES

1. D. Portales, "Los Retorcidos Caminos de la Información Política," in *La Política en Pantalla*, ed. D. Portales, G. Sunkel, M. E. Hirmas, M. Hopenhayn, and Hidalgo (Santiago: Cesoc, 1989).
2. Juan Pablo Egaña, *El Trabajo Informativo de los Canales 7 y 13* (Santiago: Ilet, 1988).
3. Ceneca-Flacso, *Encuesta de Consumo Cultural* (Santiago: Ceneca-Flacso, 1988).
4. Giselle Munizaga, *El Discurso Publico de Pinochet* (Santiago: Cesoc-Ceneca, 1988).
5. G. Sunkel, "Puesta en Conversación," in Portales, et al., *La Política.*
6. Maria Eugenia Hirmas, "Campañas de Gobierno en TV" (Unpublished work presented at the Third Chilean Congress of Sociology, Santiago, Chile, September, 1989).
7. *Estudio Cualitativo. Análisis de Mensajes del Gobierno* (Santiago: Diagnos, 1988).
8. *Dignidad. Una Estrategia para Ganar la Democracia* (Santiago: CIS, 1988).
9. This conclusion is substantiated by the findings of the public opinion polls cited in notes 13 and 14.
10. Tony Schwartz, *The Responsive Chord* (Garden City, N.Y.: Anchor Books, 1974).
11. The judgment is based on the polls cited in notes 13 and 14 and on the author's experience as a participant in "focus groups" that discussed campaign strategies during the campaign.
12. The effectiveness of the broadcast messages was confirmed by the polls cited in notes 13 and 14.
13. "Informe Sobre una Encuesta Acerca de la Propaganda Electoral en el Gran Santiago" (Santiago: Diagnos, 1988).
14. Universidad Cumplutense de Madrid-Ceneca-Cerc. "Informe Encuesta TV-Plebiscito-Cultura Politica. Realizada entre el 27 de Octubre y el 7 de Noviembre, 1988" (Santiago: Ceneca-Cerc, 1988).

15. Ibid.
16. "Renovación Nacional Escuchó en Silencio, Crudo Analisis," *Fortin Mapocho*, 6 November 1988.
17. The largely unfavorable reaction could be seen in the daily newspaper and radio analysis during the campaign and in the polling results cited in note 14.

6

Brazilian Television in the 1989 Presidential Election: Constructing a President

Venicio A. de Lima

The 1989 presidential election was the most important event in recent Brazilian political history.[1] More than one year after the final electoral round was held on December 17, 1989, analysts remain puzzled by questions such as (1) What factors enabled a young and previously unknown professional politician (Fernando Collor de Mello) from the small northeastern state of Alagoas to win? (2) How was it possible for a leader of a metalworkers' union (Luis Inacio Lula da Silva) to challenge the front-runner, to make it to the second electoral round, and to receive almost 32 million votes? (3) What patterns were developed in the Brazilian presidential election that might set the pace for elections in other Latin American countries during their transitions to democracy?

Elections are extremely complex and dynamic processes, differing radically in their logic according to a wide range of variables. It is therefore very difficult precisely to determine the factors that explain the behavior of the majority of voters. The traditional paradigms of political analysis, positivist in methodology and behaviorist in theory, are too limited to account for the broad scenario of representation in the election process. Elections are inseparable from the political culture in which they occur, and to understand a political cutlure one must consider a broad range of phenomena—beliefs, expectations, discussions, ceremonies, rituals, symbolisms, gestures, memories, myths. In contemporary mediacentric societies, the understanding of politics transcends the boundaries of political science, media, and cultural studies. In this complex environment, comparative political analysis offers a great challenge to researchers, for the concepts, definitions, and theory of this discipline are still emerging.

The presidential election of 1989 happened in a context unprecedented in Brazilian history. Taking place twenty-five years after the

1964 military "coup d'état" and almost thirty years after the last direct presidential election, it had the following special features:

1. No other elections for the executive or legislative branch of government, at either the regional or local levels, took place at the same time.
2. For the first time, illiterates were allowed to vote. (Illiterates and semiliterates account for more than two-thirds of the voting population.) Also newly enfranchised were persons between the ages of 16 and 18 (close to 3.3 million people or a little more than 4 percent of voters).[2]
3. It was the first Brazilian election to take place in two rounds. When none of the candidates received an absolute majority in the first round of voting on November 15, the two candidates receiving the most votes participated in a runoff on December 17.
4. It was also the first to take place in a country "integrated" by a modern cultural industry. In this industry, television stands out. And among television networks, the "virtual monopoly"—an expression first used to refer to Globo by former Communication Secretary Said Farhat in 1980—of TV Globo dominates, with an audience fluctuating between 60 percent and 84 percent on any given day and at any given time.[3]

TELEVISION: THE KEY FACTOR

This chapter deals mainly with the first of the three questions suggested at the outset, arguing that in Brazil, where traditional political institutions such as politicians, political parties, unions, and Congress have historically been weak, the reasons for Fernando Collor's success in the 1989 presidential election can be found in the political scenario of representation that was constructed in and by the media, especially television through *novelas* (popular Brazilian soap operas), newscasts, polls, and marketing. This agenda was developed over a period of years but reached its culmination after June 1988, when the National Constituent Assembly decided on the election date. Well before September 15, when the free radio and TV electoral time (*horário gratuito*) was provided by law to all candidates, and at least six months before the first electoral round on November 15, the scenario had been delineated. Collor's greatest ability was to identify himself, by means of an efficient marketing strategy, with the political scenario. Adjusting his public image to the media's "ideal profile" of a candidate, he gradually integrated himself into the modern establishment (national and/or associated), becoming the only candidate able to embody and represent its interests. It was in this way that he gained establishment support and acquired the votes to guarantee his victory.

The following sections develop this argument both theoretically and empirically.

MEDIA AND CONTEMPORARY POLITICS

A perusal of articles listed in the *International Political Science Abstracts* indicates how little has been done to explore the role of the media in contemporary politics. Most of the research focuses on the understanding of "classical" political institutions such as political parties, the state, and the military or broad topics such as authoritarianism, regime transitions, and corporatism. On the other hand, the history of political communication theory and research in the West has been strongly influenced by the dominant communication paradigm prevailing in the United States in the past forty years.[4] The "limited effects" model and the reduction of political communication research to campaign studies equated with marketing product campaigns composed the framework within which most of the findings in the field were posited.[5] Furthermore, there seems to be very little interaction between the two disciplines or their practitioners.

Some evidence had emerged in mainstream American communication research by the mid-1950s that indicated a need to move toward a new framework that would replace short-term behavioral effects with long-term cognitive effects.[6] This new line of inquiry opened the way for the development of the theory of the "agenda-setting" power of the media.[7] However, despite these and other suggested new directions, political communications research and theory, mainly in the U.S. tradition, remained innocent and essentially favorable regarding the media and politics as independent institutions in democratic societies.

It can be said that the beginnings of a paradigm shift in political communications research coincided with the consolidation of communication industries, especially commercial television, by the late 1960s and early 1970s, both in European and third-world societies,[8] even though a large number of the latter were then under military authoritarian (nondemocratic) political regimes.

The return to the concept of powerful media made possible an increased awareness of the key cultural (ideological) place of the media in the political and electoral processes of Western liberal democracies.

Some authors were concerned with the power of the media to produce "that which is rendered/constituted as public," thereby transforming the public into "elements of conformity in political activity."[9] Others described the eruption of "videopolitics" as a phenomenon in full expansion, where a new "touch-button man," molded by the screen and related to the world through visual language, enters into contact with political power via television.[10] Still others, such as Paletz and Entman, remarked that

> television [entertainment and advertising] teaches its audience about the options their society offers, the norms it enforces; about the expectations, values and standards of judgement [societies] apply and should apply to life. In this way, television goes beyond the provision of reassurance, vicarious participation, diversion, escape; it socializes.[11]

Also Meyrowitz points out that

> television as an environment is shaping and reshaping national character and contemporary patterns of feeling and thought. . . . Television is the context within which most of us perceive the world, within which we think about politics, about entertainment, about news, almost anything.[12]

Studies have, in addition, emphasized the rediscovered importance of political mythology and the imaginary as opposed to the implicit rationality of mainstream political science paradigms;[13] the presence of myths in media culture;[14] the structural constraints of different media genres, melodrama or news (the "newsmaking" approach);[15] and the impact of media technology in contemporary culture.[16]

The current body of literature in this area has emerged from (1) diverse social, economic, cultural, and media environments such as the United States, Great Britain, France, Italy, Brazil, and Argentina; (2) diverse academic disciplines such as anthropology, sociology, political science, social psychology, and communication studies; and (3) diverse theoretical paradigms such as liberal-functionalist, anthropolitical-structuralist, technological-determinist, Marxist, and so forth.

More recently, some postmodern theorists have also strongly asserted that in contemporary culture reality is replaced by media-created images.[17] This position, however, lacks a theory of the subject and without such a theory it is devoid of utopian possibilities and cannot further the discourse of social change.[18] It therefore ends up proclaiming "the death of politics" in the same way the new conservative theoreticians proclaim "the end of history."[19] Media and politics thus return in the

1990s to the same innocent relationship they had under the limited effects model that dominated the field of political communication more than thirty years ago.

What is missing in this seemingly circular movement from limited effects to some postmodern discourses is a dialectical view of the relationship between media and politics. Such a view can be found in Hall's concept of "scenarios of representation," which is grounded in Gramsci's notion of hegemony. Hall points out that

> how things are represented and the "machineries" and regimes of representation in a culture do play a constitutive, and not merely a reflexive, after-the-event, role. This gives questions of culture and ideology and the scenarios of representation—subjectivity, identity, politics—a formative, not merely an expressive, place in the constitution of social and political life.[20]

Since representations in contemporary culture are mainly created by and through the "machineries and regimes" of the media, they are able to establish a political scenario that not only reflects existing political institutions but also constructs new ones. This is done within the rules and norms defined and structured by the media themselves, as technological forms, as channels of discourse, and as social institutions, or what Gramsci calls "private hegemony apparatuses."[21] Television occupies a central position as a "machinery and regime" of representation since it constitutes the most trusted source of news, information, and entertainment.[22] Its specific narrative structure and language constrain both news and entertainment, and it has developed particular genres (such as the *telenovela*, or soap opera) that are suitable to its own "regime" of representation and popular with large audiences.

The media are becoming a privileged site in which the struggle for knowledge and meaning—that is to say, the struggle for power—is delineated and fought in contemporary cultures. Because the media both construct and reflect the different scenarios of representation in which questions of class, race, gender, desire, pleasure, and identity are defined, they are therefore able to "reconstruct" politics. It is exactly in this way that the media reveal their power in contemporary cultures. They define the thematic agenda and establish the structural limits within which the entire electoral process (not only "political campaigns") will be performed. The ubiquitous media construction of a broad spectrum of images and values (representations) that are reflected or represented in the news, situation comedies, action dramas, soap operas, *novelas*, movies, and sports events most frequently determines, a priori, the chances of success or failure for a political candidate in contemporary liberal democratic elections. The media have the power to define the limits of a candidate's possibilities by presenting him or her as more or less suited to the era of videopolitics.

The scenario of representation is articulated within what Hall calls the "dominant or preferred meaning," which corresponds to a "dominant or preferred reading."[23] Because it is an expression of the media's cultural hegemony, however, the existence of such a preferred reading does not necessarily imply a "diabolic conspiracy," even though the political scenario is purposely constructed and explored through the planned political marketing of the competing candidates. Indeed the scenario of representation is the space in which cultural hegemony[24] is contested, and, as such, it must be "continually renewed, re-created, defined and modified" to the extent that it is "continually resisted, limited, altered and challenged by pressures that are not its own."[25]

The following discussion of the 1989 Brazilian presidential election is designed to clarify this theoretical framework as well as some of its implications for research and analysis of the relationship between media and politics.

TV GLOBO AND BRAZILIAN POLITICS

Seventy-three percent of the households in Brazil had at least one TV set by 1989,[26] and the four major national TV networks (Globo, Sistema Brasileira de Televisão, Bandeirantes, and Manchete) covered respectively 99.39 percent, 89 percent, 87.98 percent, and 70 percent of the households by April 1989.[27] Also in 1989, an average of 95 percent of all Brazilians declared that they watched TV regularly.[28] In a country that holds world records for adult illiteracy, where the main newspapers have an average daily circulation of only about 300,000 copies, and in which radio has never been a national medium of communication, television has become incontestably the principal means of public communication since the early 1970s.

Available data for the six major Brazilian metropolitan areas by the middle of the electoral year (July through September of 1989) revealed that TV Globo maintained an audience of 59 percent or better at any given time and over 84 percent during prime time (8:00 to 10:00 P.M.). This is the time slot of "Jornal Nacional" (a national network newscast) and of "Novela das Oito" (a melodrama airing at 8:30 P.M.), programs that have been among the ten national rating champions for the past twenty years.[29] Thus, to speak of media in Brazil necessarily means to speak of TV Globo.

In order to understand the real dimension of the "disproportionated social space"[30] occupied by TV Globo in Brazil—the fourth-largest and one of the world's most-watched television networks—it is worth remembering that it is part of a solid economic and financial conglomerate of more than 100 companies with annual budgets estimated at around 2 billion U.S. dollars, owned and directed by Roberto Marinho. The constitutive role of TV Globo's "machineries and regimes" and its direct involvement in Brazilian social and political life is well known and has been the focus of previous studies.[31]

In regard to the 1989 presidential election, it is not difficult to identify the Globo empire's position and its important role in articulating the interests of a significant sector of the Brazilian establishment. Through the *O Globo* newspaper's editorials, the network's traditional "official" voice, Globo clearly opposed the progressive candidacies of Leonel Brizola and Luiz Inacio Lula da Silva and designed an explicit and public profile of its ideal candidate, politically conservative and "modern" in economic policy, favoring widespread privatization of state-owned enterprises and the total opening of the economy to foreign investment and trade.[32] In late July 1989, Roberto Marinho granted an interview to the newspaper *Folha de São Paulo,* and even though claiming not to have made a "definitive decision," he stated his (and thus Globo's) clear preference for Fernando Collor de Mello.[33]

Collor de Mello was only 39 years old at the time. Young, handsome, an athlete with a black belt in karate, he was a journalism graduate and married (a second marriage) to a twenty-three-year-old woman. Son and grandson of members of the traditional political elite of both the south and the northeast of Brazil, he was appointed by the military regime to be mayor of Maceió, the capital of the state of Alagoas, in 1978. In 1982, he was elected to the Congress by the Partido Democratico Social, or Social Democratic Party (PDS), which supported the military. Moving to the Partido do Movimento Democratico Brasileiro, or Party of the Brazilian Democratic Movement (PMDB), he was elected governor of Alagoas and inaugurated in March 1987. Collor had had strong links with Globo since 1978 when he became president of his father's regional media empire—the Arnon de Mello Organization—which is the biggest multimedia group in Alagoas, controlling the major state newspaper (*A Gazeta de Alagoas*), thirteen radio stations, and TV Gazeta, an affiliate of TV Globo. Collor's brother was for several years regional director of TV Globo in Recife and São Paulo. Marinho himself was a partner of Collor's father, with whom he bought the property on which the first TV Globo building was built in Rio de Janeiro. Collor was therefore a journalist and a communication industry executive who had both commercial and personal (family) ties to the Globo empire. It came as no surprise, then, when the campaign revealed that Globo's support for Collor was not only editorial but was also reflected in the actions of the Globo empire and its economic and political allies.[34]

The historical fragility of Brazilian democracy made it possible for TV Globo to develop a political scenario of representation not only within the logic of the media (especially television) but also within the political logic of the commitment granted to one candidate by the nation's most powerful media mogul.

THE *NOVELAS*

It is beyond the limits of this chapter to discuss the enormous historical and cultural importance of melodrama and *novelas* (through radio and TV) in Latin American societies and specifically in Brazil. TV Globo's *novelas* were an important component in the construction of the political scenario for the 1989 presidential election. Their importance can be attributed to four factors: (1) the space occupied by *novelas* in the regular Globo programming (a minimum of four hours daily); (2) the exceptional ratings (an average of above 70 percent for the 8:30 P.M. prime-time *novela*); (3) the nature of the audience, which is national and cuts across social categories, age groups, income differences, and professions; and (4) the immense power of the *novelas* to constitute and organize a specific representation of reality.

Studies have shown that *novelas* are so-called administered fiction. They follow the rules of industrial cultural production and are subject to a series of constraints: commercial interests such as merchandising, sound track creation (national and international), and advertising; responses from the audience measured on a day-by-day basis through specialized polling and ratings; and the characteristics of scriptwriters, actors, and producers. TV Globo produces its own *novelas* and monopolizes its writers, directors, and actors by keeping them under permanent contract. *Novelas* usually have at least two writers and might have as many as four different directors and two or three production teams. What results from this complex process is a bricolage, a fragmented product, whose production is driven by a basic thematic impetus. The control of the narrative development thus escapes from the hands of the writers, the actors, the producers, and the audience. (Some writers, especially those few who still manage to write entire scripts themselves, keep some level of control.) The audience also intervenes in the process but within narrow narrative possibilities without producing real changes in theme.[35]

The question is who decides what the theme of a *novela* is going to be, when the series will be scheduled, and what time slot it will occupy in the programming (*novelas* last for an average of six months)?

Writers under contract (and others) submit summaries of *novelas* that might be developed. All summaries follow the pattern of melodramatic narrative but vary in thematic content. According to Ortiz and colleagues, the decision process involves (1) the commercial department, (2) the director of programming production, and (3) the TV Globo *direção geral* (top management).[36]

It is a contention of this chapter that the choice of the *novela*'s thematic content is a key element in the construction of the political scenario. As is the case with any other industrialized cultural product, *novelas* are structurally similar but set different agendas and help to construct or reflect different political scenarios according to their thematic emphasis. This is what happened in the 1989 Brazilian presidential election. In 1988 and 1989, eighteen *novelas* were being aired by TV Globo in different time slots. Five of them were shown for the second or even third time at an early afternoon slot and one—in a very unusual and unique way—was shown for a second time even though it had just finished its first presentation.

Three particular *novelas*, aired sequentially or simultaneously during 1988 and 1989, had a central role in constructing the political scenario. They were "Vale Tudo" (Anything Goes), 8:30 P.M., which played for almost eight months from May 16, 1988, through January 8, 1989; "O Salvador da Patria" (Savior of the Country), 8:30 P.M., which played for more than seven months from January 9 through September 16, 1989; and "Que Rei Sou Eu?" (What King Am I?), 7:00 P.M., which also played for more than seven months, from February 13 through September 16, 1989, and was aired again in a special time slot at 5:00 P.M., usually not used for *novelas*, beginning October 22, 1989 and going through January 1990.

In their basic narrative themes, all three *novelas* either directly or indirectly portrayed Brazil as a kingdom of political corruption run by professional politicians and politics as a contaminated social space. The solution for the country's problems could come, not from "traditional" politicians and politics in these *novelas*, but only from outside since traditional politicians were irremediably lost. A study of those three *novelas* published before the election shows how without distinction, any and every political activity, the state, politicians and public servants were identified with corruption, waste, incompetence, lack of work, and corporatism. Because of these identifications all politics began to be seen as an activity exercised against the interests of the citizens. The public servants of the state, politicians, and workers were universally transformed into "maharajahs,"[37] thereby, enemies of society.[38]

The disqualification of politicians and politics by the media did not restrict itself to television or to the *novelas*. It was in fact a long-term process, already identified by political scientists in Brazil.[39] It helped construct the scenario for the national launching of an "outsider," a young, unknown, modern "hero," "savior of the country," who would in the end win the 1989 presidential election: Fernando Collor de Mello.

THE NEWS AND THE POLLS

Under the prophetic title, "One Man's Political Views Color Brazil's TV Eye," the *New York Times* published on January 2, 1987, parts of an interview with Roberto Marinho in which he asserted, referring to TV Globo's evening news, "Jornal Nacional": "We provide all the necessary information, but our opinions are in one way or another dependent on my character, on my convictions, and on my patriotism. I assume responsibility for all the things that I direct."[40] Marinho lived up to his word: "Jornal Nacional" and the rest of the TV Globo news programs (and the newspaper *O Globo*) not only reflected his personal political beliefs during the electoral process but also gave more and more favorable space to the conservative candidate whom he was supporting.

The construction of the political scenario by and through TV Globo news had at least two aspects: the disproportionate amount of favorable coverage given to Collor as compared to all other candidates and the weekly announcement (or the "omission") of the poll estimates of what candidates were ahead and who would be the contenders in the second electoral round.

COLLOR-FUL NEWS COVERAGE

It is well known that as soon as he took office as governor of Alagoas on March 1987, Collor received national network coverage and that TV Globo transferred a special reporter from Brasília to Maceió to cover "the region" in May 1988. Between March and May 1988, Collor also appeared on TV Globo's prime-time news programs such as "Globo Reporter" (similar to CBS's "60 Minutes") and "Fantástico" (a Sunday night weekly news program). The data indicate that Collor's presence on all TV Globo news programs between July and August 1989 was significantly greater than that of any other candidate.[41]

The disproportionate and favorable coverage given to Collor was notorious—so much so that it became a campaign theme in denunciations by at least four candidates: Brizola and Lula (progressive); Ulysses (centrist); and Aureliano Chaves (conservative). In fact, Marinho's public support of Collor's candidacy (July) was evident in Collor's overexposure and the simple exclusion of negative campaign incidents. Surveys conducted by Lima at the University of Brasília for the months before the two electoral rounds also support this claim.[42]

THE ANTICIPATED WINNER

From the middle of April, when Collor surpassed Brizola and was reported in first place, the aided-recall voting intention polls carried out by IBOPE (Instituto Brasileiro de Opinião e Estatística) under contract with Globo and reported on "Jornal Nacional" occupied a central role in the news coverage of the campaign. Because Collor had remained in first place in the announced poll results since April (seven months before the first round), the question in the political scenario constructed by Globo was, "Who is going to be Collor's contender?" The poll results were made public as if one of the winners of the first round had already been determined, and in this manner, Collor was publicly constructed as the winner. Lima suggests two points related to electoral polls: the possibility of the "bandwagon effect" and the serious ethical question linking Collor to "to IBOPE since IBOPE was under contract by" and was also "voluntarily" advising Collor.[43]

A study carried out in nine northeastern states by IPESPE (Instituto de Pesquisas Sociais, Politicas e Económicas, or Institute of Social, Political, and Economic Research) and the graduate political science program at the Universidade Federal de Pernambuco was published in May 1990. Among other findings, it was clear that

> the polls directly influenced the decisions of the voters. Approximately 41.5% of those interviewed revealed that they were "very" or "somewhat influenced" by poll results. Forty-three percent thought that poll results were "very important" when choosing a candidate

who "has a good chance of winning." The influence of polls was greater, however, among those with the least schooling: 44.2% of those who have completed only primary school acknowledged their influence, while among the voters with college degrees only 21.1% acknowledge them."[44]

POLITICAL MARKETING

There are various estimates of Collor's total campaign budget.[45] They are, however, all high compared with any standard. In June 1989, Eduardo Collor de Mello, Collor's cousin and one of his campaign coordinators, estimated the total campaign expenses at around 1 billion dollars.[46] The specialized magazine *Midia & Mercado* (Media and Market) estimated the direct marketing costs alone at close to 130 million dollars; *Isto É/Senhor* (a weekly news magazine) suggested 150 million dollars as a "conservative calculation"; and the marketing coordinator of another candidate's campaign estimated those costs at between 250 and 400 million dollars.

Information indicates that at least since December 1987, the objective of Collor and his inner circle was to make him a viable presidential candidate. Collor sought and got national media coverage even before he took office as governor of Alagoas. At different times, he hired a polling company (Vox Populi); an agency for economic planning and financial consulting (ZLC); four advertising agencies (Saldiva & Associados in 1988 and Setembro, DNA, and Opçao in 1989); and a computer and information service (CAP Software).

Collor knew from public opinion polls that "government corruption" was considered nationally to be one of the country's worst social problems. He began to explore that issue as candidate for governor in 1986 and was elected by running a moralistic campaign under the nickname of "the maharajah's hunter." Knowing also that professional politicians had been the focus of popular distrust in successive public opinion polls for years,[47] Collor began to construct for himself the public image of an "outsider"; that is, an image of someone who practices politics without being a professional politician.

The results of Collor's long-range political marketing strategy did not take long to appear. In the end of June 1987, Vox Populi carried out a national public opinion poll on the image of the new governors, asking the question, "Which governor do you most admire?" Collor received 12 percent of the favorable responses while the governors of the powerful states of Rio de Janeiro and São Paulo reached 7 and 8 percent. By

January 1988, Vox Populi conducted another national poll on political and electoral themes. According to *Jornal do Brasil*, the "maharajahs" fill an entire chapter in the Vox Populi report.[48] Among those who knew Collor, his "fight" against the "maharajahs" was singled out as his main positive quality.

The immediate result of the Vox Populi report was the production by the ad agency Saldiva & Associados of the 1988 annual radio and TV program of the Partido da Juventude (Youth Party), which would be aired in May by all radio and TV stations. Collor, who was still affiliated with the PMDB party, appeared for 47 minutes in the one-hour program as an "invited" guest.[49] The electoral judge of Rio's Tribunal Superior Eleitoral (TRE), the regional electoral court, did not allow the television program to show the then-governor of Alagoas, but the judge did not prohibit the program to be aired by radio. Collor spoke repeatedly of the fight against "maharajahs"; suggested that he did not have the style of a professional politician; insisted on his youth "like 65% of the Brazilian population which is less than 45 years old"; and affirmed that "today the Brazilian problem is a moral question and the moralization of public service in this country is not being given adequate attention."[50] Upon referring to the need for administrative reform, Collor also touched on the theme of "privatization," which would later move to center stage in his discourse as candidate.

The program began a practice that would be repeated in 1989, that is, the legally doubtful appearance of Collor in the annual radio and TV programs of political parties to which he was not even affiliated.[51] It also indicated the total "match" between, on the one side, Collor's style of discourse and marketing strategy, and, on the other side, the polls and the political scenario that was being constructed in the media for the 1989 election.

The ad agency Setembro supervised the production of the next program to be aired in March and began by changing the name of the party itself from PJ to the new PRN (Partido da Renovação Nacional, or Party of Reconstruction). Although the polls had indicated that the party's name was not important for the voter, "the new name was created in the lab based on the characteristics with which Collor intended to identify himself."[52] The PRN program was created within a TV logic, which even included "commercial" breaks. The program portrayed Collor talking about the "moral, political, and ethical crisis" and of course criticizing the "bad politicians and the maharajahs." The words used repeatedly by Collor were "character," "dignity," "honor," "courage," and "justice."

Money, audacity, and loopholes in the electoral laws made it possible for Collor to continue this strategy. The next radio and TV program to be utilized was that of the obscure and unknown PTR (Partido Trabalhista Renovador, or Labor Reconstruction Party) in April. The objective this time was to show "the Brazil that succeeded" and to portray Collor in "the Indiana Jones style, preaching his ideas in blue jeans and a sports shirt. . . . The key words of the program were the same as before, adding a new *motto*, austerity. 'We want a new Brazil,' chanted a chorus of young people."[53]

Previous legal requests for the suspension of the upcoming annual radio and TV programs of the PSC (Partido Social Christão, or Social Christian Party) was supported by Brizola's PDT (Partido Democratico Trabalhista, or Democratic Labor Party) but rejected by the superior electoral court (TSE), and the strategy was repeated again. TV star Mayra Magri, or Camila, the problematic girl of the "O Salvador da Patria" (The Savior of the Country) *novela*, was the main attraction of the program, in which Collor dealt with themes such as ecology, public deficit, corruption, and ethics. Commenting on the PSC program, *Folha de São Paulo* stated, "It is certain that Collor has already established himself as a representative of the discourse of privatization and efficiency."[54]

The next IBOPE poll announced by TV Globo's "Jornal Nacional" confirmed Collor in first place with 43 percent of aided-recall voting intentions, almost four times Brizola's 11 percent and more than five times Lula's 8 percent. Collor's popularity was attributed to the following themes, in this order: his association with youth and the young, his courage and determination, the fight against the "maharajahs," the success in the government of Alagoas, and the opposition to the federal government. Collor's position was so comfortable that he refused to participate in TV debates sponsored by the Bandeirantes and Manchete networks (not carried by Globo) before the first November 15 round of voting.

Collor's campaign was "produced" within a coherent marketing strategy of image construction that included everything from his gestures (fingers forming V for victory) and his discourse ("my people") to the colors (those of the national flag) and the music surrounding him. For one full week, he was trained with a video from the U.S. National Education Media Center, produced by Jack Valenti—former White House consultant and, now president of the Motion Picture Association of America—on how to speak with confidence and style. Under the supervision of Setembro, the ad agencies DNA and Opção produced the radio and TV programs of the PRN, PTR, and PSC parties as well as the programs that were used during the free time provided on radio and television to all candidates by the Tribunal Superior Eleitoral, under the law, beginning September 15. Those two ad agencies were also in charge of the production of more than 108 miscellaneous political marketing items including signs, bumper stickers, buttons, ads, outdoor displays, and manuals.

THE SCENARIO OF REPRESENTATION

By June, the political scenario within which the 1989 Brazilian presidential election was to be played out had already been constructed. *Novelas*, the news, the polls, and the political marketing strategies were the "machineries and the regimes" of this construction. There was the TV scenario itself, which valued attributes that conformed to a media logic, including youth, beauty, modernity, sportiness, and courage. There were also the specific elements of the political scenario. The narrative of the *novelas* portrayed politics and politicians as negative. The state was construed to be corrupt and inefficient, and so were its public servants. TV Globo news programs were faithful to the political beliefs of mogul Roberto Marinho and called on the country to unite to support Collor, who was represented as modern, optimistic, and an "outsider." The 1988–1989 crisis in the Western European countries covered daily by TV news provided the ideal background to reinforce the discourse elevating privatization over socialism. Through the media's eyes, Fukuyama's "end of history" was in sight.

This was the scenario of representation in which Collor was launched nationwide through "Jornal Nacional" and the legally dubious use of the annual programs of the PJ, PRN, PTR, and PSC parties. Guided by opinion polls, Collor, the professional politician, son and grandson of politicians, was able to create an image of himself as the moralistic "outsider," fighting corruption (the "maharajahs" and the federal government). As a young, handsome athlete, he also fit TV models of desire and pleasure.

Collor preached the privatization of the state in the name of efficiency and modernity, opening the way for the alliances that would make him acceptable to the Brazilian establishment.

Finally, it is necessary to emphasize that although this scenario of representation was built over a long period and was very well constituted by mid-1989, it would not stand by itself. Its maintenance required a permanent and complex struggle. As indicated earlier, scenarios of representation operate within a hegemonic construction and must therefore be "continually renewed, recreated, defended, and modified" because they are "continually resisted, limited, altered, and challenged."[55] Collor, the "elite" candidate, won the election in the second round with 43 percent of the vote, but Lula, his opponent, and a labor leader, had 38 percent of the total vote. The almost 32 million who voted for Lula were certainly struggling toward a counterhegemonic political scenario, and, given Brazilian political "elitist tradition," this is an extremely significant accomplishment that must be seriously studied if it is to be totally understood.

CONCLUSIONS

Some basic questions can be raised from the argument advanced here. The first is theoretical, with implications for conducting research about the relationship of media and politics; the second is legal, referring to both the Brazilian electoral and communication laws and the functioning of the Electoral Justice; and the third is political, reconsidering the nature of democracy that can be constructed in Brazil and in other Latin American countries.

If the argument presented here is correct, it would once again show that analysis of the media's message—programming—isolated from its context is of little real value. Stuart Hall alerts us that there can be no communication theory separated from "(a) a general social theory; (b) a developed cultural theory; and (c) a properly historicized model of social formations." Theories in which these conditions do not occur, remain "sociologically innocent."[56] In the case of the 1989 Brazilian election, an analyst who tries to understand the role of the media in Collor's victory by studying the "political campaign," commonly considered to be the free radio and TV programs presenting the candidates' platforms and carried after September 15, runs the risk of concentrating on the wrong subject.

A point that could be raised about this analysis is that it does not follow the contemporary research and theoretical trend to displace the axis of the analysis from the production of the message to its reception; that is, to the process of the construction of meaning by the audience. How does one reconcile the return to the concept of the media as powerful, with the rediscovery of the active audience or of cultural resistance? The notion of a "scenario of representation" advanced in this chapter allows for a dialectical view of the media's role as both reflexive and constructive. In the case of the relationship between television and elections, the election results are the most precise indicators of the voters' construction of meaning; that is, of their overall cognitive response and of their "activity" as a media audience. Furthermore, Brazil is a country that "jumped" from a pre-Gutenbergian condition (very low levels of literacy and print media circulation) to a condition in which the most-advanced technical sophistication of images predominates. There is little or no knowledge about the cognitive effects of this media "jump." It must also be remembered that "an active audience" does not necessarily mean a "critical audience" or indicate "resistance"[57] and that the construction of meaning is possible only within the structural limits of the hegemonic process.[58]

It becomes clear upon studying the 1989 election that the Brazilian electoral laws are poorly enforced and also have serious loopholes. For example, it is possible for a single candidate to utilize the annual political party programs on national radio and television to promote himself or herself in the presidential race; it is possible for the same public opinion polling agency to work for both a television network and one of the candidates; it is possible for the results of the electoral polls to favor a particular candidate; and there is no "right to respond" outside of the free electoral time on radio and TV, such as on TV news programs. Add to all of this the incredible slowness of the superior electoral court (TSE) in reaching a final decision on fundamental questions raised during the electoral process in order to enforce the law.

The 1989 election made clear the urgent necessity of democratizing communication legislation. The new Brazilian constitution of 1988 (title VIII, chapter V) provides some instruments that could improve the current situation: It forbids the existence of a monopoly or oligopoly in the media; it establishes the complementarity of public, private, and state broadcasting systems; it establishes the regionalization of cultural, artistic, and journalistic production; and it establishes the creation of a Council of Social Communication as an auxiliary office of the National Congress. Various bills are presently on their way through both the Senate and the House, designed to give administrative form to these constitutional provisions. The hope is that this regulation will become operational and that the advances of the new constitution will not turn into dead letters, as has been the tradition in Brazil.

It is important, at this point, to consider some of the implications of our argument on the free electoral broadcast time, or *horário gratuito*. There is no doubt that the *horário gratuito* continues to be an important part of the electoral process, above all for the small parties. The fact that Lula was able to double his voter preference (from 7 percent to 14 percent) during the *horário gratuito* period in the first round indicates its importance.

A debate is now in progress in the National Congress between the holders of broadcast licenses and the political parties over the possible alternatives in the legislation on the free electoral hour. There has to be a better way to incorporate vital political information into the viewing habits of the radio and TV audiences.

Finally, the 1989 Brazilian election leads to a reconsideration of the concept of democracy. What kind of democracy is possible in contemporary mediacentric cultures, where political scenarios are necessarily reflected and constructed by the media, especially television? Has Collor's election now become the paradigm for electoral processes in other Latin American countries, as the Brazilian 1964 military coup set a trend for the whole southern cone?[59]

Despite all the differences, Brazil and other Latin American countries share a common characteristic: They are mediacentric transnational consumer cultures. The central position of commercial television in all Latin America unites otherwise quite different societies in the sense that they are all dominated by "machineries and regimes" that constitute and reflect scenarios of representation in which people live and make sense of their lives. Even though there are different histories and traditions among Latin American cultures, the widespread adoption of private television and its commercial and consumerist scenarios seems to herald collapse of difference and the adaptation of a method of political practice that makes it urgent to intensify the struggle for critical citizenship.

Democracy in contemporary mediacentric cultures should be reconsidered as a utopian political project to be achieved in the historical process of the construction of opposing scenarios of representation. Subjectivity, identity, and politics must constitute and reflect the concrete cultural hegemonic struggle of empowered citizens toward societies in which real difference and diversity will prevail in class, race, gender, desire, and pleasure.

This is the challenge before those who study media and politics in Brazil and elsewhere: to help build a democracy where the will of the majority prevails over the "competence" of a media-constructed political scenario of representation.

NOTES

1. Paper presented to the 41st Annual Conference of the International Communication Association, Chicago, May 1991. The research for this paper was supported by a grant from the Brazilian National Research Council (CNPq). Sections of this paper were also presented in a slightly modified way by Venicio A. de Lima and Susan S. Reilly as

"Constructing the Political Scenario: Television, Elections, and the Quest for Democracy" at the Fourth International Television Studies Conference, London, July 1991.

2. Tribunal Superior Eleitoral, "Eleitores Brasileiros em 1986/Estimativa de Eleitores entre 16 e 18 Años," (1989).

3. "Caderno de Midia," *Imprensa* 26 (October 1989).

4. Steven H. Chaffee and J. L. Hochheimer. "The Beginnings of Political Communication Research in the U.S.: Origins of the 'Limited Effects' Model," in *Mass Communication Review Yearbook*, vol. 5, ed. M. Gurevitch and M. R. Levy (Beverly Hills and London: Sage, 1985); Stuart Hall, "Encoding/Decoding," in *Culture, Media, Language*, ed. S. Hall et al. (London/Birmingham: Huntchinson/CCCS, 1980).

5. Jesse G. Delia, "Communication Research: A History," in *Handbook of Communication Science*, ed. C. R. Berger and S. H. Chaffee (Beverly Hills and London: Sage, 1987).

6. Kurt Lang and Gladys Lang, "The Mass Media and Voting," in *The Process and Effects of Mass Communication*, ed. W. Schramm and D. F. Roberts (Champaign: University of Illinois Press, 1974).

7. B. C. Cohen, *The Press, the Public and Foreign Policy* (Princeton, N.J.: Princeton University Press, 1963).

8. Elisabeth Noelle-Neumann, "Return to the Concept of Powerful Mass Media," *Studies of Broadcasting* 9 (1973). Renato Ortiz, *A Moderna Tradição Brasileira* (São Paulo: Brasiliense, 1988).

9. Albino Rubim, "Comunicação, Espaço Público e Eleições Presidenciais," *Textos de Cultura e Comunicação* 24 (1989).

10. Giovanni Sartori, "Video-Power," *Government and Opposition: Journal of Comparative Politics* 24 (Winter 1989).

11. David Paletz and Robert Entman, *Media, Power, Politics* (New York: The Free Press, 1981).

12. Joshua Meyrowitz, "Television's Covert Challenge," *Dialogue* 4 (1989).

13. Raoul Girardet, *Mythes et Mythologies Politiques* (Paris: Seuil, 1986).

14. Roger Silverstone, *The Message of Television* (London: Heinemann, 1981); Roger Silverstone, "Television Myth and Culture," in *Media, Myths and Narratives—Television and the Press*, ed. James W. Carey (Beverly Hills and London: Sage, 1988).

15. David Thorburn, "Television Melodrama," *Understanding TV—Essays on TV as a Social and Cultural Force*, ed. Richard P. Adler (New York: Praeger, 1981).

16. Raymond Williams, *Television—Technology and Cultural Form* (New York: Schocken, 1975).

17. Jean Baudrillard, *For a Critique of the Political Economy of the Sign* (St. Louis, Mo.: Telos Press, 1978).

18. Peter McLaren, "Postmodernity and the Death of Politics: A Brazilian Reprieve," *Educational Theory* 36 (1986). Neil Larsen, "Postmodernism and Imperialism: Theory and Politics in Latin America," *Postmodern Culture* 1 (September 1990).

19. Francis Fukuyama, "The End of History," *The National Interest* 16 (Summer 1989).

20. Hall, "Encoding/Decoding."

21. Gramsci quoted in *Selections from the Prison Notebooks of Antonio Gramsci*, ed. Quintin Hoore and Geoffrey Powell Smith (New York: International Publishers, 1971), p. 261.

22. Douglas Kellner, *Television and the Crisis of Democracy* (Boulder: Westview, 1990); *Anuário Brasileiro de Midia, 1990/1991* (São Paulo: Meio & Mensagem).

23. Hall, "Encoding/Decoding."

24. T. J. Jackson Lears, "The Concept of Cultural Hegemony: Problems and Possibilities," *The American Historical Review* 90 (1985).

25. Raymond Williams, *Marxism and Literature* (New York: Oxford University Press, 1977).

26. Instituto Brasileiro de Geografia e Estatística. Pesquisa Nacional por Amostra de Domicílios, 1989.

27. "Caderno de Midia," *Imprensa*.

28. *Anuário Brasileiro*.

29. "Caderno de Midia," *Imprensa*.

30. Michele Mattelart and Armand Mattelart, *The Carnival of Images* (New York: Bergin

and Garvey, 1990; orig. 1987).
31. Venicio A. de Lima and Murilo Ramos, "A Televisão no Brasil: Desinformação e Democracia," in *Da Distenção à Abertura: As Eleições de 1982*, ed. David Fleischer (Editora da Universidade de Brasília, 1988); Venicio A. de Lima, "The State, Television and Political Power in Brazil," *Critical Studies in Mass Communication* 5 (1988); Venicio A. de Lima, "O Medo de Votar e Perder," *Correio Braziliense* 24 July 1989.
32. Roberto Marinho, "Convocação," *O Globo*, 2 April 1989.
33. Neri V. Eich, "Robert Marinho Torna Explicito Apoio a Collor," *Folha de São Paulo*, 26 July 1989.
34. Venicio A. de Lima, "Televisão e Política; Hipótese Sobre a Eleição Presidencial de 1989," *Communiçãcao e Política* 9 (April–June, 1990): 29–54.
35. Mattelart and Mattelart, *Carnival of Images*; Renato Ortiz et al., *Telenovela: Historia e Producão* (São Paulo: Brasilense, 1989).
36. Ortiz et al., *Telenovela*.
37. The word *maharajah*, literally *an Indian prince*, became a catchword in the 1989 Brazilian presidential election. Collor used it to refer to any overpaid (real or imaginary) politician or civil servant who lived as lavishly as an Indian prince without working much. "Maharajahs" became the number-one public enemy and Collor, the "maharajah hunter." As early as March 23, 1988, (twenty months before the first electoral round), *Veja*, the most popular Brazilian weekly magazine, ran a seven-page cover story on the theme. The cover pictured Collor under the heading: "Collor de Mello—the hunter of maharajahs."
38. Rubim, "Comunicação."
39. Maria do Carmo Campello de Souza, "The Brazilian 'New Republic': Under the Sword of Damocles," in *Democratizing Brazil*, ed. Alfred Stepan (New York: Oxford University Press, 1989).
40. Alan Riding, "One Man's Political Views Collor Brazil's TV Eye," *New York Times*, 12 January 1987, A-4.
41. Lima, "Televisão e Política."
42. Ibid.
43. Lima, "O Medo de Votar e Perder."
44. Leticia Lins, "Pesquisa Mostra Memoria Curta de Eleitor Nordestino," *Jornal do Brasil*, 27 May 1990.
45. This section is based on a much more detailed account of Collor's political marketing in Lima, "Televisão e Política." All data and bibliographical references are to be found there. See also Teodomiro Braga, "Como se Faz um Presidente," *Jornal do Brasil*, 19 December 1989.
46. J. C. Cancellier, "Campanha de Collor Custa US $1 Bilhão, Revela Primo," *Correio Braziliense*, 29 June 1989.
47. Venicio A. de Lima, "O Descredito do Poder Legislativo," *Revista de Cultura Vozes* 78 (1984).
48. *Jornal do Brasil*, 19 December 1989, Special Edition, p. 2.
49. Brazilian electoral laws (Lei 4.737/65 and Lei 5.682/71) require from radio and television stations (which are state concessions) the annual free broadcasting of an hour-long program on the party's principles and propositions. The laws are quite clear, however, that those annual broadcasts cannot be used to announce any particular party candidate for any public office. In addition, in the sixty days prior to the elections, radio and television stations are required to broadcast two hours of political messages from the candidates of all parties according to their representational percentage in Congress. Paid political advertising on radio and television is forbidden.
50. *Jornal do Brasil*, 14 May 1988, p. 5.
51. The majority leader of the powerful PMDB political party—Senator Ronan Tito—charged in a Senate session in May 1989 that there had been "financial transactions" between Collor and the PRN, PSC, and PTR parties in order for him to appear as a "guest" in their annual radio and TV programs. Brizola's PDT party immediately moved against Collor in the Tribunal Superior Eleitoral (superior electoral court). As

late as March 1991 (sixteen months after the first round of the election was held), there had been no final decision by the court.

52. *Jornal do Brasil*, 19 December 1989, Special Edition, p. 3.
53. Braga, "Como se Faz um Presidente."
54. Nelson Sá, "Garoto Problema," *Folha de São Paulo*, (19 May 1989).
55. Williams, *Marxism and Literature*.
56. Hall, "Encoding/Decoding."
57. David Sholle, "Resistance: Pinning Down a Wandering Concept in Cultural Studies Discourse," *Journal of Urban Studies* 1 (1990).
58. Hall, "Encoding/Decoding."
59. Ronaldo Munck, *Latin America—The Transition to Democracy* (London: Zed Books, 1989).

7

The Brazilian Case: Influencing the Voter

Joseph Straubhaar, Organ Olsen, and Maria Cavaliari Nunes

The role of the media, particularly television, in Brazilian politics is striking and hotly debated. There is a tendency among scholars and the general public to see television, particularly TV Globo, the dominant network, as a decisive, even determining factor in the outcome of political campaigns. In fact, the fear of television's power led to certain significant reforms in Brazil's 1988 constitution, specifically the creation of the *horário gratuito* (free electoral campaign time given to each party on television and radio) to make sure that all candidates and parties have access to the electronic media. This was an attempt to further the overall democratization of Brazilian politics, to ensure that neither the government nor the media industry could have exclusive use of television and radio to shape the images of candidates and issues.

In 1989, Brazil held its first direct elections for president since 1960. All citizens were required by law to vote or justify their absence. The election was held in two rounds: an initial round in November in which all twenty-two announced candidates participated and a runoff in December between the two who got the most votes in the first round. In both stages, several potentially decisive factors competed to persuade voters. First, as we shall see, television news, debates, and free political advertising time seemed to dominate other sources of information. However, direct personal contacts with political parties, campaign organizations, unions, and the Church, as well as discussions with local opinion leaders, family, and friends also seemed important.

One of the key issues to examine in the 1989 Brazilian campaign is the impact of the *horário gratuito* (free electoral campaign time on radio and television) on the election process. The *horário gratuito* was quite successful in its goals: Both final-round presidential candidates, Lula (Workers' Party) and Collor (Partido de Reconstrucão Nacional, or

PRN), defined themselves through the precampaign and campaign *horário gratuito* television access programs. Indeed, Lula's campaign succeeded to the degree that it did (gaining 47 percent of the final vote) at least in part because of the *horário gratuito*, for Lula did not have the external resources of Collor, who was backed by TV Globo and therefore had favorable TV exposure outside of the *horário gratuito*.

There are several related issues to consider in examining the role of the media in political power in Brazil. The first issue, an ongoing academic debate, concerns the relative power of the media over their audiences. What assumptions can one make about the ability of the media, particularly television, to shape the thinking of individual audiences and voters? Does the influence of the media tend to be strong or weak? Second, how much competition does television get from other media and other sources of information in the process of forming images in the minds of audiences and thus influencing the decisions of voters? Does the television industry truly have as much power in relation to other sources of cultural formation and information as a number of scholars assert? Third, to what extent do various groups enable individuals to interpret the media? As Barbero asks, how do groups help individuals mediate the media?[1] This chapter focuses primarily on the second question, which we address through survey data. However, a brief consideration of the other questions will lead to a better understanding of our findings.

THEORETICAL PERSPECTIVES

Most studies, whether focused on structural/institutional issues or audience behavior, show television to be the dominant medium in the politics and culture of Brazil. But just how dominant is it?

Several lines of thought and research envision the media, particularly television, as very powerful. The Frankfurt school of sociology, which has been very influential in Latin American analysis of cultural industries, saw the media, or "cultural industries," as having great power over their audiences. Marxist and neo-Marxist scholars in Europe and Latin America likewise tend to see the media and the culture they support as an ideological superstructure determined by the economic relations of production and the relations of classes. The British-American school of thought referred to as "cultural studies" contains a lively controversy over whether the media or audiences are more powerful. Some theorists in this debate observe that media messages contain a preferred reading, the message that powerful institutions intend them to have, but Morley, Fiske, and others have shown that audiences frequently make alternative or even oppositional readings of television or other messages, rejecting the preferred reading. Some behavioral effects theories, such as Gerbner's cultivation theory, tend to see the media as powerful, cultivating a number of strong images and behaviors in heavy viewers. However, most behaviorally oriented researchers see media effects as limited. Umberto Eco critiqued the Marxists and other strong-effects theorists as "apocalyptic" and the behavioral scientists as "integrated" (with the dominant interests in the media system). Similarly, Barbero critiqued both Marxist/neo-Marxist and behavioral schools of thought for being overly functionalist and concentrating on the presumed media effects rather than looking at how people make sense of the media and what groups and traditions help people mediate media content.[2]

The lines of theory that show most current application and value in the Brazilian setting focus on active audience reception and class differences within the active audience.[3] Interesting U.S. scholarly approaches to the active audience, such as the theory of uses and gratifications, tend to diminish the overestimation of television as the "main source" of information and news;[4] these approaches are used less by Brazilian and other Latin American researchers because they do not give sufficient weight to structural factors such as social class. More attention is being paid to cultural studies theories, such as those of Hall; to class-focused audience research, such as that by Bourdieu; and to the incorporation of research about broadcast media structures with audience research.[5] In fact, this chapter begins its examination of the effect of television on the Brazilian elections with a review of the structural or institutional situation of Brazilian television. However, by combining analysis of institutions with audience analysis, we hope to further debunk some lines of critical theory in both Brazil and the United States that tend to see broadcast media institutions, particularly those in such powerful positions as TV Globo in Brazil, as virtually omnipotent in creating and maintaining political trends and candidacies.

TELEVISION: THE DOMINANT MEDIUM

Both structural/institutional and audience behavior analyses show television to be the dominant information medium in Brazil. Non–mass media channels of organizational and interpersonal communication, however, are also very important.

Television's dominant position is the result of policies enacted during the era of the military government (1964–1985), which subsidized the television infrastructure, including microwave and satellite relay systems, and encouraged the purchase of TV sets with favorable credit and policies. Government support helped the TV Globo network grow into a quasi monopoly, which, until recently, held 60 to 80 percent of the audience.[6] The network still routinely wins over 50 percent of the viewership.

The military governments used television to control information. The military, political, and police authorities censored television news and even entertainment shows. With *abertura* (political opening), government intervention declined after 1978. Under the civilian New Republic, begun in 1985, television news was permitted a more active role in covering politics and an increased role in elections by virtue of the access provided to the candidates.[7]

Although formal military and government control over television diminished, the owners of the major television networks maintained their own political interest and alliances. Roberto Marinho, owner of the Globo radio, TV, and newspaper empire, remained a crucial supporter of the new civilian regime, which relied on TV Globo for support of its economic plans and other projects in television news coverage. Today, however, Marinho and TV Globo no longer dominate television. Competition has grown with the addition of three other television networks: TV Manchete, owned by magazine publisher Adolpho Bloch, which in 1990 finally bested TV Globo in prime time with a *telenovela* (prime-time serial) called "Pantanal," about the west of Brazil; Sistema Brasileira de Televisão, owned by TV personality Silvio Santos, who has bested Globo in Sundays with variety shows aimed at the lower middle and working class; and TV Bandeirantes, owned by the Saad family, which predates Globo and has specialized in news and sports shows for smaller audiences. More competition will come with new UHF channels scheduled to specialize in music, news, and foreign language programs. Those will further diversify ownership and control, admitting Editora Abril (Brazil's largest publishing house), Radio Jovem Pan of São Paulo, and other major media companies into television competition. Editora Abril had sought such entry in vain during military rule.

Notwithstanding the increased competition, TV Globo still often gets up to 70 percent of the total Brazilian TV advertising budget, which is very large for a third-world nation (over 60 percent of total advertising has gone to television for over a decade). When the last military regime began to lose legitimacy during the 1984 opposition campaign for direct presidential elections, TV Globo shifted adroitly to provide close coverage of the subsequent successful presidential campaign of Tancredo Neves (who died before he could be inaugurated) and the government of his vice-presidential running mate, José Sarney.[8] TV Globo also moved early to support Fernando Collor's candidacy in 1989. Now, however, TV Globo must increasingly share its power with other television networks.

The role of television is enhanced by the weaknesses in other media structures and limits on audience access to other media. Radio remains important, particularly for the 20 to 30 percent of the population without regular access to television. Newspaper circulation consists of only about 3 million daily issues among a population of over 140 million, and the top news magazine, *Veja* (published by Editora Abril), has a circulation of about 900,000 weekly. Even if each newspaper or news magazine is read by an average of two to three people, the reach of the print media remains quite limited.

Television is the only truly national news source, since newspapers and radio are local or regional. News magazines are national but reach only the middle class and elite, and even among these groups the readership is limited. According to a 1981 study[9] of better-educated audiences (with a secondary education or more) in four Brazilian cities, TV Globo's "Jornal Nacional" ("National News") was the only information source shared by most of them, followed distantly by the national news magazine *Veja*, then by regional newspapers and radio. Some residents of Brasília read Rio and São Paulo newspapers, but even the media in those large urban centers are heavily regional. Despite increasing competition, TV Globo's "Jornal Nacional" dominates geographic coverage among television newscasts. In 1989, it routinely drew over 60 percent of the television audience, ranking among the top three or four TV programs, and continuing to dominate all other news sources in regular exposure.[10]

Free radio and TV advertising time given to candidates (*horário gratuito eleitoral*) and televised debates among the candidates were also major forms of television information in the 1989 presidential elections. Candidates in the first round were given free air time during both afternoon and prime time in proportion to the size of their congressional representation. They could produce and air whatever they wished. In the second round, the two finalists were given equal blocks of time. Contrary to some expectations, the public did watch the free electoral advertising time. Over 80 percent of the TV audience watched at least once in a two-week sample period, and almost 60 percent watched three or more times, according to studies by the Instituto Brasileiro de Opinião e Estatística (IBOPE) in November 1989.

This free political advertising prevailed over other means by which time on television and radio had been provided previously. Rules under the military (pre-1985) had fluctuated. When relatively open access to television in some elections led to opposition victories, as in 1974, the military reduced exposure in subsequent elections to the display of mug shots with party identifications. Under the 1988 constitution, however, parties and individual candidates were granted access to daytime and prime-time hours on radio and television; the purchase of political advertising time was forbidden.

Several live debates were held during first-round and runoff elections, with clips used in candidates' free political advertising. Debates were summarized in newscasts. Some observers felt the edited summary by TV Globo of the final debate between Lula and Collor was slanted toward the latter, who eventually won the election. The broadcast became controversial when TV Globo's news director resigned in protest.

THE RELATIVE INFLUENCE OF TELEVISION
ON PUBLIC OPINION

The dominance of television as a source of political information among the mass media was confirmed by a national sample survey of 2,680 in October 1989 by IBOPE. The survey also showed television as part of a complex environment in which personal and organizational sources mediate information,[11] and personal sources often complement or offset the dominance of television news.

In the October survey, respondents were given a list of information sources and asked to indicate which three they used most. The source voters most frequently said helped them choose a candidate was conversation with family and friends (41 percent). The next most frequently cited source was the free advertising time on radio and television (34 percent). Other choices were conversations with colleagues at work or school (27 percent), candidate debates on television (26 percent), television news about candidates (20 percent); newspapers (15 percent), and radio news (10 percent). Sources mentioned less frequently were neighborhood associations (6 percent), the Catholic church (5 percent), union activists (5 percent), public opinion polls (5 percent), and radio commentators (5 percent). Twelve percent said that they used none of these, and 8 percent did not know. Although three of the top five channels of information are related to television, two of the top three sources are interpersonal and organizational.

Barbero notes several key mediating factors beyond the mass media in the formation of opinion and culture.[12] His research emphasizes the importance of families, church groups, neighborhood groups, and ethnic groups in mediating traditional, non–mass media forms of communication and in providing forums for the discussion and analysis of the mass media themselves. His notion is similar to that of the two-step flow,[13] although with a more refined view of the localized and decentralized mediating role of the opinion leader.

One of the questions we now wish to explore is the interaction between the media and the combination of personal and organizational sources of information in forming voting intentions and in receiving and processing political polling information. The use by individuals of interpersonal sources often takes the form of families and colleagues discussing information from television newscasts. Studies have shown, for example, that such discussions can radically reinterpret the television news organizations' intended reading of events and statements. For instance, Carlos Eduardo Lins da Silva's study of the reception and interpretation of news in two Brazilian working-class communities, one in economically underdeveloped northern Brazil and one in the industrialized south, showed that news coverage of strikes by TV Globo, intended to be negative, was interpreted according to the interests and experience of the two communities.[14] Workers in the south were upset about the obviously misleading coverage, and workers in the north wondered whether it was time to try organizing a strike.

CAMPAIGN STRATEGIES AND INFORMATION SOURCES IN THE 1989 ELECTION

From this review of research and theory, one might expect that Brazilian voters seeking political information would use a mix of mass media and interpersonal sources such as family, friends, and colleagues, along with organization channels such as the Catholic church, unions, and neighborhood associations. These last three groups have been singled out by many observers as important communication networks on the grassroots level. In the 1989 election, Lula of the Workers' Party was supported by most of the unions and by the progressive wing of the Catholic church. These groups, as well as many neighborhood associations, were very active at the local level in mobilizing support for Lula.

In contrast, Collor, the eventual winner, waged a campaign of modern political marketing, relying on polling and market research to design themes and television to communicate with voters, especially since he did not have a strong party base. Collor benefited from an early lead based on precampaign media exposure. He dominated the information space in the precampaign free television time given to political parties. In the first stage of the free political time, each party was allotted one hour between March and May 1989. Through negotiation, Collor won control of the time of three minor parties, and most analysts (see Lins da Silva in this book) feel this contributed significantly to his rapid rise in the polls. Critics worried that both Collor's cumulative media exposure and his continuing lead in the opinion polls would generate a bandwagon effect for him.

A study by *Folha de São Paulo* of a national sample on August 19 and 20, 1989, indirectly supports the notion that Collor benefited, at least initially, from television coverage. Of those whose primary information source was television, 46 percent preferred Collor over Leonel Brizola (the next strongest then with 13 percent), Paulo Maluf (7 percent), and so on, whereas the Collor-Brizola margin was smaller among those relying primarily on radio (Collor, 31 percent; Brizola, 17 percent), newspapers (28 percent; 17 percent), or magazines (20 percent; 21 percent). A confounding variable in the relationship is that lower-class voters both preferred Collor and relied more on television, so class might have caused both results.

Lula employed a strong television campaign as well, using the Workers' Party's television production unit, TV dos Trabalhadores (Workers' TV). But he also relied heavily on groups willing and able to engage in extensive door-to-door, factory gate, parish, and other local personal or organizational campaigns. We observed an extensive personal contact campaign by those groups in São Paulo, and we saw extensive media coverage of similar campaigns around Brazil, stretching remarkably far into rural areas, principally due to the "progressive" Church. Lula's political strategists were looking at both mass media, particularly television, and a rising set of grassroots organizations that campaigned at the personal level.

Information Sources and Candidate Preference

When sources of information are compared among voters preferring Collor or Lula in October (for the first round of elections in November), patterns tend to confirm the candidates' strategies. Collor's prospective voters tended to rely heavily on television, except for TV debates (which Collor boycotted in the first round), while Lula's voters were more likely to use union, Church, and organizational channels, while also using mass media (table 7.1).

Analysis of the data in table 7.1 reveals several trends. All voters

Table 7.1
INFORMATION SOURCES FOR SUPPORTERS
OF EACH CANDIDATE

	Collor	Lula	Brizola	Covas	Maluf	Guimarães
Talking with friends/ family	44%	38%	43%	37%	39%	43%
Political advertising	37	39	31	41	40	32
Talking to colleagues	28	30	29	29	23	26
Television news	23	22	19	25	24	21
TV debates between candidates	18	34	31	43	37	19
News in newspapers	13	16	14	29	26	14
Seeing candidates in rallies	18	16	18	14	12	19
Radio news	13	8	11	6	11	12
Radio commentators	5	5	5	6	5	7
Information by the Church	4	6	4	4	7	6
Information by labor leaders	3	13	5	7	4	9
Neighborhood associations	7	8	7	7	5	7
Poll results	7	4	3	9	6	3

NOTE: Up to three sources could be chosen from the list.

tended to rely on conversations with family and friends, as noted earlier. But, for supporters of Lula, Covas, and Maluf, the free radio and TV advertising time proved slightly more important than conversations with family and friends. TV and radio political advertising was cited notably less by supporters of Brizola and Guimarães, who were not seen as being as effective on television.

Televisions news was also cited less by Brizola supporters, probably because of Brizola's repeated accusation that TV Globo, the dominant channel in TV news, was biased against him. In contrast, supporters of Covas, Lula, Maluf, and Brizola cited TV debates much more often than supporters of Collor and Guimarães. The former were seen in press commentary as doing well in the debates, whereas Collor boycotted the first-round debates and Guimarães was perceived in the press as doing badly.

Connections also emerge between candidate support and social class in the use of information sources. Covas and Maluf supporters tended to be middle class or higher. This finding correlates with a greater reliance on newspapers, which table 7.2 shows to be more prevalent among the better educated. Radio news is more important for the

Table 7.2
INFORMATION SOURCES BY LEVEL OF EDUCATION

	Primary	Middle	Secondary	University
Talking with friends/family	41%	43%	40%	34%
Political advertising	30	35	39	42
Talking to colleagues	23	29	33	30
Television news	21	20	19	23
TV debates between candidates	13	28	41	55
News in newspapers	8	17	22	42
Seeing candidates in rallies	12	18	18	14
Radio news	12	11	6	6
Radio commentators	4	6	6	4
Information by the Church	6	5	4	0
Information by labor leaders	3	6	9	3
Neighborhood associations	4	10	7	3
Poll results	4	6	7	6

NOTE: Up to three sources could be chosen from the list.

lower classes, as reflected in table 7.2, but the overall pattern of the relationship between radio and support for various candidates is not clear.

Information by Church sources was most important for Lula and Guimarães, both of whom had the backing of the "progressive" Catholic church, and Maluf, who was backed by more conservative Catholic and Protestant groups. Lula, who first emerged as a labor leader, was clearly preferred by those who relied most on information from labor sources.

Interestingly, poll results were not a primary source of information for many voters—they ranked at the bottom of the listed choices. However, those who most frequently cited polls supported Collor, who had a commanding lead in the polls, and Covas, who was climbing in the polls.

Information Sources and Voter Demographics

Although some information sources were common to almost all groups, there was considerable variation among voters. Education was the most powerful variable in explaining the use of information sources. This matches research findings from other countries, such as France[15] and Colombia[16] where education (or cultural capital, as Bourdieu puts it) is strongly linked to media use, information patterns, and cultural tastes. Economic class, measured by income, showed patterns quite similar to those of education, hardly surprising since both are linked to social class. Since self-reporting of incomes in Brazilian surveys is considered less reliable than self-reporting of education, the latter has been used here as the primary indicator of social class.

Analysis of table 7.2 shows that, again, the two sources used by almost all Brazilians, regardless of education, were discussions with family members and television news. Education made little difference in the use of TV news as a principal source. It also made little difference in reliance on family members as a source, except that the best educated rely on family members less. Lower educational groups were less likely to report reliance on colleagues.

Groups with more education were slightly more likely to cite electoral propaganda on TV and radio as a major source. The better educated were more likely to cite television debates and newspapers, while the less educated more often cited radio news and Church leaders.

Data in table 7.3 suggest that gender made some difference in the use of political information, but its effect was modified by work outside the home, especially for women. Whether or not they work outside the home, women rely more than men on family and friends and slightly more on the Church. Women and men who work outside the home show a similar tendency to cite colleagues and TV debates as information sources.

As has been observed in a number of third-world countries since Lerner's work in Turkey, some of the most striking differences in

Table 7.3
INFORMATION SOURCES, GENDER, AND WORK OUTSIDE HOME

	Men Who Work Outside Home	Women Who Work Outside Home	Men Who Don't Work Outside Home	Women Who Don't Work Outside Home
Talking with friends/family	38%	38%	42%	45%
Political advertising	33	34	34	36
Talking to colleagues	32	22	32	18
Television news	20	16	20	23
TV debates between candidates	26	24	32	23
News in newspapers	17	16	14	14
Seeing candidates in rallies	16	18	16	12
Radio news	10	8	9	11
Radio commentators	5	6	5	5
Information by the Church	4	4	6	6
Information by labor leaders	5	7	6	4
Neighborhood associations	6	8	8	6
Poll results	6	8	4	5

Table 7.4

INFORMATION SOURCES AND URBAN/RURAL DENSITY

000's/MUNICÍPIO	Rural Areas		Small Towns		Larger Cities	
	<10	10–20	20–50	50–100	100–500	500+
Talking with friends/family	41%	46%	41%	31%	43%	40%
Political advertising	27	41	34	31	39	35
Talking to colleagues	29	29	28	20	25	29
Television news	23	16	17	22	19	23
TV debates between candidates	16	19	24	33	31	32
News in newspapers	10	11	12	18	20	22
Seeing candidates in rallies	13	14	15	15	18	14
Radio news	11	8	11	11	8	10
Radio commentators	5	4	3	3	7	5
Information by the Church	5	5	6	6	4	4
Information by labor leaders	5	2	3	5	7	7
Neighborhood associations	6	4	5	8	8	7
Poll results	6	4	3	6	5	6

media habits and media effects are between those in relatively rural as opposed to urban environments.[17] Our study gauged differences in city size and urban-rural differences in terms of the number of voters located in the county (*município*), a political unit somewhat larger than the average U.S. county or township. Although *municípios* vary in size and hence in population, they are a relatively good measure of differences among rural, small town, small city, medium-sized city, and relatively large city.

Analysis of information in table 7.4 suggests that, as with education, there are relatively few differences among rural areas, small towns, and urban settings in the use of certain key information sources such as family and friends, colleagues, TV news, and radio news. The latter is perhaps surprising, since radio is thought to be a rural medium in some third-world nations, but radio is also a key medium for the urban working class and the poor in Brazil. There are major differences among rural areas, small towns, and urban settings in the use of other key information sources. Those in smaller towns and rural areas made less use of the radio and TV election advertising, newspapers, and information from labor leaders.

The Viewing and Use of Political Advertising

Most Brazilians watched the free political advertisements fairly frequently during the week preceding the survey. Those with primary education or less, or in smaller towns or rural areas, were least likely to watch (table 7.5).

Most Brazilians were also relatively attentive to political advertisements, as demonstrated in table 7.6. Those with less education were, again, least likely to be attentive.

Respondents showed a tendency to pay attention only to a candidate they had already picked. That may be relevant to the notion of a bandwagon effect from polling, but it is equally relevant to using mass media to reinforce a selection determined primarily through interpersonal or organizational means, such as the Church or unions. Again, the least educated were more likely to use political advertising in this way, as shown in table 7.7.

Table 7.8 demonstrates that less-educated Brazilians were also more likely (39 percent) than the best educated (25 percent) to cite the political ads on electoral free time as very useful in picking a candidate. Most Brazilians found the free political advertisements useful in making a decision, as indicated in table 7.9.

A key issue in press coverage of the 1989 election was whether the political advertising was oriented toward negative campaigning or toward constructive messages about the candidates' own programs. Many

Table 7.5
LEVEL OF EDUCATION AND THE WATCHING OF POLITICAL ADS

	Education			
	Primary	*Middle*	*Secondary*	*University*
Did not watch in last 7 days	37%	24%	18%	18%
Watched 1–3 days	27	38	41	38
Watched 4–6 days	12	19	18	21
Watched 7 days a week	22	19	22	22

Table 7.6
URBAN/RURAL DENSITY AND THE WATCHING
OF POLITICAL ADS

	Rural Areas		*Small Towns*		*Larger Cities*	
000's/MUNICÍPIO	*<10*	*10–20*	*20–50*	*50–100*	*100–500*	*500+*
Did not watch in last 7 days	40%	31%	27%	28%	25%	20%
Watched 1–3 days	27	34	34	32	37	36
Watched 4–6 days	11	17	16	15	16	19
Watched 7 days a week	19	18	21	22	22	25

Table 7.7
ATTENTION TO POLITICAL ADS AND EDUCATION

	Education			
	Primary	*Middle*	*Secondary*	*University*
Pay a lot of attention to political ads	50%	50%	57%	53%
Pay medium attention	28	31	33	33
Pay little attention	14	12	6	7
Don't pay attention	7	7	4	6

Table 7.8
SELECTIVE ATTENTION TO POLITICAL ADS AND EDUCATION

	Education			
	Primary	*Middle*	*Secondary*	*University*
Attend only to the candidate one intends to vote for	20%	21%	14%	8%
Attend equally to all	67	62	70	73

Brazilian commentators felt, for example, that heavy negative campaigning by Collor in the last two weeks of the final round in December greatly contributed to his victory.

In October, voters perceived political ads as tending to be negative, as demonstrated in table 7.10.

It is clear from the data in table 7.11 that those who considered the political ads as primarily positive (offering proposals rather than attacks) tended to find the ads more useful. Those who saw the political advertisements as negative found them less useful.

The Effect of Free Political Advertising Time in 1989

It is clear that the effect of free political advertising time in the 1989 Brazilian presidential elections was substantial. The survey showed the radio and television political advertising to have been the second most frequent source of information for choosing a candidate, as previously demonstrated—relatively more important in smaller towns and among the better educated. Contrary to some cynics' original expectations, the Brazilian audience stayed tuned for the political advertising time block. The survey showed several measures of the high degree of interest. In addition to the measures already reported, TV sets stayed on during this time block; the number of days watched in the last week was fairly

Table 7.9
USEFULNESS OF FREE POLITICAL ADVERTISEMENTS
IN DECISION MAKING

Usefulness of Advertisements	Percentage of Voters
"Help a lot"	37%
"Help somewhat"	23
"Help a little"	17
"Don't help much"	7
"Don't help at all"	14

SOURCE: IBOPE October 1989 survey.

Table 7.10
PERCEPTION OF ADVERTISEMENTS AS PROPOSALS OR ATTACKS

Proposals versus Attacks	Percentage of Voters
"All proposals"	8%
"More proposals than attacks"	31
"Evenly divided between proposals and attacks"	17
"More attacks than proposals"	30
"Only attacks"	7

SOURCE: IBOPE October 1989 survey.

high; and most viewers watched at least sometimes, watched much of the program, and paid attention (IBOPE October 1989 survey).

Despite the relative popularity of the *horário gratuito* revealed in our October 1989 survey and the relatively large audience for the *horário gratuito* shown by IBOPE audience research, the 1989 campaign ended with many people questioning the way the programs had been used. Despite the antipathy to negative campaigning that our survey revealed, the campaign by Collor and, to a lesser degree, by Lula had become quite negative.

Television debates were controversial during the 1989 campaign but also seem to have been widely viewed. Television debates tied for third most frequent information source (with colleagues) in the overall sample. Debates were the main source for the wealthiest and the better educated and tied (with conversations with family) for first among the middle class and those with secondary education. However, the rules for debates, particularly restrictions on participation (or refusal to participate, as with Collor in the early debates), and the selective editing of debates for use within political advertising and newscasts remained controversial, in fact becoming more controversial as the importance of the

Table 7.11
UTILITY OF ADS SEEN AS POSITIVE OR NEGATIVE

Opinion of Ads as Sources of Information	All Proposals	More Proposals	Divided	More Attacks	All Attacks
"Help a lot"	48%	41%	40%	29%	33%
"Help somewhat"	14	28	23	24	20
"Help a little"	18	14	20	17	13
"Don't help much"	6	5	7	9	7
"Don't help at all"	14	9	9	19	24

debates to voters has been clarified. Many analysts noted, in particular, that heavily edited news coverage of the debates by TV Globo was used to manipulate the images created in the second debate of the final round to the detriment of Lula.[18] This interpretation receives empirical support. Daily tracking polls by IBOPE showed that support for Lula, which had been slowly growing, leveled off and began to fall slightly after the second debate and TV Globo's showing of its controversial edited version.

FREE POLITICAL ADVERTISING TIME IN 1990 STATE AND LOCAL ELECTIONS

Some research done during the 1990 election campaigns indicates that the *horário gratuito* was working less well in state and local races than it had in the 1989 presidential contest. In research by DataFolha published in September 1990, the *Folha de São Paulo*, many São Paulo voters said that they never (32 percent) or rarely (9 percent) watched the political advertising, although some watched daily (18 percent) and many now and then (40 percent).[19] This represents a substantial decline from the previous year. More negatively yet, in the DataFolha poll, 49 percent said they were against the broadcast of political advertising (*propaganda eleitoral*) while 39 percent favored it. Many (24 percent) liked it as it is, simulcast on all stations at the same time; 41 percent felt that coverage should be alternated among all stations on different days; and 28 percent insisted that it should not exist at all.

A limited number of interviews with media professionals, academics, and political campaign people by one of the authors in August and September 1990 indicated that although most still consider the free political advertising a good idea, state and local races present a severe problem to the current approach. In the limited amount of time available to each party, the need to present a number of candidates for a variety of offices fragments the informational space, resulting in a rapid presentation of faces that say only a few words. The professionals feel that the parties have not used their time well and that only a few campaigns have been able to relay coherent ideas and images to the voters by radio and television in 1990.

CONCLUSIONS

In political terms, the most interesting question is the relative success of the *horário gratuito* in diminishing the potential manipulation of television's power by either the government or the television industry. Some have concluded that television was manipulated by both TV Globo and Collor to secure his election.[20] However, by opening the presidential campaign—and therefore giving a relatively radical opposition candidate, Lula, unprecedented access to prime-time television audiences—the *horário gratuito* had quite a striking effect. The performances of Lula and Collor during the *horário gratuito* boosted both their campaigns. We argue that Lula got as far as he did only as the result of astute use of both the *horário gratuito* and the strength and reach of the organizations that backed him. However, the potential for manipulation by the television industry was not neutralized, as TV Globo's successful "editing" of the images in the last debate shows. Nevertheless, we would argue that this potential was moderated both in principle and in fact by the forum for reply that the *horário gratuito* provided.

While the Brazilian approach to promoting a more even competition among candidates by giving parties free political advertising time still seems an intriguing step in the right direction, it is problematic for local races. It seems to work best when the races are at the presidential or gubernatorial level and when parties focus their energies on a few candidates and themes. Still, it seems to have helped consolidate the democratic transition by giving more parties and candidates a more direct channel to voters.

The other principal conclusion, on a more theoretical level, is that this study further reinforces the concept that the role of television and other mass media as information sources has to be considered in relation to a larger information system in which interpersonal sources such as family, friends, and colleagues, as well as organizational sources such as the Church, unions, and neighborhood groups, also have significant roles. The media, particularly television, are powerful, but only relatively so. They are not a hypodermic needle, capable of injecting opinions, attitudes, and values into the audience.

Despite television's relative dominance of the political process in Brazil, other sources of information clearly competed strongly with it. Even though some of the discussions with families, friends, and colleagues cited as major sources of information for those interviewed by this study were undoubtedly centered on news provided by TV Globo and other television industries (created with clear preferred readings favoring Collor), we can conclude from the relative strength of Lula's performance that oppositional readings were being made by many voters. Further, our study gives some suggestions as to how oppositional readings were made, not only by individuals bringing their experiences to bear but also by ideas communicated by the Church, unions, and local organizations, either directly to voters or through their colleagues and families.

NOTES

1. J. M. Barbero, "Communication from Culture: The Crisis of the National and the Emergence of the Popular," *Media, Culture and Society* 10 (1988).
2. For a case study, see V. A. de Lima, *Media and Democracy: The Construction of a Brazilian President* (Chicago: International Communication Association, 1991). The Frankfurt school is discussed in T. W. Adorno, "Television and the Patterns of Mass Culture," in *Mass Culture*, ed. B. Rosenberg and D. W. White (Glencoe, Ill.: The Free Press, 1957); the Marxist/neo-Marxist view in C. E. Lins da Silva, "Transnational Communication and Brazilian Culture," in *Communication and Latin American Society*, ed. R. Atwood and E. McAnany (Madison: University of Wisconsin, 1986); and the British-American approach is addressed in J. Fiske, *Television Culture* (New York: Methuen Press, 1987). The "preferred reading" is addressed in S. Hall, "The Rediscovery of Ideology: Return of the Repressed in Media Studies," in *Culture, Society and the Media*, ed. M. Gurevitch et al. (London: Methuen Press, 1982); the opposing viewpoint is taken in D. Morley, *The Nationwide Audience: Structure and Decoding* (London: British Film Institute, 1980), and Fisk, *Television Culture*. For cultivation theory, see G. Gerbner et al., "Some Additional Comments on Cultivation Analysis, *Public Opinion Quarterly* 44 (1980): 408–10. (Cf. Violence Profile series in *Journal of Communication* 1976–1980.) For a view of media influence as limited, see J. Robinson and M. Levy, *The Main Source: Learning from Television News* (Beverly Hills: Sage Publications, 1986). The critiques by Eco and Martin-Barbero appear, respectively, in U. Eco, *Apocalittici e Integrati* (Milan: Bompiani, 1964), and Barbero, "Communication from Culture."
3. N. G. Canclini, "Culture and Power: The State of Research," *Media, Culture and Society* 10 (1988); Barbero, "Communication from Culture."
4. Robinson and Levy, *The Main Source.*
5. Hall, "The Rediscovery of Ideology"; and P. Bourdieu, *Distinction: A Social Critique of the Judgement of Taste* (Cambridge: Harvard University Press, 1984).
6. S. Mattos, "Government and Advertising Influences on Brazilian Television," *Communication Research* 11 (1984): 203–20; and J. Straubhaar, "Brazilian Television: The Decline of American Influence," *Communication Research* 11 (1984): 221–40.

7. J. Straubhaar, "Television and Video in the Transition from Military to Civilian Rule in Brazil," *Latin American Research Review* 24 (1989): 140–55.

8. Straubhaar, "Television and Video."

9. U. S. Information Agency, *Media and Information Sources in Brazil* (Washington, D.C.: Government Printing Office, 1982).

10. "Metade dos Paulistanos Rejeita Horário Eleitoral," *Folha de São Paulo*, 10 September 1990, sec. A, 10.

11. Barbero, "Communication from Culture."

12. Ibid.

13. E. Katz, "The Two-Step Flow of Communication," in *Mass Communications*, ed. Wilbur Schramm (Champaign: University of Illinois Press, 1960), 334–66.

14. C. E. Lins da Silva, *Muito Alem do Jardim Botanico* (São Paulo: Summus, 1985).

15. Bourdieu, *Distinction.*

16. Barbero, "Communication from Culture."

17. D. Lerner, *The Passing of Traditional Society* (Glencoe, Ill.: The Free Press, 1964).

18. de Lima, *Media and Democracy.*

19. "Metade dos Paulistanos," *Folha de São Paulo.*

20. de Lima, *Media and Democracy;* Marques de Melo.

8

The Brazilian Case: Manipulation by the Media?

Carlos Eduardo Lins da Silva

The Brazilian presidential election on November 15, 1989, offers a unique opportunity to test theories about the influence of mass media in politics. This was the first time in Brazilian history that the mass media played a central role in a presidential election. TV Globo, the country's largest network, with an average audience of 65 percent, had a preferred candidate, who in fact won the election. At first glance, this would seem to confirm the thesis that TV can manipulate society at will. Let us therefore take a closer look at the media's role in the presidential campaign, which has been discussed in the preceding two chapters.

One cannot endorse the thesis of TV manipulation without a rigorous analysis of the three different ways the media presented politics during the campaign: in the free electoral hour (on radio and TV), in normal coverage by the press and the broadcast media, and in the series of debates among candidates (on TV only).

The form of presentation that reached the largest audience was the free electoral hour. In the first stage of the election, from January to May, any registered political party received one free hour on prime-time national radio and TV. During these five months, equal time was given to all parties, including some that were mere vehicles for ambitious individuals who lacked programs, proposals, or supporters. This was one of the many aberrations in the Brazilian electoral law created after the military period. Under the pretense of democracy, everyone was given equal standing, whether a major Congressional party or a "microparty" born of some desire to strike a high profile or to make deals with authentic politicians needing TV time.

In a shrewd political move, presidential candidate Fernando Collor de Mello, ex-governor of the small, poor northeastern state of Alagoas and a heretofore obscure figure, managed to take over the time slots of three tiny parties. He could thus address the electorate three times in

Table 8.1
BRAZILIAN POLITICAL PARTIES

PRN	Partido de Reconstrução Nacional
PTR	Partido Trabalhista Rural
PSC	Partido Social Comunitário
PDS	Partido Democrata Social
PT	Partido do Trabalhadores
PSDB	Partido da Social Democracia Brasileira
PMDB	Partido do Movimento Democrático Brasileiro
PFL	Partido da Frente Liberal
PTB	Partido Trabalhista Brasileiro
PDT	Partido Democrático Trabalhista
PSD	Partido Social Democrata
PCB	Partido Comunista Brasileiro
PL	Partido Liberal

three months. None of his competitors got more than one opportunity to address the national electorate in this period.

Collor was featured on the PRN's program on March 30, on the PTR's program on April 27, and on the PSC's program on May 18. Over this same period, Collor jumped to a lead in the polls, rising from 17 percent on April 16 to 42 percent on June 3. In late March, his rating had been only 9 percent. He remained at about 40 percent until September. By then, many observers predicted that he would win an absolute majority in the first round (the law required a runoff between the two candidates with the most votes if none got over 50 percent).

There is no doubt that these three television programs in March, April, and May contributed decisively to Collor's eventual victory. This effect was due less to the programs' high quality than to their projection of the image, name and slogans of a previously unknown candidate. However, no number of TV appearances would have given Collor the election if his image and ideas had not responded to the electorate's hopes and aspirations. The best evidence is that after the beginning of the second phase of campaign programs on September 15, Collor went down in the polls and not up (to 33 percent in September and 26 percent on October 5, according to DataFolha), confounding the predictions of most analysts. This decline occurred because Collor's image as an innovator had deteriorated during the campaign, partly because his "antipolitical" image had lost its novelty. His exposure on TV was correlated with his strength in the polls only during the initial period when he rose from anonymity to stardom. In fact, none of his first three TV programs rated among the highest in this initial phase. The right-wing PDS got the largest audience with 74 percent; followed by PT (left), 72 percent; and PSDB (center-left), 67 percent. The PTR got 62 percent; the PSC, 62 percent; and the PRN, 61 percent.

Why, then, did Lula (PT), Maluf (PDS), or Covas (PSDB) fail to perform better in the opinion polls if their programs got a larger audience? Because the electorate was already familiar with their faces and their messages. Moreover, their parties had already alienated the voters by having had to govern the largest cities and states. Brazilians who had voted for them, hoping for miraculous changes, were disillusioned when rapid change did not come.

The second phase of the campaign started on September 15. All twenty-two presidential candidates appeared twice a day, on both radio and TV, but a new criterion for allocating time was introduced. Each candidate had air time proportional to the size of his party's delegation in Congress. Parties without a congressional representative had one minute. Experience soon showed that the candidate with most TV time did not necessarily have the most success. Ulysses Guimarães (PMDB) had more than twice as much time as Collor and Lula combined. Aureliano Chaves (PFL) had 60 percent more time than the total for Collor and Lula. But Ulysses and Aureliano ended with significantly fewer votes than Collor, Lula, Brizola, and other candidates. Aureliano received only nine votes for each second on the air. The exotic Enéas, by contrast, from the minuscule PRONA, got 203 votes for each of his seconds on the air.

Another myth soon disproved was that the most expensive and sophisticated TV productions prevail in the long run. The PMDB, led by an excellent team, spent thirteen times as much on its programs as the PRN and nearly a hundred times more than PT. But the PMDB candidate suffered an overwhelming defeat. Although the PMDB, PFL, and PDS programs were as good as those of the PRN and PT, this factor did not determine voter preference. Previous experience had already demonstrated that high-quality TV programming does not guarantee electoral success. In the 1985 mayoral election, for example, the program quality for both Eduardo Suplicy (PT) and Fernando Henrique Cardoso (PMDB) surpassed that of Jânio Quadros (PTB), yet Jânio was elected.

Nor did audience size have anything to do with the final vote. Although the number who watched the free programs was more or less equal, the DataFolha opinion polls indicated that on average the PT programs had the lead (61 percent against 59 percent for PDT, 59 percent for PSD, 59 percent for PCB, 58 percent for PFL, 58 percent for PDS, 57 percent for PRN, and 56 percent for PSDB). It is likely that the humorous tone of the PT programs, especially the satires of TV Globo aired in the first round, boosted their audience.

Yet Lula, the PT candidate did not win. Nonetheless, he gained steadily in the opinion polls after the campaign began on TV. Before September 15, he was at 6 percent. An October 5 poll showed an increase to 10 percent. By November 12, Lula was up to 15 percent and seemed likely to be Collor's opponent in the second round. A second candidate who benefited from access to free TV time was Guilherme Afif (PL), who emerged from obscurity to vie for a leading spot.

Further evidence that Lula and Afif benefited most from the free TV time can be seen in the DataFolha polls on which candidate voters considered most effective on television. Collor was always first, while Lula and Afif shared second, with percentages invariably higher than their ratings in the current opinion polls. Each of the other candidates, including Collor, had very similar figures by both measures.

The most obvious lesson here is that voters preferred candidates who presented a fresh image. The best-known political faces, those most identified with past and present federal governments—Ulysses, Aureliano, Maluf, Covas, Brizola—were at a disadvantage regardless of their TV programs. It should be further noted that during the entire free TV programming there was little change in voters' preference. Also very few people changed their voting intentions. The reinforcement effect could be seen in all polls: Voters who had already chosen a candidate tended to consider his TV performance the best, thus strengthening their original preference.

Also disproven by the free political hour was the myth that popular artists or personalities can attract votes simply by appearing on a program. Collor had no support from any TV stars except for the singer Simone and actresses Cláudia Raia and Marília Pêra. All the other stars supported Lula, Ulysses, Covas, Brizola, or Roberto Freire (PCB). In the second round, they all supported Lula. PT's jingles sung by TV stars were as popular as those of TV Globo by the end of the year. Yet Collor won the election.

The free TV programs in the second round reinforced the impressions from the first. Lula's programs consistently surpassed those of Collor from both a technical and an artistic standpoint. In fact, Collor became virtually unrecognizable, especially in the first five days of the second round, to those who had followed his campaign from the beginning. Long, boring speeches, with Collor at medium distance in a style resembling Brizola's (PDT), replaced his earlier short slogans and clear messages full of effective images and impressive technical effects, such as showing voters "coloring in"—a pun on the candidate's name—on the last day of the first round. Yet this inferior quality did not give Lula the victory.

Neither Collor nor Lula reached the second round because he was more telegenic than his competition, although this may have been a factor. Similarly, Lula lost despite having better programs in the second round, although their high quality may have contributed to his strong vote. Both Collor and Lula consolidated their images as social reformers, whether they were or not. This is why they got to the final round. Collor said what most people wanted to hear, and he won.

There was one incident in the free electoral hour during the second round that many observers will forever believe to have clinched Collor's victory: Lula's ex–common-law wife declared, on Collor's TV program, that her former husband had once offered her money to have an abortion. It was one of the most regrettable campaign events from an ethical viewpoint, but although none of the pollsters moved fast enough to measure the incident's effect on the final result, it was probably negligible in terms of trend reversal or vote definition. A commonsense analysis indicates that it may have worked against Collor with more intellectually sophisticated groups and hurt Lula with working-class groups. The extent to which Lula was psychologically shaken by this event will always be argued, as will the degree to which it accounts for his poor performance in the second of the two debates between him and Collor (Lula had done well in the first). Either way, it seems too subjective a factor for us to evaluate precisely.

One thing can be confirmed, however. If this episode harmed Collor with the more educated electorate, it further erodes the myth that "opinion makers" (the urban, formally educated middle classes) are decisive in elections. The principal print commentators—who represent the opinions of this influential group—supported Lula, Covas, Brizola, or Freire in the first round and Lula in the second round. When Collor's rating in the polls began to fall from about 40 percent in September, especially among voters with higher education, many analysts predicted that this fall would continue unchecked, since the view of the "opinion makers" would have an inevitably multiplying effect. But it did not happen.

Further proof that the "opinion makers" were not as influential as generally predicted came from the TV debates during the first round. These programs were watched by only a minority of voters, almost all from among the "opinion makers." They condemned Collor for boycotting these debates. But it seems not to have affected the first-round vote. In the second round, Lula defeated Collor in the first debate, by most observers' calculation. Collor narrowly won the second. Yet Collor won the election by a wide margin. Brazil proved George Gallup, Jr., right when he wrote, after twenty-eight years (1960 to 1988) of measuring the effects of hundreds of debates on American elections: "The debates . . . have tended to reinforce the convictions of voters who were already committed."[1]

The factors that lead voters to choose one candidate over another, more than debates or TV advertising, are ideology, class interests, pressure from family and friends, and the belief that a candidate's personal qualities are best for the position sought. Debates rarely change votes, as has been proved since the famous first debate between Nixon and Kennedy.[2]

Those who like conspiracy theories believe that TV Globo had conducted a huge operation to place its future candidate in the presidency ever since 1987, when it gave heavy coverage to then-governor Fernando Collor's crusade against corrupt public servants ("maharajahs") in Alagoas. According to this view, the plot even included the scripts of the popular TV Globo soap operas "Que Rei Sou Eu?" (What King Am I?) and "O Salvador da Pátria" (The Savior of the Country). The supposed goal was to induce the voter subliminally in favor of Collor. Perhaps Roberto Marinho (the owner of TV Globo) was incredibly Machiavellian, but could his plotting have reached this level of sophistication?

A somewhat more plausible explanation is that Collor's extraordinary political sensitivity picked up on the elemental feelings of many voters—the desire to fight corruption, for instance—feelings that soap opera screenwriters were capturing at the same time. This would account for the common discourse in Collor's speeches and the soap opera scripts.

There can be no doubt that the coverage by TV Globo and *O Globo* newspaper (with the second-largest circulation in Brazil) favored Collor, whom Globo owner, Roberto Marinho, had declared to be his candidate. It is unlikely, however, that this coverage decisively influenced the final result. First, the bias was subtle, with occasional exceptions. The biographies of the two candidates as presented on TV Globo's heavily watched Sunday game and variety show "Fantástico" of November 20 were examples of gross partiality. The same could be said of the coverage of the second debate on "Journal Nacional" on December 20 and of many headlines in *O Globo* newspapers. However, these were short-lived fragments in the audience's memory and did not create a coherent campaign to promote one candidate to the detriment of the others.

Collor was also aided by the fact that, unlike most other candidates, he did not hesitate to descend to unadulterated demagoguery. He was more than ready to promise the quick and miraculous solutions that less-informed voters look for. It was a tactic that served him well.

It is not surprising that Collor did so well among voters who declared they had no interest in politics (about 50 percent according to the DataFolha/Cedec poll of September 28, 1989). For them, Collor's anti-political discourse was perfect. For others, who saw in Lula and Brizola the red menace, Collor's conservatism was sufficient. And for those identified with "Reaganism" and "Thatcherism," Collor's extreme free-market message fit like a glove.

The fact that Globo and other TV networks, as well as the print media, gave Collor more coverage than other candidates was due more to journalistic criteria than to political favoritism. Collor led the polls, he was the least known of the leading candidates, and he had held office for much less time; he therefore had to be given more space by the media.

Increased media attention does not necessarily translate into an advantage, however. Whether a candidate profits from media exposure depends on whether he uses the opportunity for positive or negative messages, how the news is received by the voter, and how consistent the candidate's views are with the voter's. The effect of a candidate's media exposure on voter preference is clearly a complex phenomenon that has more to do with fixing an image than persuading voters.

Every week, DataFolha measured the time given to each candidate in the principal TV news programs. Although Collor had more coverage overall (true also in the Brazilian and international newspapers), at specific times Ulysses, Aureliano, or Silvio Santos had more. The space given each candidate depended primarily on their newsworthiness at the moment. When the second campaign round began, Lula had more coverage on all the TV networks except TV Globo, but even Globo gave roughly equal time to each during the first week after the first-round vote. At that point, Lula, not Collor, was more newsworthy.

The print media, which reached a much smaller audience, were reasonably nonpartisan during the campaign, with the obvious exception of *O Globo*. The other dailies probably clarified issues for the more educated readers, just as they may have originated some assignments for the TV networks. But it is unlikely that they caused any dramatic changes in voter behavior.

The most important conclusion is that the media have become an indispensable forum for transmitting the candidates' ideas and personalities to the voters. Although the rallies drew large crowds and were more important than expected in the 1989 campaign, they did little to help clarify issues for the public. The viewers at the rallies were invariably the active supporters of the candidate in question and did not need to be persuaded. Indeed, the use of rally scenes on TV became more important than the rallies themselves.

In spite of their growing importance, the mass media are still far from capable of determining election results. Elections are decided by the candidates' ability to project an image compatible with voters' aspirations, their ideological (political, moral, ethical) beliefs, their material interests, and the pressure exerted by their family and friends. The media represent only one field—albeit the most important one—where the contenders do battle. There are other fields: party organizations, campaign funding rallies, sponsoring committees, and caucuses of regional leaders, to name a few. In the end, however, the decisive factor in elections is the identification between voter and candidate.

NOTES

1. George Gallup, Jr., "The Impact of Presidential Debates on the Vote and Turnout," in *Presidential Debates: 1988 and Beyond*, ed. Joel L. Swerdlow (Washington: League of Women Voters, 1988), 34–42.
2. Elihu Katz and Jacob Feldman. "The Debates in the Light of Research: A Survey of Surveys," in *The Process and Effects of Mass Communication*, ed. Wilbur Schramm and Donald F. Roberts (Champaign: University of Illinois Press, 1974), 701–54.

9

The Mexican Case: The Media in the 1988 Presidential Election

Ilya Adler

Thousands of studies have been conducted around the world on the role of the media in electoral processes. These studies, which have produced rich theoretical frameworks, assume a political system that follows the norms of liberal democracy, combining notions of economic capitalism and democratic rule. This is symbolized in the right of the people to freely elect their rulers. It is the latter assumption that guides research into issues regarding the media's role in elections, including

- The manner in which the media shape the issues and perceptions of a political campaign
- Media practices and biases in reporting these processes
- The relative importance of different media in shaping opinion
- The impact of political advertising
- Access to the media by candidates and parties
- Strategies used by political forces to manipulate the media
- The way the media facilitate or impede the democratic system

The importance of the media can be attributed to their critical role in promoting the public's participation in electoral processes. The media are assumed to inform the choices of the citizens, supposedly the ultimate decision makers.

This chapter reports selected findings and conclusions about the role of the media in the 1988 Mexican presidential campaign, with special attention to the Partido Revolucionario Institucional (PRI), or Institutional Revolutionary Party.[1] The chapter begins with a brief description of the democratic and hierarchical duality of the Mexican political system and examines its relation to the Mexican media. The major candidates and the media's role in that election are reviewed.

Two analyses of the role of the media in this election are presented. The first focuses on the features of the media that relate to their role in a democratic process. The second deals with the role of the media in a hierarchical system. We begin by distinguishing between these two levels of analysis.

DEMOCRATIC-HIERARCHICAL DUALITY

The nature of the Mexican political system is a source of debate among political scientists, most of whom focus on the contradiction between a democratic and an authoritarian system. The former is based on individualism and a social representation rooted in the sovereignty of the individual through the structure of law and votes. The latter is hierarchical, reflecting the image of society as a whole, comprising various vertically interrelated segments.[2] In this view, social representations are the product of negotiation between the segments or factions.

In the traditional Mexican political system, a democratic, individualistic discourse is used to articulate an essentially hierarchical system. Contrasting individualistic (democratic) and hierarchical (authoritarian) forces are reflected in the contradictory forms of socializing and competing discourses. For example, to assure themselves of speedy or privileged services in public institutions, Mexicans will arrive at an office and mention that someone important has sent them (*vengo de parte del Licenciado X*) or that someone important has arranged the meeting for them (*un arreglo*).

This duality has also been noted in other Latin American societies. In his analysis of the Brazilian political system, DaMatta observed these two contrasting and competing discourses and found that the hierarchical dominated.[3] When Brazilians find themselves obstructed by a legal matter, they negotiate a solution (*jeitinho*, or compromise), or if they cannot negotiate, as may be the case, for example, when getting a traffic ticket, they often allude to the familiar, *Você sabe com quem está falando?* (Do you know with whom you are speaking?) This statement gives the impression that the person receiving the ticket knows someone who is higher up the hierarchical ladder and can therefore pull rank on the ticketing police officer. It would not be unusual for the officer to defer to the person who says this (assuming the person can manage to convince the policeman that he or she is of higher rank). Thus, although the democratic spirit specifies that a traffic ticket is due, the hierarchical system prevails in one-on-one encounters.

The Mexican political system is similar. The duality is reflected in many instances of both formal and informal political discourse—after all, the very name of the ruling party, the Institutional Revolutionary Party, is a contrast in terms and in reality. The party may formally operate under assumed, general democratic principles of law and order, but the way in which individuals maneuver within the system is hierarchical.

Analysis of the media in a dual political system depends on the ability to consider both elements equally and simultaneously. If we want to offer a critical analysis of the media's role in a democratic system, we would be interested in issues of fairness of coverage, openness of the media to different candidacies and opinions, journalistic responsibility, and the like. If we analyze the media from the hierarchical perspective, we must begin from the viewpoint of the system, attempting to explain how the media maintain the existing political hierarchies that guarantee the continuity of the structure as a whole.

This contradiction is reflected in the way the media are organized and have traditionally operated in Mexico. For example, Mexican laws on the media are based on democratic principles: Freedom of expression is constitutionally guaranteed, and the media are mostly owned by private interests. However, Mexican media do not have the legal constraints typically found in liberal democracies, such as libel and slander laws, which, while enacted as safeguards of other individual rights, tend to inhibit freedom of speech.

Mexican media operate in a manner that reflects an ordered hierarchy, controlled by powerful forces of government and private business. Although most media are privately owned, it is commonly known that the owners are in the same social elite as those in government, and they work closely to maintain their status, order, and credibility through mutual agreement or the trade of favors. Thus the contrast between formal regulation of the media and their informal (or negotiated) operation has led to widely differing scholarly conclusions about the degree of press freedom in Mexico, especially in the relationship between the media and government. Merrill, Carter, and Alisky state that "the Mexican mass media traditionally do not criticize the President of the Republic directly, but do sometimes criticize his cabinet ministers."[4]

In a later study, Merrill describes Mexico as a country with "little control" of the press by government, enjoying a ranking similar to West Germany and the United Kingdom.[5] In one of the few systematic historical studies of the content of the Mexican press, Montgomery found that the press becomes more critical of the government in times of social stress; she thus concludes that Mexico enjoys a high degree of press freedom.[6]

But other scholars and journalists who have studied how Mexican media operate have arrived at very different conclusions. Adler and Riding document in detail the many ways government institutions exercise control over the press through co-optive measures, including monetary offers to journalists and editors.[7] As Adler notes, these actions find little resistance among many members of the media:

> Editors are not only aware of this, but condone it, and in many cases, demand it. First, the system [of bribes] allows them to pay reporters unrealistically low salaries. Second, many editors actually receive a "share" of the payment. Lastly, a reporter who is not willing to follow the system may cause a loss of revenue in publicity. According to almost all the journalists interviewed, writing a piece critical of the government without the editor's knowledge and approval is nearly impossible. Television does not escape the system either, and it is known among communicators that popular news programs "sell" time for government news.[8]

Thus the media in Mexico, as hierarchical organizations, demand the right to be free and the opportunity to be corrupt! This is one more manifestation of the inherent contradiction in the Mexican political system.

THE CANDIDATES

Traditionally, the PRI's process of nominating its presidential candidate is one of the best-kept secrets in the country. The top leaders of the party, representing various sectors within the PRI, negotiate with the incumbent president to select the party's nominee. However, it is widely believed that the president has the final say, and for this reason, the PRI nomination is popularly referred to as *el dedazo* (the "big finger"), meaning that by pointing his finger, the president can decide the nominee.

Before the 1988 nomination, a small but important faction within the PRI began publicly calling for a more democratic and open nomination. This faction was led by Cuauhtémoc Cárdenas Solorzano, a former governor of the state of Michoacán, and, more important, the son of Lázaro Cárdenas, a founder of the PRI and one of Mexico's best known and beloved presidents (1934–1940). This stature made Cárdenas's challenge to the traditional system difficult to ignore or minimize, but his faction, known as "the Democratic Current," was unable ultimately to influence the nomination—at least in the 1988 elections.

Because he believed he could not work within the PRI, Cárdenas left the party and became an opposition candidate under the coalition of leftist parties called the National Democratic Front (Frente Democrático Nacional). His name recognition made him an important contender from the start. The most organized and largest leftist party, the Mexican Socialist Party (Partido Mexicano Socialista, or PMS), however, had already nominated Herberto Castillo. He stayed in the race until June 1988, when increasing pressure from his own party, which saw a unique opportunity to create an alliance, forced him to support Cárdenas. Thus, by election day, Cárdenas was supported by all the parties of the left, as well as by many elements within the PRI, such as peasants and union members, who were attracted by his nationalist and populist positions or who believed the PRI had gone too far to the right.

Meanwhile, the Partido de Acción Nacional (PAN), traditionally the most important opposition party, had nominated Manuel Clouthier ("Maquio"), a charismatic self-made entrepreneur known for his publicity stunts. PAN was identified with business interests and espoused a free-market philosophy, proposing a reduction in the size of government and less intervention in the economy.

Two other candidates ran in the elections, but neither gained much support. They were Ibarra de Piedra, a Troskyite who had years earlier made a name for herself by publicly decrying the "disappearance" of her son for political reasons, and Gumercindo Magana, who had the support of the small but active sector tied to conservative Christian democratic groups.

MEXICAN MEDIA AND THE ELECTORAL PROCESS

The formal structure of the mass media in Mexico is similar to that found in most liberal Western democracies.[9] Most print media are privately owned but are often linked to political figures or to large business concerns that use them to create alliances with powerful groups.[10] Countless newspapers and magazines are published throughout the country, but only a few have national distribution. This study used only newspapers and magazines from Mexico City, where the federal government is located (table 9.1).[11]

Television and radio, as is the case in other countries, are more formally and directly regulated by the government through licensing. In addition, a number of radio and television stations are operated directly by the government. The only public television network is run at the federal level, but many regional radio and television networks are operated by the states. Because of the political monopoly of the PRI, these public stations usually show little independence from either government or party politics. Publicly owned radio and television stations

Table 9.1
SELECTED DATA ON MEXICAN MEDIA

Dailies	
Excelsior	Circulation: 175,000–185,000 Key points: Considered the leading newspaper, widely read by the political class. Offers a wide range of information and commentaries.
El Norte	Circulation: 100,000 Key points: Largest newspaper of Monterrey, with good reputation among journalists for being "clean," with a probusiness leaning.
La Jornada	Circulation: 25,000 Key points: Founded by dissidents of *Unomasuno*, it is the preferred paper of intellectuals, with a progressive leaning. Considered to have a small but politically important readership.
Unomasuno	Circulation: 70,000 Key points: Until the advent of *La Jornada*, it was the paper of the left. The original director, Manuel Becerra Acosta, was a former director of *Excelsior*.
El Universal	Circulation: 225,000 Key points: The senior paper of Mexico City, very successful financially and considered center and usually progovernment.
Weeklies	
Siempre	Circulation: 100,000 Key points: A traditionally important political magazine read by the political class. Editorially tends to be identified with the PRI, but it allows regular critical pieces.
Proceso	Circulation: 200,000 Key points: Its director, Julio Scherer, is considered the most influential journalist in Mexico. He founded *Proceso* when, as director of *Excelsior*, he challenged presidential power and was forced to leave. Considered to be the most critical publication in Mexico, enjoying a good reputation among journalists.
Television	
Imevision	Key points: Government owned, it reaches most cities in Mexico.
Televisa	Key points: The giant consortium has a virtual monopoly over private television and is the most important producer of television programming. Politically, it tends to be identified with a pro-U.S., probusiness view. Although Televisa is a private consortium, its connection to political leadership is well known and as we shall see later, was made public by Televisa's president.

SOURCES: *World Media Handbook* (New York: United Nations Department of Public Information, 1990); Raul Trejo Delarbe, ed., *Las Redes de Televisa* (Mexico City: Claves Latinoamericanas, 1989).
NOTE: All papers are Mexico City, except *El Norte*, which is from Monterrey.

are also operated by institutions of higher education, such as Channel 11, which is run by the Instituto Politécnico (Politechnical Institute).

Most electronic media are private, as in the United States. However, unlike U.S. television and radio, the electronic media of Mexico have no limits to the number of stations that can be owned by a single organization. Thus the giant Televisa consortium in Mexico has a virtual monopoly on private television. Its communications empire extends to radio, films, sports, cable television, records, publishing houses, museums, and other related organizations. It is fitting that in one of the best-known studies of the conglomerate, Televisa is referred to as the "fifth estate."[12]

By law, political parties have limited access to free air time, but this is a small portion of the total time the electronic media devote to electoral matters. Parties are allowed to buy air time, although stations can refuse them. Furthermore, neither television nor radio is required to honor the so-called "fairness doctrine." This U.S. tradition was dropped as a legal requirement by the FCC in 1989, but its basic assumption that news accounts should cover "both sides of an issue" continues to be a mainstream journalistic value. For example, the opposition party may be permitted to broadcast a speech immediately following a presidential speech. In Mexico, there is no legal recourse to the notion of fairness for challenging the news judgment of stations.

THE ROLE OF THE MEXICAN MEDIA IN DEMOCRATIZATION

The 1988 Mexican elections purportedly demonstrated a strong push toward greater representation, at least as reflected in the development of a multiparty system. If so, how important were the media in bringing about this change? Did the media consequently show a greater degree of freedom despite the political monopoly of the PRI? Were the media important in strengthening opposition parties?

The study on which this chapter is based analyzed journalistic coverage of the elections, with particular attention to the news rather than political propaganda, in the belief that the news should play a responsible role in democracies, informing and educating by reporting on important changes and new trends as they develop.[13] Factors that might indicate a greater media role in influencing the democratic process include the degree to which news about opposition parties was reported and the content and tone of news about the candidates.

Although the new openness of the Mexican print media during the campaign is significant, it could hardly be the basis for mass political mobilization in a country where most citizens do not read newspapers. In Mexico, the press is a vehicle for the political class,[14] and although many newspapers are published, their circulations are modest. *Excelsior*, the leading political newspaper in the country, claims to have a circulation of roughly a quarter-million but probably does not exceed 200,000, according to information given to us by present and former journalists of the newspaper. Television reaches a wide audience as the worldwide news source of choice.[15] Best known among Mexican television news broadcasts is Televisa's "24 Hours" (24 Horas). The radio industry is not as monopolistic as television and print. Nonetheless, opposition parties were largely shut out of radio broadcasts.

Randomly chosen contents of *Excelsior*, with selected coverage by *Proceso, Siempre,* and *La Jornada;* "24 Hours"; and some radio interviews were studied here. Although there are many other news outlets in Mexico, the ones used in this analysis are considered among the most important, in terms of both audience reach and political impact. In addition, journalists from all media who covered the election provided additional material about then-current and groundbreaking journalistic practices.

Campaign Coverage in the Print Media

We analyzed a sample of articles appearing in *Excelsior* on twenty-four days randomly chosen between January and May 1988, reviewing for each day the average amount of space devoted to each of the candidates' campaigns, the average number of op-ed pieces about the campaign, and the average number of stories about each candidate. Photographs were not included in these computations (table 9.2)

The PRI campaign received more coverage in *Excelsior* than all other campaigns combined, with more than 50 percent of the total reporting on the presidential campaign process. This volume, however, can hardly be explained by newsworthiness alone. Everyone then in Mexico knew that the 1988 elections were important because of the strength of the opposition parties. The emergence of political forces might have been deemed especially newsworthy because it represented "something new." For example, the 1980 candidacy of John Anderson in the United States, which ultimately gained about 5 percent of the votes, received an impressive amount of coverage in both print and electronic media.[16]

The only newspapers that extensively and regularly covered the campaigns of political parties other than the PRI, especially those of Cárdenas and Clouthier, were *Excelsior, El Universal, La Jornada,* and *Unomas-*

Table 9.2
AVERAGE DAILY COVERAGE* IN *EXCELSIOR* OF
PRESIDENTIAL CANDIDATES IN THE 1988 MEXICAN
PRESIDENTIAL ELECTION FROM A SAMPLE OF
TWENTY-FOUR DAYS (JANUARY–APRIL 1990)

Candidacy	Column Inches of News Stories	Number of News Stories	Number of Op-Ed Pieces
Salinas de Gortari	98.5	4.0	2.3
Cárdenas	30.1	1.1	0.4
Clouthier	30.3	1.2	0.2
Castillo	28.4	0.9	0.3
All Others	5.0	0.3	0.1
Coverage of Elections by Political Columnists All Candidacies: 89.4**			

*This includes editorials, op-ed pieces and letters to the editor. It does not include political columnists.

**The writing of political columns makes it difficult to create exclusive campaign categories. However, in a limited sample drawn on a paragraph-by-paragraph basis, the PRI campaign was the main focus in 75 percent of the cases.

uno. Excelsior gave significantly more coverage to opposition parties than it had given in previous campaigns. *Proceso,* a weekly magazine important in the recent history of Mexican journalism as a forum for critical coverage of Mexican politics, printed an interview in which opposition candidates interviewed agreed that in comparison to electronic media, print media provided significant space to their campaigns. Cárdenas, the former PRI leader who became the opposition candidate most threatening to the the party's hegemony in the presidential elections, characterized press coverage of his campaign as "objective and truthful, but scarce." In the interview published by *Proceso* on March 7, 1988, he stated, "While the press publishes one story a day on the opposition candidates, if that much, the official candidate [Salinas de Gortari] gets many pages."

The press did break new ground by printing criticism of the official candidate, Salinas de Gortari. For example, *Siempre,* one of the most important political weeklies in the country, wrote on October 14, 1987, immediately after the candidacy of Salinas de Gortari was announced:

> The nomination fell on Carlos Salinas de Gortari, who was up until now, Secretary of Planning and Budget. And the irony is that we seem to have reached such extremes [in Mexico] that it is no longer required of him [the candidate] to possess a solid preparation nor great knowledge about the issues.

To publish harsh criticism of the person expected to be the next Mexican president was considered by journalists and observers a "break with tradition." As one informant journalist noted, "The tradition in Mexico is that there are three 'sacred' subjects journalists dare not criticize: the Virgin of Guadalupe, the Army [Estado Mayor], and the President. Obviously, we have broken with one taboo."

Of the print media analyzed in this study, *Proceso* was the most relentless in its critical coverage of the PRI campaign and the lame duck presidency of Miguel de la Madrid Hurtado. It was also the only national print outlet that regularly covered the media as a campaign issue, devoting many articles to details of PRI methods, some corrupt, of procuring the support of the media.

Campaign Coverage by "24 Hours"

The news program "24 Hours," anchored by the best-known Mexican television journalist, Jacobo Zabludovsky, has long enjoyed first place in the ratings and is seen throughout Mexico, as well as on many Spanish language television stations in the United States. Ideologically, Televisa is aligned with big business and is strongly pro-U.S. and antileft, as documented extensively by Gutierrez Espindola.[17] Its conservative rightwing tilt is especially evident in its coverage of international news and often does not correspond to the official government position on international issues. Perhaps because its programming is perceived by the public as independent from the government in international news, Televisa programming, and in particular "24 Hours," has received high ratings.

At the same time, Televisa is vulnerable. From the right, it is attacked as a monopoly and as protecting the PRI's privileges in coverage and news angles. From the left, it is the target of critics who advocate a publicly owned television industry. Televisa is therefore likely to be aligned with government positions, especially relating to the institution of the presidency.

In the early stages of the 1988 campaign, the president of Televisa, Emilio Azcarraga, declared that "Televisa is with the PRI," surprising journalists and intellectuals with its open endorsement. Discussion centered on how the endorsement might have hurt the candidacy of Salinas de Gortari, as well as speculation about reciprocal favors from the PRI. The statement was interpreted by some as proof that the PRI had lost touch with its traditional populist base and had become identified with the interests of big business. Nevertheless, until the campaign

Table 9.3
DISTRIBUTION OF COVERAGE BY "24 HOURS" OF PRESIDENTIAL CANDIDATES DURING THE 1988 MEXICAN PRESIDENTIAL ELECTIONS (APRIL 4–JUNE 24, 1988*)

Candidate	Number of Stories	Average Length of Story	Total Time
Salinas de Gortari	74	1 min./55 sec.	141 min./40 sec.
Cárdenas	10	55 sec.	8 min./51 sec.
Clouthier	7**	31 sec.	4 min./ 9 sec.
Castillo	9	50 sec.	7 min./30 sec.
Ibarra de Piedra	7	38 sec.	4 min./23 sec.
Magaña	3	48 sec.	2 min./23 sec.

*Only news that directly covered the campaign was included. Excluded from the table are general election stories (technical, etc.) or general political stories unrelated to the campaign.
**Not included is one particular story that lasted 7.5 minutes; it is discussed at length in the text.

started, "24 Hours" was regarded as a more independent television news source than government-owned stations (table 9.3).

In nightly editions of "24 Hours" between April 4 and June 24, 1988, more than 80 percent of the time devoted to the campaigns was focused on the PRI candidate. Coverage of opposition parties was infrequent, and the occasional stories were short. There was a hierarchy in the distribution of time assigned to the opposition candidates. The difference between the time allotted the PRI candidate and all the others, however, was such that all the opposition candidates appeared equally important, or equally unimportant. Especially noteworthy was the reduced coverage of Clouthier (even less than that of Castillo) although as the candidate of the traditionally strongest opposition party, Clouthier might have been considered more newsworthy. But reduced coverage of Clouthier's campaign was no accident.

Effective analysis of television news includes examination of both audio and visual elements, because the message transmitted and received is derived from both components.[18] Stories on the PRI usually contained long sound bites from candidate Salinas de Gortari, while the voice in stories about opposition candidates was usually that of the anchorperson or reporter. In only two stories on Cárdenas was his voice actually used.

The tone used in reporting on the candidates differed sharply. Stories about Salinas de Gortari were usually read enthusiastically, and he was always referred to with the reverence accorded a president. Stories about the opposition were read in a flat voice, and the candidate was sometimes referred to as "another candidate."

Sarcasm was sometimes evident in stories about opposition candidates, especially Cárdenas. In one instance, a news story reported a speech Cárdenas had given in which he stated, "My government will be pluralistic and there will be room for representatives of all the parties . . . but not for those of the PRI." The camera switched to the anchorperson, who raised his eyebrows and added, "Not so pluralistic."

Differences were also noted between the visual images used in news stories of the PRI and those of opposition candidates. In most cases, visuals of Salinas de Gortari showed large and enthusiastic crowds or showed the candidate in command. By contrast, visuals for opposition candidates usually showed few supporters, and in the case of Cárdenas, often focused on students, giving the impression that his candidacy attracted only the "young and educated." Few of the images depicted peasants or workers attending Cárdenas's rallies, although it was well known that in some parts of the country he held significant strength among those groups.[19]

Eventually, "24 Hours" became an issue of the campaign, and opposition parties uniformly criticized its rather exaggerated bias in favor of the PRI. The opposition criticism could not be easily dismissed, because dissent came mostly from the candidate of PAN, a party that represents private free-market ideology and has a strong following among many groups that otherwise identify themselves with the economic philosophy of Televisa.

Frustrated by PAN's inability to secure time on television and radio, Manuel Clouthier made the allocation of media time a campaign issue. With the support of other opposition parties, PAN organized Resistencia Civil, a formal boycott of Televisa, especially "24 Hours." One sticker displayed on many cars around the country read, "Don't Watch 24 Hours Because It Doesn't Tell the Truth" (*No Vea 24 Horas Porque No Dice La Verdad*). Clouthier routinely appeared throughout the country with his mouth covered by adhesive tape to symbolize the electronic media blackout he charged had been imposed on him and his party.

When the opposition parties persisted in making the electronic media an issue of the campaign (and one that was reported by selected print media, such as *La Jornada*, *Proceso*, and *Excelsior*), Televisa attempted to answer the accusations. Zabludovsky, in one newscast, read the entire text of a paid op-ed advertisement that had been published in various newspapers and was signed by Alcoa de la Vega, secretary of the Union of Workers in Mexico's television and radio industry. It took Zabludovsky 7.5 minutes to read the entire text, giving the impression that the opinions expressed by the op-ed ad were part of a factual news story. The last words of the text, read in a careful, slower pace, stated, "Mr. Clouthier is not fooling anyone. Thus ends the public statement."

In another broadcast, Zabludovsky explained and defended the journalistic criteria Televisa used to cover the opposition:

> We studied the procedures in other countries. In Italy, the four most important [television] channels have distinct political orientations and function accordingly, favoring their preferred party. . . . In the United States, the political parties can buy as much air time as they want. In Televisa, we believe that the political parties should be assigned air time in the news in proportion to the quantity of votes that they received in the last elections.

In the same editorial, Televisa demonstrated how, by this formula, Cárdenas may actually have received more coverage than was fair. Zabludovsky concluded by stating that the "respect" owed to the audience did not allow Televisa to give in to the opposition candidates' demands. The credibility of "24 Hours" appeared to have been hurt as a result of the controversy.

Radio Coverage

We were unable to systematically tape radio news programs during the campaign. Instead, radio journalists who had worked on the campaign were interviewed, and radio coverage of the campaigns in selected sites in the state of Veracruz and Mexico City were taped.

Because control of the radio industry is not as monopolistic as that of other media, opposition candidates were, in a few instances, interviewed freely or able to buy commercial time. Some talk shows gave significant air time to opposition candidates; however, even this coverage was minute in comparison to the time and scope given to Salinas de Gortari's campaign. In Veracruz, for example, each of the three candidates was allowed access to radio interviews, but the official candidate received full coverage of all his campaign events. The opposition parties, especially PAN, protested their lack of access to radio.

Nevertheless, both Clouthier and Cárdenas regarded radio opportunities as very important. In Veracruz, when Cárdenas was interviewed in the regionally known news program, "Ocho en Punto" (Eight O'Clock on the Dot), he stated

> I have had, I must say, the important opportunity to campaign on radio. That is, there have been many stations in different parts of

the nation, which, in my opinion, performed their duties, opened their doors to us and allowed us to reach their audiences, as is happening here. But, on the other hand, if we look at what official television has done, it mentions almost nothing about what we are doing every day. With us, sometimes it's "candidate X was in this town," and that's it.

While disc jockeys or radio reporters could not deviate from the "official" guidelines, callers were frequently able to offer sharp criticism or state their support for opposition parties. One radio reporter said, "Basically, when the official candidate is in town, you have to be careful. But once he is gone, they [the PRI] don't pay that much attention to what we do. Things happen very fast in radio."

As the first medium to broadcast the name of the official PRI candidate, radio was critical in the *destape,* or "uncovering," when the official candidate is announced. There is highly charged speculation surrounding the announcement, because the name of the candidate is kept secret. However, in the hours preceding the official announcement that Salinas de Gortari was the candidate, one radio station aired what became known as the "false uncovering" (*destape falso*). In a taped interview, Alfredo del Mazo, believed by many to be favored as the candidate, referred to and extended congratulations to Sergio Garcia Ramirez, another possible candidate, as the party's nominee! Such a blunder by an important politician like Alfredo del Mazo was the topic of much discussion, even after the elections.[20] Many journalists placed such importance on this affair because it gave radio the status of a player, not just a transmitter in Mexican politics.

Radio grew in significance during the campaign because it occasionally became a conduit for public expression through talk shows and interviews with opposition candidates. But it is important to note that it was the strength and persistence of the opposition candidates that ultimately forced radio stations to grant them greater access.

THE ROLE OF THE MEDIA IN THE HIERARCHICAL SYSTEM

The campaign, in our estimation, is a process in which two fundamental political rituals take place. One ritual plays out the drama of uncertainty (ambiguity), which in turn serves to ratify the importance and dominance of negotiations and engages members of the political class in an ongoing activity of interpretations that ultimately define "reality." The candidate becomes the symbol by which uncertainty is resolved as he travels around the country. A second ritual involves the transformation of the candidate of choice into a national symbol with kinglike qualities. (This is well illustrated in the "scenario creation" of Brazilian soap operas as described in Venicio de Lima's chapter in this book.) We found that the role of the print media was mainly instrumental in the ritual of uncertainty (and negotiations) and television was used mainly to transform the candiate-negotiator into the president-king of the republic.

The Conventional View

Many researchers have concluded that the media in Mexico are best described as a communications tool supporting the hegemonic domination of the powerful class, a combination of capitalists and other leaders of the PRI. Its members, if not emerging from the entrepreneurial class, find in this coalition the possibility of becoming future members of this class. This analysis is based on the influential work of Gramsci, who developed the theory of hegemony to explain how capitalism manages to survive in liberal democracies without using physical threat.[21]

If this analysis applies to Mexico, it follows that Mexican media have taken a leading role in indoctrinating the population to accept social inequalities as natural. Some studies have suggested a correlation between viewing commercial television in Mexico and a more materialistic, individualistic, and pro-U.S. preference.[22] These studies do not, however, provide enough evidence to conclude that the PRI, as a unique political institution that uses a different discourse from that of commercial television, is able, through the media, to convince people to vote for its candidates. If media coverage gave the PRI an electoral advantage, how can we explain the recent strength of the opposition?

If the media are to be persuasive in elections, they must have some credibility among their audiences. The relationship of source credibility and persuasion is complex, and there is substantial evidence that the credibility of the initial source is important in determining impact.[23] Previous research on the general credibility of the Mexican media dismisses them as credible sources of information.

In a survey of a sample of government workers in Mexico City, Adler found that more than 80 percent of respondents polled believed that the press was not credible when covering issues affecting the Mexican government or the PRI.[24] Recent observations in Eastern European countries with highly censored and controlled media tend to show that press control does not automatically create believers.[25] If anything, therefore, the Mexican elections could be considered, in terms of rallying votes for the dominant party, a significant failure of the power of the media.

The print media manifested their independence during the 1988 presidential campaign, in part by indicating that they were not wholly committed to PRI interests. During the campaign, a dramatic rise in the circulation of critical publications such as *Proceso* and *La Jornada* seems to support the theory that a demand exists for a more independent, critical press. Despite the increased public interest, critical comments were the exceptions, and the media did not significantly change their practices. As in former elections, media attention focused mainly on the campaign of the PRI candidate.

Journalists interviewed during the campaign indicated that press coverage for the PRI was secured through a very expensive system of co-optation in which reporters, editors, publishers, photographers, and other media representatives received ample reward for devoting their space and time to the PRI candidate. These rewards often supported the newspapers and magazines, according to interviews. In exchange, the press was expected not only to give ample coverage to the PRI campaign but also to accept photographs and news bulletins furnished directly by the PRI campaign and publish them as news reports (*gacetillas*). Few publications could claim that they were not participants in this co-optation. *La Jornada*, for instance, which represents the interests of the left, was often difficult to find in Mexico City during the campaign, precisely because it gave ample coverage to the candidacy of Cárdenas. Nonetheless, it has been reported that *La Jornada* accepted *gacetillas*. Many reporters for *La Jornada* resented this practice, and as a compromise, the publishers agreed that *gacetillas* would be published in a different typeface so that at least the journalistic community would know.

A Different View

The PRI campaign, including its use of the media, was more than a series of strategies to elicit votes. Past PRI campaigns, even those that were uncontested, were very similar in style and size to the 1988 campaign. For example, former president Lopez Portillo, who ran unopposed in 1976, received more coverage in *Excelsior* than Echeverría in 1970 and roughly the same as de la Madrid in 1982.[26] The PRI also continued to assign great importance to newspapers and magazines, and the majority of reporters following the 1988 PRI campaign represented print media. This focus on print media hardly suggests a vote-eliciting mentality, since Mexicans, like citizens in most other countries, get their news from television and radio. Although Mexico has many newspapers and magazines (more than fifteen dailies in Mexico City, for example), print media penetration in the general population is not high. Therefore, the important question is, What is the rationale for the PRI's expensive and exhausting preoccupation with the media, especially the print media, if this effort is not to secure votes?

The Presidential Campaign

To answer this question, it is essential first to describe the role of the presidential campaign in the Mexican political system. In Mexico, two important questions traditionally exist regarding presidential elections: Who will be the PRI candidate, and once that is known, what he will do and with whom will he ally himself when he is in power?

The PRI incorporates diverse groups and organizations as well as leaders who espouse a variety of ideologies and interests. To guarantee that each group represented by the PRI has a chance to find a place in the government, the Mexican political system is presidential, and the president serves only one term. The presidential system ensures that a large number of jobs will be assigned to new people every six years, and therefore those groups that do not find their place in one administration always hope to be part of the next. As soon as the party's nominee is announced, interest shifts to how the new power structure will be organized, how each actor will be placed in the next administration.

The Campaign as Political Ritual

During the campaign, the PRI candidate—often referred to as "the official candidate"—travels to every region of the country, where a series of events and ceremonies, best described as political rituals, is organized. Social rituals, of which political rituals are a type, are especially important in moments of ambiguity that border on potential disruption of the social order.[27] In political campaigns, Mexican media provide arenas for these political rituals so they can be shared with the larger public.[28]

The campaign rituals symbolically represent two fundamental processes in the political cycle. During the campaign, new alliances are established and defined. The establishment of a new governing coalition is expressed in conflict and resolution during these rituals. Campaign rituals secure the presidential nature of the political system: They transform the person-candidate into an almost mythical figure of king-president, who represents an understanding of the problems and concerns of the people as well as a vision of the solutions.

The Media and Political Ritual

In recent years, some media scholars have begun looking at the role of the media in significant social rituals. Elliott's excellent study of press rites in Great Britain illustrates how the press is used to maintain social relations.[29] In this analytical framework, the press is an integral part of society; production and audience are not separate components. The repetitive, or ritualistic, manner in which certain stories are covered (about terrorist acts, for example) is explained by what anthropologists have proposed as a central function of many rituals: the desire to bring about a sense of togetherness, especially in times of ambiguity.

The ritualized nature of the campaign is duplicated in the media, which become an additional component in the rituals of the campaign. A ritualized reporting of the campaign takes place. At each important stop during the 1988 PRI campaign, the press typically published statements made by regional leaders and common folk, outlining their needs and problems. The candidate's speech then addressed these problems and offered solutions.

When the candidate visited a town, local newspapers published advertisements and editorials from various groups (such as unions and associations) giving their welcome and support to the candidate and "next president" of Mexico. Political commentators filled pages of print that provided additional interpretations of events occurring on the campaign trail. The publicity, in the form of advertisements, television and radio programs, banners, posters, buttons, and scenic arrangements, were much the same at each of the campaign stops, often being transferred from one stop to another. This cycle was repeated from city to city, region to region, day in, day out.

The Importance of Interpretation

In Mexican politics, facts are scarce while interpretations proliferate. Nowhere is this more evident or far-reaching than during the presidential campaign. These interpretations are fundamental to an understanding of the political system.[30] Interpretations (and their link to the process of political negotiations) begin during the campaign and reflect the negotiations between the candidate and different sectors and leaders at both the national and regional levels. Thus, in each event of the campaign, both conflicts and resolutions are represented. The seating order of leaders, the speeches made by the candidate and other leaders during these campaign ceremonies, the presence or absence of personalities on the campaign trail, are all facts interpreted in terms of alliances and relations between the candidate and diverse groups around the country.

Two examples demonstrate the importance of this process. Gomez-Tagle offers data from a recent election for the Chamber of Deputies and the three former Chamber elections.[31] After a careful follow-up of those cases in which the opposition parties challenged the election results, Gomez-Tagle concludes that

- Without a doubt, vote fraud by the PRI had taken place in some districts.
- Nevertheless, one could not prove to the Electoral Commission that vote fraud had occurred.
- Although vote fraud could not be proven, in some cases the Electoral Commission recognized irregularities and declared those elections void.
- Nevertheless, decisions to declare the elections void were the result, not of direct pressure by any particular electoral district, but of a global negotiation between the PRI and each party.
- In many cases, the fraud that occurred had not been necessary to guarantee the PRI victory.

This ambiguity is central to the political culture. For example, in the issue of vote fraud, a frequent scenario in Mexican politics, opposition parties (as well as PRI candidates vis-à-vis their own party) are forced to negotiate with the PRI. In this case, the deputy of the PRI who has won a seat in the Chamber of Deputies cannot claim this victory as a personal triumph but most admit a debt to the party apparatus. Thus, in the electoral process itself, "there is a system of accountability and verification of votes which guarantees that interpretations will prevail over facts, and that the process of negotiation will prevail over individual sovereignty."[32]

The Media and the Process of Interpretation

For the political class, correct interpretation is a central issue because it means identification with the leaders to whom power and privilege will be granted in the new administration. Since interpretation is not an easy task, the political class needs guidance from both formal and informal sources of information. The press, but not the electronic media, provides an important source for interpretations of how the new administration is being shaped and how alliances are being built. Therefore, it is not as important that the facts are correct as that the interpretations are on target.

Journalists assigned to cover the PRI campaign were often charged to provide readers with interpretations about the relevant power struggles dramatized in the rituals. As one informant journalist noted,

> Frankly, the newspapers don't really have to send reporters just for the purpose of covering the events of the campaign.We get all the information, with photos, directly from the PRI, so that the only important thing we have to do in the campaign is to report on those subtle symbols that may reveal who is going to be in—or who will be out—in the new government.

This role allows members of the political class who cannot or are not invited to be present at campaign ceremonies to figure out how the power game is proceeding. Through the press, the political class can reduce its uncertainties. For this reason, political columnists, particularly those who chronicle political life and the campaign, are an elite among the press corps. Most reporters covering the PRI campaign are guests of the PRI, with their expenses paid by the PRI and their incomes supplemented. The political columnists are considered special guests with special status. They get better hotel rooms, have more access to the candidate, and are granted more favors. These columnists are well known and regularly read by members of the political class.[33] A similar role is played by some journalists, who are neither guests nor, apparently, financially supported by the PRI. They follow the campaign and interpret the events, as did journalists representing the weekly magazine *Proceso* in the 1988 campaign.

The political chroniclers fill their columns with revealing facts of the campaign, and through these hermeneutic exercises help direct and shape "authorized" versions of the facts. The press can thus be viewed as the organ by which both "facts" and "interpretations" are presented to the political class.

This status is reserved for the press, not for the electronic media, because the vast amount of information that the political class requires can be accommodated only by print media. For example, a photograph of the candidate shaking hands with a given personality quickly becomes a lead story about the state of negotiations among groups pictured, or it may signify a position of relative power to the person who appears "close" to the candidate. One photojournalist remarked that he frequently received generous monetary offerings from people in return for a photograph showing them shaking hands with the candidate. Photos that show the magnitude of public manifestations, lists of pictures of the "special guests" (politically significant persons) who attend those events, and the like, are all valued pieces of information.

Our analysis of the political columns in *Excelsior* that targeted "significant" themes in the campaign revealed the following:

- The presence or absence of national and regional leaders on the campaign trail, especially stressing those who were seen often or those presumed to wield political power.
- Who is talking to whom—almost "gossip," in which the simple fact that two politicians are seen together or greeting each other is presumed to have meaning.
- Dissent within the party. This is not a common theme; however, it appeared often in the case of "La Quina," the leader of the Oil Workers' Union, in which much speculation centered on his supposed "secret" support for Cárdenas.
- Lists of candidates for Congress and Senate, the most-discussed topic often interpreted in terms of who were close associates and supporters of Salinas and who were members of the "system." Much of this discussion involved the ability and power of the candidate and his close associates, as well as key leaders of the PRI, to place their people on the list. These references were then interpreted as the result of negotiations, which were also "graded" in terms of the degree of relative power they reflected. Much attention was devoted to the Working Sector of the PRI, which was generally considered (interpreted) not to have favored the selection of Salinas de Gortari.

Uncertainty as Power

Uncertainty (ambiguity) is also a useful source of power for the candidate. Organizational sociologists have long recognized that uncertainty becomes an important source of power for individuals or subunits within organizations.

Crozier's analysis of the French tobacco-processing industry suggests that work in this industry is so highly mechanized and standardized that little is left to chance.[34] The only important area of uncertainty within the organization is the possibility of machine breakdown. He found that mechanics who could successfully deal with this eventuality enjoyed considerably more power than would be predicted on the basis of their formal position in the organization. He concluded that subunits that cope more effectively with uncertainty are more likely to acquire power. Similarly, Goldner reported that the industrial relations unit in a manufacturing organization maintained its base of power by "its use of the union as an outside threat."[35]

Uncertainty and the Media

In interviews during the 1988 campaign, some reporters underscored the "contradictions" (ambiguity) present in the candidates' speeches. For instance, at times, Salinas spoke "with all candor" that the one-party system was a thing of the past. He would at other times stress his adherence to the "goals of the Mexican Revolution." This was sometimes interpreted as a warning against a quick, reformist interpretation of his oft-stated program of modernization.

Contradictory messages kept people wondering and presumably unable to act—especially if they would be affected by the candidate's ideology. The press is a fundamental instrument in the diffusion of these messages of uncertainty. For example, in one of the speeches he made in Puebla on February 19, 1988, Salinas de Gortari stated, "In politics, alliances carry a price. Those that are made with my party will see a positive response in actuality. Those that are made against my party will, also in actuality, have to live with the consequences." This statement was made in a speech to the Mexican Union of Electricians and the all-important Oil Workers' Union. Commentaries in the critical press had indicated that the leaders of the Oil Workers' Union were unhappy with the nomination of Salinas de Gortari and his policies.

In the days that followed, columnists, as well as other politicians, interpreted Salinas de Gortari's remarks. He was criticized because the speech seemed to contradict the new democratic spirit with which the candidate was presumably identified, and some questioned whether he truly wanted to "hear Mexico speak," his campaign slogan. Was this statement a message to the opposition or to members of the PRI, targeted by the candidate because of their lukewarm support? Those who defended the candidate simply noted that it was not unusual for candidates to reward those who had supported them. One journalist interviewed by the author pointed out that some PRI members who wrote their interpretations in the newspapers had been identified with factions of other PRI leaders, and Salinas's statement enabled him to keep attention focused on himself:

> It doesn't really matter what he meant. At the time, the country
> was busy figuring out the potential impact that the candidacy of

Cárdenas was having on the traditional base of support of the PRI, especially in the organized labor sector. As soon as he [Salinas] said those words, everybody started to talk about what he meant by it. He kept them very busy for quite a few days.

Thus, the press disseminates the campaign rituals to a larger audience, serves as an arena where messages create ambiguity (both as an exercise of power and a facilitator of the negotiation process), and is a source of interpretation of campaign events. Ambiguity is served by a style of journalism that might be termed "user-unfriendly." A reader must have great knowledge about who's who to understand both the events and the interpretations found in the press. For example, the frequent publications by commentators never reveal if the author is a journalist, a politician, or a private citizen.

Indeed, research on how politicians interpret the press indicates that only those with much experience in Mexican politics find newspapers useful. Others find them too difficult to decode without the help of "experts."[36] An example was provided by an ex-journalist and public affairs specialist who worked for a Mexican government ministry on a newsletter in which newspaper articles were translated into "straight facts" for the American public. She often found that the articles were clouded with such uncertainty that many times the actual information was wrong:

> I think the journalists themselves were wary of interpreting or reporting the facts wrongly; their articles were written with such ambiguity that should the journalists have printed the wrong information, they could easily have said that the reader interpreted the information incorrectly. This made it difficult to extract factual information from the articles, but left journalists with an "escape," should an angry politician accuse them of misinterpreting what he had said. The only way I could be fairly certain the facts were correct, was if they were repeated at least five times in separate articles.

The Candidate as National Figure

The PRI campaign served to construct the person of the president of the republic. During the campaign, the candidate traveled through the country and received endorsements, heard complaints, accepted petitions, and spoke with diverse persons and groups who demanded privileged positions of negotiation with the candidate. In this process of listening to regional problems, the candidate became identified with all parts of the country. Simultaneously, because of his willingness to listen, he was identified with solutions to regional problems.

As the candidate traveled through the country, references were always made to his particular connection with each region. In Puebla, he was presented as a fellow "Poblano" because at some point in his life he had worked in that state; in Veracruz, he was a "Veracruzano" because his mother was a teacher in that state; in Tlaxcala, he was identified with that state because he had conducted his field research there as a student. These images of the candidate as belonging to every region of the country were repeated by the local media during each of the campaign stops.

The candidate's identification with each region was, however, manifested most symbolically in the ritualized hearings (*audiencias*) in which he listened to local concerns and pledged his commitment to solve problems. In these elections, the PRI used both television and radio as important forums for such hearings. The slogan adopted by the candidate, "Let Mexico Speak Out" (*Que Hable México*), was used in every region where the candidate appeared on television and radio to answer questions from the general public. These carefully staged ceremonies were used to convey the candidate's sincere desire to "hear the people" and make an endless list of commitments.

In addition to regular broadcast appearances Salinas de Gortari made to answer callers' questions, local television and radio stations often dedicated the entire day to covering all the local events of the campaign. Popular disc jockeys were recruited to give this coverage a festive spirit, and local personalities from both the political and entertainment world acknowledged the importance of the visit. The image was clear: This was not the visit of a presidential candidate as much as the visit of the president-king making a stop to meet his people and offer himself as the answer to their problems.

Television images during these stops were carefully staged to present the candidate as godlike and demonstrate the wide support of the general population. His words were reported as if they were divine and were almost always followed by shots of ever-present large crowds of supporters. The manner in which he was portrayed as delivering his speeches, the photo angles, the portrayal of the candidate as identifying with all the regions of the country, transformed him into a national symbol.

Media as Symbols and Instruments of Power

Some people interviewed believed that because television and radio are the most widely used news media, the campaign exploited them to secure votes. It could be that this was the intention, but if anything, this may have had a boomerang effect. The PRI seemed to have overlooked the fact that a certain degree of media credibility is required for effective persuasion. Televisa's uncritical, outspoken support of the PRI and automatic derision of opposition candidates is one example of how television's credibility was thrown into question during the campaign. But as one expert in media-government relations told me, "It doesn't matter, does it? They [the electronic media] pleased the one person [Salinas de Gortari] they needed to please!"

The media, of course, cannot be viewed as outside forces in the political system. They represent their economic and political interests, which are also part of the negotiation process. For many newspapers and magazines, the campaign represents the single most important source of income, not only during the campaign, but in the future as well, because the campaign establishes the relationship of media with the new administration. Most publications offer the official candidate their unconditional support from the very start of the campaign, exercising a rigid self-censorship, because they wield little power to survive economically without the resources that the campaign (and the future administration) provides. Journalists know that the president can ultimately dictate to other government institutions whether or not a TV station or radio or publication is to be favored with government income during his administration.

In 1976, *Excelsior* confronted presidential power under the administration of Luis Echeverría and found it too strong. Ultimately, the system of co-optation brought with it the threat of financial sanctions. As a result of the power struggle, *Excelsior* was forced to "fire" its editor, Julio Scherer, who then began to publish the well-known weekly *Proceso*. The fact that *Proceso* has managed to survive without traditional sources of revenue (government publicity, bribes, and so on) is a noteworthy chapter in the history of Mexican journalism. That does not mean, however, that other publications could duplicate the success of *Proceso*.

The more important newspapers and magazines, such as *Excelsior* or *Siempre*, did publish harsh criticisms of the candidates, especially in the beginning of the campaign. These criticisms themselves became a hot topic of interpretation. For example, many of the politicians believed that the harsh criticism of the PRI candidate by *Siempre* in the beginning of the campaign was simply a negotiating ploy, a way of securing greater resources for its owner and staff. Other interpretations suggest that the publisher, who was dying, was mentally unstable or wanted to leave a mark in journalism, or that the publisher of *Siempre* had a personal dispute with Salinas de Gortari. Whatever the reason, the reactions to these criticisms proved once again the dominant role of interpretations in Mexico. Likewise, when television stars appeared with the official candidate in the campaign events, this was interpreted as the general support that Televisa was giving the candidate and not the personal support of the stars themselves.

Given the importance of the media in shaping "facts" and constructing the image of the president, media outlets are necessarily seen as important instruments of power. The meaning that members of the political class assign to the media lies in its symbolic manifestation of power. From the moment of the *destape*, it is expected that the candidate will secure favorable treatment in the media and successfully shape the form and content of the media's campaign coverage. Furthermore, it is expected that the candidate will dominate the news.

During the first few weeks of this campaign, following the announcement of Salinas de Gortari as candidate, the lame-duck president, Miguel de la Madrid, still dominated the front page of newspapers and lead stories of television and radio newscasts. This was interpreted by specialists in press-government relations as a sign of political weakness of the candidate. An expert told us, "If he [Salinas de Gortari] can't get his name in the top story of the front page [*ocho columnas*], then there isn't much he will be able to accomplish [in his administration].

Ultimately, the political class interprets control of the press not so much in terms of how effective media are in persuading the general public as in symbolizing the minimum requirement of the president—his ability to wield power.

CONCLUSIONS

In this overview of the role of the media in the 1988 presidential elections, we have tried to present two distinct lines of analysis. In the process of redemocratization, there was, without a doubt, a new openness that had not existed prior to 1988. But on the whole, the majority of the media did not change its practices and generally continued to conduct its reporting in the traditional way.

The print media chosen for this analysis are primarily the leading print outlets in Mexico. *Excelsior* should not, therefore, be considered a typical example of press coverage around the country. Print news outlets such as *Excelsior* are concerned about maintaining high readership and therefore cover events of importance even at the cost of offending the ruling party. Their prestige also gives them enough journalistic muscle to be more open and critical. But they are the exceptions. Had this analysis included other, more representative, newspapers, the hegemonic presence of the PRI would have been far greater.

If Mexico is to become a stronger democracy, it is likely that the structure and practice of Mexican journalism must undergo fundamental changes. Perhaps the role of the press will diminish considerably, or at least, fewer resources might be allocated to the press from the campaigns and their players. A stronger democracy will also require a more independent press, one that can truly reflect the changes taking place. A healthy democracy undoubtedly requires responsible news media. In Mexico, as elsewhere, the question will be the ability of journalists to gain that independence, which will require, among many things

- Realistic salaries to journalists so that they need not be co-opted
- More independence for news divisions of television and radio stations
- The breakup of the monopolistic nature of the television industry as a whole

Changes might even include granting journalists partial power to regulate their own profession, because there is little doubt that the kind of unregulated journalism that works to a satisfactory degree in other countries has not worked in Mexico. As Hernan Uribe writes in his *Journalism Ethics in Latin America*, in Mexico "freedom of expression has become, in reality, the freedom of the rich."[37]

But from the point of view of the traditional (hierarchical) political system, the media serve important functions that explain why the PRI spends so many resources and pays so much attention to them even though vote getting is not the principal preoccupation.

The press, on the one hand, has an important role in the rituals of the campaign through which the drama of political negotiations and alliances is played. The press is also an arena for members of the political class who are participants in and affected by the formation of the new power structure. Therefore, the press makes it possible to extend those rituals to other political players who cannot be present at campaign events. Through the press, the political class can indirectly participate in the drama of ambiguity and resolution that the campaign represents.

On the other hand, the electronic media, especially television, concern themselves with campaign rituals that build the image of the president. The strong presidentialism of Mexico's traditional political system requires that candidates assume a like image: They must be portrayed as knowledgeable, concerned, and above all powerful.

These contrasting roles assigned to the press and the electronic media make it necessary to analyze both forms. The analysis from the perspective of rituals explains their distinct place in the "traditional" system, which seems to be rooted in strongly held political cultural traits. Perhaps future campaigns will require a different role for the media, but any changes that might take place will no doubt be affected by the residuals of tradition. That is why understanding this tradition becomes all the more necessary.

NOTES

1. This chapter is based on data collected from a larger ethnographic study of the 1988 PRI campaign by Larissa Lomnitz, Claudio Lomnitz, and Ilya Adler in "El Fondo de la Forma: La Campaña Presidencial del PRI en Mexico, 1988," *Nueva Antropologia* 11 (1990): 45–82.
2. Louis Dumont, *The Political Forms of Modern Society: Bureaucracy, Democracy, Totalitarianism* (Cambridge, Mass.: MIT Press, 1986).
3. Roberto Da Matta, *A Casa e a Rua: Espaço, Cidadania, Mulher e Morte no Brasil* (São Paulo: Brasiliense, 1985).
4. John Merrill, R. Carter, and M. Alisky, *The Foreign Press: A Survey of the World's Journalism* (Baton Rouge, La.: Louisana State Unversity Press, 1972).
5. John Merrill, "Government and Press Control: Global Views." In L. John Martin and Ray Eldon Hiebert, eds., *Current Issues in International Communication* (White Plains, N.Y.: Longhan, 1950), pp. 110–112.
6. Louise F. Montgomery, "Stress on Government and Press Criticism of Government Leaders: Mexico 1951–1980," *Gazette,* 34, no. 3 (1984): 163-173.
7. Ilya Adler, "Media Uses and Effects in a Large Bureaucracy: A Case Study in Mexico" (Ph.D. diss., University of Wisconsin-Madison, School of Journalism and Mass Communication, 1986); Alan Riding, *Distant Neighbors* (New York: Alfred A. Knopf, 1985).
8. Adler, "Media Uses and Effects."
9. For a review of the Mexican broadcasting industry and its role and importance in Mexican politics, see Raul Trejo Delarbre, ed., *Las Redes de Televisa* (Mexico City: Claves Latinoamericanas, 1988); Fátima Fernandez Christlieb, *Los Medios de Difusion Masiva en Mexico* (Mexico City: Juan Pablos Editor, 1984); Miguel A. Granados Chapa, "La Radio en Mexico: Otros Comentarios," *Prensa y Radio en Mexico* (Faculted de Ciencias Politicas y Sociales, Centros de Estudios de la Comunicacion) 1 (1978): 45; among others.
10. Fátima Fernandez Christlieb, *Los Medios de Difusion Masiva en Mexico* (Mexico City: Juan Pablos, 1984).
11. For an in-depth analysis of the relationship between the state and the broadcasting industry in Mexico, see Elizabeth Mahan's "Mexican Broadcasting: Reassessing the Industry-State Relationship," *Journal of Communication* 35 (1): 60–75. In this analysis, Mahan shows how the relationship tends to give Televisa the upper hand.
12. Raul Delabre, ed., *Televisa: El Quinto Poder* (Mexico City: Claves Latinoamericanas, 1985).
13. By propaganda, we mean paid ads that filled the papers, usually in the form of statements of support by various public and private associations, institutions, party factions, and so on. A more difficult distinction deals with party-sponsored propaganda that appears as regular news stories—called a *gacetilla*. Because they are not "obvious," such stories were treated here as part of the news. However, the reason photos were excluded from the analysis is that the author had reliable information that these were, on the whole, completely packaged by the party and were considered propaganda.

14. Adler, "Media Uses and Effects."
15. Adler, "Media Uses"; *World Media Handbook* (New York: United Nations Department of Public Information, 1990).
16. Michael Robinson and Margaret A. Sheehan. *Over the Wire and on TV: CBS and UPI in Campaign '80* (New York: Russell Sage Foundation, 1983).
17. José Gutierrez Espindola, "Información y Necesidades Sociales/Los Noticieros de Televisa," In Delarbe, *Televisa.*
18. Doris Graber, "Content and Meaning: What's It All About?" *American Behavioral Scientist* 33 (2): 135–52.
19. These descriptions of Televisa's coverage are based on monitoring of the broadcasts done by Lomnitz, Lomnitz, and Adler in the larger ethnographic study, "El Fondo de la Forma."
20. Jorge Herrera, *La Radio el PRI, y el Destape* (Mexico City: Diana, 1988).
21. Antonio Gramsci, *Prison Notebooks,* ed. Quinton Hoare and Geoffrey Nowell Smith (London: Lawrence and Wishart, 1971.) First published in six volumes between 1948 and 1951.
22. A. Martin del Campo and M. Robeil Corella, "Commercial Television as an Educational and Political Institution: A Case Study of Its Impact on the Students of Telesecundaria," in *Communication and Latin American Society: Trends in Critical Research, 1960–1985,* ed. R. Atwood and E. McAnany (Madison, Wis.: University of Wisconsin Press, 1986).
23. See Michael Singletary, "Components of Credibility of a Favorable News Source," *Journalism Quarterly* 53:316–19. Also see Leo Jeffres, *Mass Media Processes and Effects* (Prospect Heights, Ill.: Waveland Press, 1986), especially pages 195–200 for a detailed discussion on media credibility.
24. Adler, "Media Uses and Effects."
25. In Eastern Europe, decades of tightly controlled media and ideological indoctrination did little to secure favorable votes for Communist candidates once free elections were held. The point here is not that the media have no effect on electoral outcomes but that such effects cannot be assumed simply on the basis that one party or one dominant class has a greater ability to disseminate its messages.
26. Petra Secanella, *El Periodismo Politico en México* (Mexico City: Prisma, 1984).
27. Arnold Van Genneph, *Rites of Passage* (New York: Johnson Reprint, 1969); Victor Turner, *Dramas, Fields and Metaphors* (Ithaca: Cornell University Press, 1974).
28. Other candidates obviously also traveled, but our research did not allow us to follow those campaigns and make comparisons in terms of strategies or symbolic meanings. The discussions they conducted were played out in the press (not on radio or television), and as such, they were internal discussions, within the political class, rather than discussions with the general electorate. Adler argues that the press in Mexico should be regarded as an arena where political struggles are expressed—an arena agreed on by the members of the active political class.
29. Philip Elliott, "Press Performance as Political Ritual," in *The Sociology of Journalism and the Press,* ed. H. Christian (London: University of Keele, 1980).
30. Lomnitz, Lomnitz, and Adler, "El Fondo de la Forma."
31. Silvia Gomez-Tagle, "Democracia y Poder en Mexico: El Significado de los Fraudes Electorales en 1979, 1982 y 1985," *Nueva Antropologia* 9 (3): 127–57.
32. Lomnitz, Lomnitz, and Adler, "El Fondo de la Forma."
33. Adler, "Media Uses and Effects."
34. Michel Crozier, *The Bureaucratic Phenomenon* (Chicago: University of Chicago Press, 1964).
35. Fred H. Goldner, "The Division of Labor: Process and Power," in *Power in Organizations,* ed. Mayer N. Zald (Nashville: Vanderbilt University Press, 1970).
36. Adler, "Media Uses and Effects."
37. Hernan Uribe, *Etica Periodística en América Latina* (Mexico City: Universidad Nacional Autonoma de Mexico, 1984).

CONTRIBUTORS

Editor

Thomas E. Skidmore is Céspedes Professor of History and director of
the Center for Latin American Studies at Brown University. He received his B.A. from Denison University, an M.A. from Oxford University, and a Ph.D. from Harvard University. He is the author of *The
Politics of Military Rule in Brazil, 1964–1985* (1988), coauthor of *Modern Latin America*, 3d ed. (1992), and coeditor of *The Cambridge Ency-
clopaedia of Latin America and the Caribbean*, 2d ed. (1992).

Other Contributors

Ilya Adler is assistant professor in the Department of Communications
at the University of Illinois at Chicago. He received an M.S. from
Boston University and a Ph.D. from the University of Wisconsin-
Madison. He has written a number of articles dealing with Mexican
and U.S.–Latino communication issues. He is the former editor of *La
Prensa Libre*, a bilingual weekly newspaper published in the San Francisco Bay area, and a former radio producer. He is an active consultant in the areas of international media campaigns and cross-cultural
communication, specializing in Latino/Anglo issues.

Douglas Gomery is professor, College of Journalism, University of Maryland at College Park, and former senior researcher of the Media
Studies Project of The Woodrow Wilson Center. He studies media
economics and history, and is the author of many articles, and author
or co-editor of nine books. With Philip Cook and Lawrence Lichty,
he is editor of *The Future of News* (1992) and *American Media* (1989).
Much of his work on media history is summarized in *Shared Pleasures*
(1992), *Movie History: A Survey* (1991), *The Hollywood Studio System*
(1986), which is also published in Spanish and French, and, with
Robert C. Allen, *Film History: Theory and Practice* (1985).

María Eugenia Hirmas is head of the Department of Communications at the Servicio Nacional de la Mujer (National Service for Women) in Santiago, Chile. She received an M.A. in sociology from the Universidad de Chile and her M.A. in communications strategies and policies from the Universidad Central de Venezuela.

Lawrence W. Lichty is professor in the Department of Radio/Television/Film at Northwestern University and the former director of the Media Studies Project of The Woodrow Wilson Center. He specializes in broadcasting history, news analysis, and audience research. With Philip Cook and Douglas Gomery, he is editor of *The Future of News* (1992) and *American Media* (1989). His other books are *Ratings Analysis: Theory and Practice*, with James G. Webster (1991), and *American Broadcasting: A Source Book on the History of Radio and Television*, with Malachi C. Topping (1975). He was director of media research for the 1983 PBS series "Vietnam: A Television History" and was historical consultant for "Making Sense of the Sixties" (PBS, 1991).

Venicio A. de Lima is associate professor of political communication, Universidade de Brasília, and adjunct professor of mass communication, Miami University-Ohio. He holds a B.A. in sociology and politics from the Universidade Federal de Minas Gerais (Brazil), and an M.A. and a Ph.D. in communication from the University of Illinois at Urbana. He is the author of *Comunicação e Cultura: As Idéias de Paulo Freire* (1984, 1981) and coauthor with Susan S. Reilly of *Constructing the Political Scenario: The Struggle for Critical Citizenship in Media-Centric Cultures* (in press).

Carlos Eduardo Lins da Silva is Washington, D.C., correspondent of Brazil's largest daily newspaper, *Folha de São Paulo*, and a visiting researcher at Georgetown University. He was managing editor, deputy editor-in-chief, and planning director of *Folha*, and has been teaching journalism at the University of São Paulo since 1976. A Fulbright Scholar and a former Woodrow Wilson Center Fellow (1987–88), Lins da Silva holds a Ph.D. from the University of São Paulo and an M.A. from Michigan State University.

Maria Cavaliari Nunes is assistant director of political polling at the Instituto Brasileiro de Opinião Pública e Estatística (IBOPE) in São Paulo. She received an M.A. in public opinion research from the University of Connecticut.

Organ Olsen is director of political polling at the Instituto Brasileiro de Opinião Pública e Estatística (IBOPE) in São Paulo. He received a Ph.D. in communications from Syracuse University.

James Schwoch is associate professor in the Department of Radio/Television/Film at Northwestern University. He received a B.A. from the University of Wisconsin and a Ph.D. from Northwestern. During 1991–91, Schwoch was the Ameritech Research Professor at Northwestern. His books include *The American Radio Industry and Its Latin American Activities, 1900–1939* (1990) and *Media Knowledge* (1992).

Joseph Straubhaar is associate professor of telecommunication and coordinator of the Brazil Program at Michigan State University. He received a Ph.D. in international relations from the Fletcher School of Law and Diplomacy, Tufts University, and served eight years in the United States Foreign Service, including three in Brazil.

Enrique Zuleta-Puceiro is professor of jurisprudence at the National University of Buenos Aires and professor of political science at the University of Belgrano. He holds a Ph.D. from the University of Madrid and is a Member of Honour of the Spanish Royal Academy of Legislation and Jurisprudence. He was visiting professor of government and a fellow at the Center of International Affairs at Harvard University. Zuleta-Puceiro is a political and public opinion consultant and a member of the board of the Instituto Brasileiro de Opinião Pública e Estatística (IBOPE) in São Paulo.

INDEX

SEQUENTIAL
LANGUAGE
DEVELOPMENT

A Program of
SEQUENTIAL
LANGUAGE
DEVELOPMENT

A THEORETICAL AND PRACTICAL GUIDE FOR REMEDIATION OF LANGUAGE, READING AND LEARNING DISORDERS

By

HARRIS M. BLUMBERG, Ed.D.

North Miami Beach, Florida

Illustrated by

Emily Flanagan

CHARLES C THOMAS · PUBLISHER
Springfield · Illinois · U.S.A.

Published and Distributed Throughout the World by
CHARLES C THOMAS • PUBLISHER
Bannerstone House
301-327 East Lawrence Avenue, Springfield, Illinois, U.S.A.

© 1975, by CHARLES C THOMAS • PUBLISHER
ISBN 0-398-03320-X
Library of Congress Catalog Card Number: 74-16430

*With THOMAS BOOKS careful attention is given to all details of
manufacturing and design. It is the Publisher's desire to present books that are
satisfactory as to their physical qualities and artistic possibilities and
appropriate for their particular use. THOMAS BOOKS will be true to those
laws of quality that assure a good name and good will.*

Printed in the United States of America
C-1

Library of Congress Cataloging in Publication Data

Blumberg, Harris M.
A program of sequential language development.

1. Communicative disorders in children. 2. Speech
therapy. I. Title.
RJ496.S7B59   618.9'28'55   74-16430
ISBN 0-398-03320-X

CONTRIBUTORS

MARY BURLINGTON, B.A.
SHERRI POLIAKOFF, B.S.
DONALD E. ROTH, M.S.

PREFACE

THE ABILITY TO EFFECTIVELY handle both spoken and written language should be one of the basic goals of our educational system.

Having worked in the area of exceptional child education since 1960 at the Reading Clinic of Temple University, The Pathway School in Norristown, Pennsylvania, within the Vanguard School system and presently as a Language Arts Consultant for the Florida Migratory Child Compensatory Program, Region III, I have become increasingly cognizant of a definite lack of complete and integrated programs for remediation of learning disabilities. As a teacher of children, and "a teacher of teachers" in a university setting, a diagnostician, reading specialist, and director of a clinical school, I have been constantly searching for a theoretically sound scope and sequence to use as a guideline for encompassing the four basic stages of communication development. Thus, the epigenesis of this work.

I would like to thank all the professionals with whom I have worked over the years who have contributed to this endeavor, especially, Dr. Marjorie S. Johnson; Dr. Stanley L. Rosner; the faculty and students of Nova University, Fort Lauderdale, Florida; and Florida Atlantic University, Boca Raton, Florida. I certainly appreciate all of the efforts and cooperation of the faculty and administration of the Vanguard School, especially that of Dr. Milton Brutten, Clinical Director, who helped with the program in its early stages, and of Mr. Ulysses G. Horne, Director, Region III, FMCCP, who has shown me a new horizon in education.

The contributors who have worked with me since its inception are current or former members of the faculty of the Vanguard School; Mrs. Mary Burlington, Mrs. Sherri Poliakoff, and Mr. Donald E. Roth. They have made possible what I feel is a vital and useful educational and remedial reference and guide. To them, my deepest appreciation and gratitude. Many may question why the theory and research? I feel this area is too often neglected in developing programs to meet the ever-increasing need for effective tools to use in clinical remediation.

I would like to thank Mrs. Emily Flanagan, the Art and Drama teacher at Vanguard School, who provided the illustrations for this book. The author wishes to thank Miss Shirley Lawrence, Miss Louise Bing, and Mrs. Ingrid DiMolfetta without whose service and assistance this book could not have been brought to its final completion.

Finally, the writer is appreciative of the ever-present encouragement, support, and assistance of his wife, Joan, to whom this book is dedicated.

H.M.B.

CONTENTS

SEQUENTIAL
LANGUAGE
DEVELOPMENT

CHAPTER 1

A PROGRAM OF
SEQUENTIAL
LANGUAGE DEVELOPMENT

THEORY AND RESEARCH RELATED TO THE PROGRAM

Communication, Language Development and Concept Formation

COMMUNICATION IS THE FOUNDATION of our society. Without communication the basic institutions upon which society depends would not exist. Stone (1955) notes, "In man, the most striking disturbance of higher integrated function are those concerned with the language mechanisms. It is in the use of written and spoken language that man is most clearly differentiated from higher animals. . . ."

The communication process as it is currently defined consists of four phases: listening, speaking, reading, and writing; these stages do not occur temporally but rather interact in a spiral and feedback manner. There have been many measures developed to describe speech and language development, the second phase of the sequence.

Gagne (1965) presents a theoretical hierarchy of learning tasks for acquiring language skills. These include:

> (1) signal learning; (2) stimulus-response learning; (3) chaining; (4) verbal association; (5) multiple discrimination; (6) concept learning; (7) principle learning, and (8) problem solving. There is need to investigate the ways in which these eight different types of learning are employed by normal children as they develop language skills. There is need, also, to study the ways in which central processing dysfunctions affect the employment of these learning strategies and interfere with the acquisition of language. (Chalfante and Scheffelin, 1969)

3

TABLE I

SUMMARY OF EARLY NORMAL SPEECH AND ORAL
LANGUAGE DEVELOPMENTAL STAGE

Age Months	General Characteristics	Usable Speaking Vocabulary (Number of Words)	Adequate Speech Sound Production
1-3	UNDIFFERENTIATED CRYING. Random vocalizations and cooing.		
4-6	BABBLING. Specific vocalizations. Verbalizes in response to speech of others. Immediate response approximate human intonational patterns. Tongue moves with vocalizations (lalling). Vocalizes recognition. Reduplicates sound. Echolalia (automatic repetition of words and phrases).		
12	FIRST WORD.	1-3	All vowels
18	ONE-WORD SENTENCE STAGE. Well-established jargon. Uses nouns primarily.	18-22	
Years			
2	TWO-WORD SENTENCE STAGE. Sentences functionally complete. Uses more pronouns and verbs.	270-300	
2.5	THREE-WORD SENTENCE STAGE. Telegraphic speech.	450	h,w,hw
3	Complete simple-active-sentence structure used. Uses sentences to tell stories which are understood by others.	900	p,b,m
3.5	EXPANDED GRAMMATICAL FORMS. Concepts expressed with words. Speech disfluency is typical. Sentence length is four-five words.	1200	t,d,n
4	Excessive verbalizations. Imaginary speech.	1500	k,g,ng,j
5	WELL-DEVELOPED AND COMPLEX SYNTAX. Uses more complex forms to tell stories. Uses negation and inflexional form of verbs.	2000	f,v
	SOPHISTICATED SPEECH. Skilled use of grammatical rules. Learns to read. Acceptable articulation by eight years for males and females.	2600+	l,r,y,s,z, sh,ch,zh,th, consonant blends

Printed originally as Table 6.0 in Lloyd M. Dunn, *Exceptional Children in the Schools: Special Education in Transition* (New York, Holt, Reinhart, Winston, 1963), p. 301.

Recently the fifth aspect of body language has been introduced as part of the communication process. This aspect is not dealt with as a separate aspect of the program, but is incorporated at specific appropriate points.

Dunn (1963) compiled the works of several authors to illustrate the development of speech and language. The development of patterns from simple to complex and from concrete to abstract are illustrated in the category of general characteristics. Brutten, Richardson, and Mangel (1973) state:

> Language and thought are related processes. Although there can be limited thought without language and restricted language without thought, in the normal child the two abilities must develop together. The growth of language makes it possible for thought to occur, for concepts to form, for ideas to become riches. The attainment of skills encompassing language and thought is called cognitive development.
>
> Cognition includes perception, because everything an individual knows is based on his taking in and organizing information delivered by the world to his sense organs; it also encompasses concept formation, the development of ideas, inferences, conclusions about information received by the senses. These ideas and concepts crystallize through and around words and word-combinations. Each person then has a means of sharing his thoughts with others who use his language.
>
> But in many learning-disabled children, sensory impressions do not jell into meaningful information. The result is disorders of language development and thinking processes. These difficulties are among the most widespread and serious problems of learning-disabled children.
>
> What goes wrong? The variety of these disorders is staggering.
>
> Just as some children have difficulty with visual perception, other learning-disabled children hear perfectly, but for a variety of reasons cannot understand what they hear. They have auditory-perceptual problems.

Language Development and Achievement

To further demonstrate the need for more critical and sensitive awareness of the relationship of language development to achievement, the following data is representative of findings in various sources.

TABLE II

CORRELATIONS OF CALIFORNIA ACHIEVEMENT TESTS—ARITHMETIC WITH CAT READING, ENGLISH AND SPELLING TESTS

	Lower Primary (Grade 1)		Upper Primary (Grade 2)		Upper Primary (Grade 3)		Elementary (Grade 4)		Elementary (Grade 5)	
	AR	AF	AR	AF	AR	AF	AR	AF	AR	AF
Arithmetic reasoning (AR)										
Arithmetic fundamentals (AF)	.63	.59	.65	.58	.53	.44	.56	.46	.76	.64
Reading vocabulary	.63	.44	.76	.57	.71	.35	.69	.34	.69	.68
Reading comprehension	.56	.59	.77	.62	.65	.43	.60	.49	.75	.68
Mechanics of English	.65	.59	.79	.62	.65	.43	.61	.49	.75	.65
Spelling	.58	.49	.60	.49	.62	.37	.56	.41	.61	.59

From Technical Report on the California Achievement Tests, 1963 Norms, Monterey, California, California Test Bureau, 1967; also reproduced in Lewis R. Aiken, Jr., "Language Factors in Learning Mathematics," *Review of Education Research*, 42:47 (Summer, 1972).

The findings of other investigators Martin (1964); Wallace (1968); Harvin & Gilchrist (1970); underscore the relationships between mathematical problem solving and reading ability. Thus, Martin (1964) obtained the following result from administering the Iowa Tests of Basic Skills to fourth and eighth graders. The partial correlation between reading comprehension and problem solving abilities, with computational ability partialed out, was higher at both grade levels than the partial correlation between computational ability and problem solving ability, with reading comprehension partialed. Finally, Murry (1949) cited evidence that performance on a geometry test, which one might suspect to depend greatly on spatial ability, was also closely related to the verbal abilities of certain students (Aiken, 1972).

Stauffer (1948) found that retarded readers did less well in a verbal opposites test than on a general capacity test, indicating an underlying lag in oral language development as well as the function of controlled association. Aiken, Jr. (1972), in his investigation of "Language Factors in Learning Mathematics," also discusses the relationship between Mathematical Vocabulary, Syntax and Readability.

Among investigations of the relationships between mathematical abilities and specific aspects of linguistic ability, particular attention has been directed toward vocabulary, and, to a lesser extent, syntax. The results of studies conducted some years ago (for example, Hansen, 1944; Treacy, 1944) indicate that knowledge of vocabulary is important in solving mathematics problems and consequently should be a goal of mathematics instruction. A fairly comprehensive correlational study reported a few years later (Johnson, 1949) involved administering six tests of arithmetic problems and six of the Primary Mental Abilities tests to several hundred Chicago school children. The following correlations between PMA Vocabulary and the standardized achievement tests were obtained; Stanford, Arithmetic Reasoning (.51), Chicago Survey Test in Arithmetic (.50), Stone Reasoning Test (.45). Furthermore, PMA Vocabulary correlated more highly with scores on a nonstandardized test composed of problems with numbers (140) than with scores on a test of problems without numbers (.26).

Language as it is used in this program encompasses all aspects of the communication process. There has been a vast amount of work and study dealing with language, not only in the communicative process, but with regard to acquisition. When surveying the literature, it can be safely concluded that there has been no single theory regarding how children acquire an auditory language code that is not debated or questioned (Chalfant and Scheffelin, 1969).

Carroll (1974); Chomsky (1959), (1965); Menyuk (1967); McNeil (1966), and Skinner (1967) have all considered the acquisition and use of a first language. Myklebust (1954, 1960) delineates three parts of a developmental sequence for language acquisition, consisting of inner language meaningfulness, receptive language, and expressive language. Vogel (1974) when exploring deficits in expressive language skills noted that skill in expressive language is one of the subtle language processes underlying reading problems.

Rudell (1970) supports the sequence of language development outlined in the present program. He states that the child's ability to understand language goes before and is better than his ability to produce language. Second, his language understanding appears to be directly related to his command of the grammatical lexical component of the discourse. Third, his language ability and performance appear to move through a developmental sequence during the elementary school years. His language performance is directly related to his language environment, including the available language model and opportunity for language interaction, the way he approaches situations requiring comprehension and objectives, and possibly maturation of his latent language strategies.

Menyuk (1967) synthesizes the various concepts and theories about the universal components of language:

> The syntactic component contains rules for defining classes of the language and their functional relationships. The semantic component contains rules for interpreting the meaning of lexical items and the underlying syntax structures of the sentence. The phonological component contains rules for defining the classes of sounds of the language and translating the underlying structure of the sentence into a sequence of sounds.

Theories of communication disorders continue to appear in the literature. Recently a very complex but theoretically sound rationale for communication disorders was developed and presented by John H. Meir (1971). He states "a disability in receiving, processing, storing, returning, and/or expressing data in proper sequence, seems a characteristic of a large percentage of ILD second-grade children. It is suggested that teachers and parents can remediate such disorders by systematic training of, for example, sequencing objects. Numerous methods for doing this are becoming available but a discussion of them is beyond the scope of this paper."

The Need for a Program of Sequential Language Development

The present program expands into a specific scope and sequence of a spiral development nature where continuous feedback occurs, the theories presented by the various authors cited throughout this section.

Several research projects funded by the federal government also note that there are several guidelines available for the identification and diagnosis of children with auditory perceptual and language development disabilities, but that there is a lack of methods and materials for remediating these problems. There has been more structural training in perceptual motor and visual perceptual problems than in training or developing auditory perception and language other than those emphasized in classes for the hard of hearing and deaf (Jordan, 1972).

To better diagnose children with auditory difficulties, there is need to develop more effective procedures for presenting auditory stimuli, eliciting responses, and increasing the number of response modes. Greater efficiency in selecting the way to present the auditory stimulus, the method of indicating response, and motivating the child to respond may help reduce the amount of response inconsistency.

The goal of auditory training is to help the child make active use of his hearing. Comparatively few studies exist concerning the training of auditory perceptual disorders. The literature is loaded with diagnostic studies and procedures. There are a few studies which indicated that some degree of amelioration is possible. Unfortunately, there is a lack of work regarding remedial procedures which are used or the nature of the disorders to which remediation was applied. The methods section of reported studies often consists of abbreviated lists including such topics as hearing and distinguishing sounds; listening games; listening to contrasting sounds, loud and soft, fast and slow, high and low; following directions; hearing through poetry; listening through stories; music to develop sound discrimination, and reproduction of auditory stimuli. "Despite the lack of detail in reporting remedial approaches, there seems to be clinic agreement that training should be attempted in the deficit areas" (Chalfant and Scheffelin, 1969).

These authors reviewed the problems in assessing and treating central processing dysfunctions which interfere with the acquisition and use of a first language. They raise a most important question, "What are the principles and guidelines for programming the systematic instruction of a first language?" This question can only be answered by research in the clinic and classroom, and by controlled evaluation of educational techniques.

None will know whether the learning laboratory has any substantial import on pedagogy and materials unless the schooling or educational process becomes better documented. Careful and detailed records must be kept for long periods of time of what in the program is useful in the classroom and/or clinical setting.

To date, the sequence has proved successful in providing guidelines for teachers. The sequence was presented at a workshop at two educational conferences—the 1973 Council for Exceptional Children and the 1974 International Conference of the Association for Children with Learning Disabilities. In both workshops its need was quite evident and the format found useful and understandable by the people on the firing line—teachers. Perhaps the results from K-12 can be applied to computer-based course processing.

REFERENCES

Aiken, Lewis R. Jr.: Language factors in learning mathematics. *Review of Education Research, 42:*46-47, Summer, 1972.

Berry, M. F., and Eisenson, J.: *Speech Disorders: Principles and Practices of Therapy.* New York, Appleton-Century-Crofts, 1956.

Bruininks, Robert H. and Kennedy, Patricia: Social statutes of hearing impaired children in regular classrooms. *Exceptional Children, 40*:336-341, February, 1974.

Brutten, Milton, Richardson, Sylvia, and Mangel, Charles: Language and thought development. *Something Is Wrong with My Child.* New York, Harcourt, Brace, Jovanovich, Inc., 1973, p. 36.

California Test Bureau. *Technical Report on the California Achievement Tests, 1973 Norms.* Monterey, 1967.

Carroll, J. B.: *Language and Thought.* Englewood Cliffs, Prentice-Hall, 1964.

Chalfant, James C., and Scheffelin, Margaret A.: *Central Processing Dysfunctions in Children: A Review of Research.* NINDH Monograph No. 9. Institute for Research on Exceptional Children, University of Illinois, 1969, p. 14.

Chomsky, Noam: Review of Skinner's verbal behavior. *Language, 35:* 1959.

Chomsky, Noam: Lecture at Project Literacy. Cornell University, June 18, 1965.

Dunn, Lloyd M. (ed.): *Exceptional Children in the Schools: Special Education in Transition.* New York, Holt, Reinhart, Winston, 1963.

First Steps in Language Experiences for Pre-school Children. The Duplicate Section, Department of Publications, Division of School Relations and Special Services, Detroit Public Schools' Board of Education, 1966, p. 95.

Gagne, R. M.: *The Conditions of Learning.* New York, Holt, Reinhart, Winston, 1965.

Getman, G. N.: *How to Develop Your Child's Intelligence.* Luverne, G. N. Getman, 1962.

Goldstein, K.: *Language and Language Disorders.* New York, Grune & Stratton, 1948.

Jordan, Ethel S.: Auditory, perceptural and language development training program. *Final Project Report Title III.* Boise, ESEN Grant 89-10, 70-13, 1969-1972.

Kennedy, Ann: Language awareness and the deaf-blind child. *Teaching Exceptional Children, 6:*99, Winter, 1974.

Luria, A. R.: *Higher Cortical Functions in Man.* New York, Basic Books, 1966.

McNeill, D.: Developmental psycholinguistics. In Smith, F. and Miller, G. A. (Eds.): *The Genesis of Language: A Psycholinguistic Approach.* Cambridge, M.I.T. Press, 1966.

Mittler, Peter (Ed.): *The Psychological Assessment of Mental and Physical Handicaps.* London, Methuen & Co. Ltd., 1970, p. 826.

Menyuk, P.: Innovative linguistic description of the language acquisition of children who acquire language normally and those whose language acquisition is deviant. In Newcomb, D. L. (Ed.): *Proceedings 1967 International Convocation on Children and Young Adults with Learning Disabilities.* Pittsburgh, Home for Crippled Children, 1967, p. 313.

Mykelbust, H. R.: *Auditory Disorders in Children: A Manual for Differential Diagnosis.* New York, Grune & Stratton, 1954.

Mykelbust, H. R.: *The Psychology of Deafness.* New York, Grune & Stratton, 1960.

Natkin, Gerald L., and Moore, J. William: The effects of instructional sequencing on learning from a simple knowledge structure. *American Educational Research Journal,* vol. 9, Washington, Fall, 1972.

Ruddell, Robert B.: Language acquisition and the reading process, 1-19. *Theoretical Models and Processes of Reading.* International Reading Association, 1970.

Skinner, B. F.: *Verbal Behavior.* New York, Appleton-Century-Crofts, 1957.

Stauffer, Russel C.: Certain psychological manifestations of retarded readers. *Journal Education Research,* XLI:410-417, February, 1948.

Stone, Calvin P.: *Comparative Psychology.* 3d ed. Englewood Cliffs, Prentice-Hall, 1955.

Vogel, S. A.: Syntactic abilities in language. *Journal of Learning Disabilities,* 7:103-109, February, 1974.

CHAPTER 2

RESEARCH: RELATED TO THE EIGHT SPECIFIC STAGES OR ASPECTS

Development of Accurate Auditory Perception, Discrimination, and Direction Following

IF ONE IS TO CONSIDER a sequence of language development where the first stage is listening, then any educational program must first consider hearing or the auditory system. Much work has been done in the area of physiological psychology regarding the sense of hearing, auditory stimulus, and the auditory system.

The nature of sound, physiological structures involved in hearing such as the ear, various auditory pathways leading to the brain and auditory cortex have been described and analyzed and investigated. Morgan and Stellar (1950) note that we have made great headways in both the psychology and physiology of hearing the past twenty years.

Research and the Need for a Sequential Program of Remediation

The first aspect of this program, the auditory area, has been studied as early as infancy. Trehub and Rabinovitch (1972), when investigating auditory linguistic sensitivity in early infancy, indicated that infants four to 17 weeks of age are able to detect some differences in sounds, upon which phonemic contracts are based. Cullen, Frago, Chase, and Baker (1968) studied the development of auditory feedback, specifically delayed auditory feedback studies on infant crying. They indicated that cry behavior may be under closed-loop auditory feedback control.

Yeni-Konshian, Chase, and Mobley (1968), who in the same

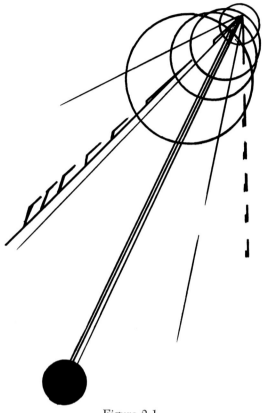

Figure 2-1

area of auditory feedback monitoring investigated the delayed auditory feedback of children between two and three years of age, concluded that there is evidence that the auditory feedback monitoring system for speech is operative in this age group, but that the speech of the younger subject was not strongly affected by D.A.F.

Age appears again to be an important aspect of auditory discrimination skills, which means maturation must be included in any search for indication of auditory disabilities. Clark and Hutchinson (1968), when investigating the auditory and visual discrimination skills of normal and articulation-defective children, concluded that the auditory and social modality tests showed significant F ratios among grade levels but not between normals and articulation-defective groups.

Flack (1973) discussed how auditory processing may be analyzed and instructional units prepared for use in learning disability classrooms for children with language disorders. Bannatyne (1973) notes that:

> psycholinguistics is the study of how the mind and brain actually process language in all its forms . . . recently several books have been written in which the authors prefer psycholinguistic exercises as a preliminary or supplementary adjunct to reading. All kinds of peripheral and filler lesson plan materials and programs are elaborated. . . . All of these are useful but few get to the heart of psycholinguistics as reading, writing, spelling and language processes which can be taught children.

The type of auditory figure ground situation in which a student is placed may impede or improve the attending ability to relevant stimuli. Stanback and Hallahan (1973) found a significant difference between the music and non-music groups in task relevant learning. The difference was in favor of the music group. They concluded music may be a stimuli aid.

Tobin and Lasky (1973) studied the types of auditory stimuli which may interfere with the performance of learning disability children. They found that linguistic competing auditory messages are most significant. (In the study, the competing messages were set up with the following procedures. Several types of messages were set up and selected on the basis of their likelihood of occurrence. To provide the type of competing message that would occur when several children are meeting simultaneously, prose reading passages and number facts requiring repetition were used.) The author concluded in summary that (1) linguistic competing auditory messages interfered with the performance of children with suspected learning disabilities but did not interfere with the performance of normal children and (2) competing auditory messages that are non-linguistic did not interfere with the performance of either group.

Recently, the question of "cultural deprivation" has come into the literature. It is this author's feelings that socio-economic disadvantagement, as a scientific issue, has "muddied the waters." These children require remediation of an auditory processing disability often resulting from a specific, or combination of etiologies. The etiology should not exclude them from programs of remediation, but more important, be a signal that the material for remediation may have to be modified according to an age-old truism—individual differences.

Gottesman (1972) examined whether differences exist in auditory discrimination ability between Negro dialect-speaking and standard English-speaking boys. The results indicate that there were no significant group differences in auditory discrimination performance on these used pairs which will be commonly differentiated in the speech of all subjects. However, both groups of standard English-speaking children were significantly higher than the group of Negro dialect-speaking children on these used pairs pronounced as homonyms in Negro dialects when they were presented contrastingly by standard English speakers.

Meier (1971) noted that:

> a disability in receiving, processing, story-relating and an expanding data in a proper sequence seems to be a large percentage of ILD conditions. This was apparent either and across all sensory models of a large percentage of the ILD children composed of about 15 percent of the population in 110 regular classes randomly selected from throughout eight states.

As noted, music has been found not only as an aid to attention to relevant stimuli, but as taught in a specifically structural manner, as a form of remediation of ILD children due to perceptual problems, specifically poor visual and auditory perception. Using visual, aural, and tactile training through practical and theory lessons over a six month period, a clinical case study indicated significant positive gains in language skills, auditory and visual perceptual abilities, sensory-motor integration, symbolic representation and memory. All these areas are found throughout the eight stages or phases of the teaching program in Chapter 3.

According to Banas and Wills (1973), new emphasis has been placed in the auditory aspect of learning. As a result of research and more effective means of measuring auditory processing, many students have been diagnosed as learning disabilities with specific dysfunction in auditory processing.

Oakland and Williams (1971) also describe these disabilities and delineate them as follows:

1. Auditory Acuity—the inability to detect the presence of sound at various levels of intensity and frequency.
2. Auditory Attention—the inability to direct and sustain attention to sounds.
3. Auditory Memory—the inability to remember and recall auditory sound patterns.
4. Auditory Discrimination—the inability to detect likeness and differences between two or more sounds.
5. Auditory Integration—the inability to collate a variety of independent sounds to form aural units.
6. Auditory Comprehension—the inability to decode and derive meaning from auditory stimuli. Comprehension often requires the fusion of attention, memory, discrimination, and integration of abilities in order to enable a person to interpret what he hears.

In one federally funded program it was reiterated that children acquire language through listening and repetition and thus the auditory system is the primary device through which language is learned. *Thus a learning difficulty is an almost unquestioned certainty, if children do not develop auditory perceptual skills in the pre-school years and do not comprehend or use language adequately.* Of 657 children in first and second grade in one school district, 346 (52%) of the children screened exhibited auditory perception problems to the extent that it would interfere with auditory learning. The screening used was the Wepman Discrimination Test. Identification was based on age norms determined by error scores in the test (Jordan 1972).

Auditory Memory Span and Direction Following

Studies and research dealing with auditory memory span are directly related to stage or phase I (Development of Accurate Auditory Perception and Discrimination—Direction Following—Listening Skills). However, much of the research in the series had been done with brain-injured youngsters (Blumberg, 1967). The importance of the findings of these studies, although as difficult to read as a novel, have direct implications in not only stage or phase I but successive stages and activities in the chapter dealing with programming.

The use of the word *retarded* in these studies pertains to achievement lag in reading and not intellectual functioning or intelligence quotients.

> A key characteristic of the performance of some brain-damaged persons is a rather severe limitation of the momentary span of attention, i.e. the amount of ideational material that can be held in consciousness at any one time. . . . This attentional deficit has obvious effects on memory functioning of spontaneous organizations of material. . . . A. A. Strauss, who has made distinguished contributions to the education of the brain-damaged, has stated that the most serious thinking handicap of the brain-damaged child is an impairment of selectivity, that is, the inability to distinguish the essential from the non-essential. . . . A study by Mathae on effects of mild brain-damaged on memory formation has shown that brain-damaged notably increases the degree of leveling. This finding adds to the evidence that the percepts and ideas recorded by the brain damaged person are less differentiated and less adaptively effective than those of the normal individual (Gardner, 1966).

The above selected statements by Gardner indicate the effect of brain injury on memory span and related functions.

There have been specific studies with retarded readers by several authors where brain-injury has not been considered as one of the variables to be controlled. Brown (1966), as well as Johnson (1956), and Stauffer (1948) have all investigated these factors.

Stauffer (1948) found that the retarded readers did less well on a verbal opposites test than on a general capacity test, indicating an underlying lag in oral language development as well as the function of controlled association.

G. Johnson (1956) found that a highly significant statistical difference at the .01 level of confidence favored the achieving reader over the retarded readers. He implied that the organization of certain auditory and visual memory span test results of retarded and achieving readers, according to the case-typing of

Temple University Reading Clinic, appeared to be justified as one means of differentiating between the two types of readers. The case-typing system appeared to be justified whether based on a relationship between the tests themselves to a lesser degree, or on the relationships between the mental age scores of the auditory and visual memory span test and the Binet mental age scores of the two types of readers.

Brown (1966) implied that tests of intelligence and memory span are relatively reliable measures to use in evaluating the capacities of severely retarded readers. Changes in reading ability seem to be somewhat related to changes in verbal capacity measures. While there may be some variation in intelligence, memory span and associative learning test-retest results, many of the psychological test patterns of retarded readers remain quite constant. However, younger children with reading difficulties may not exhibit some of the weaknesses in capacity measure that are characteristic of severely retarded reader populations.

Stauffer (1948), in his investigation of the memory span ability of his population of retarded readers, concluded that:

1. Retarded readers achieved significantly higher scores on nonverbal measures of visual memory than on verbal measures of auditory memory span.
2. Retarded readers tend to achieve higher scores with related items rather than unrelated items on verbal measures of memory span.
3. Retarded readers achieved significantly higher scores on forward span tests than on reverse span tests when digits are used to measure auditory memory span.
4. Retarded readers tend to make relatively low scores when related materials are presented arrhythmically, as measures of memory span.

G. Johnson (1956), as previously stated, investigated certain psychological characteristics of retarded and achieving readers in which he studied similar problems under specific modifications of the tests used by Stauffer. He concluded that when memory-span test results within the retarded reader and achieving reader groups are compared:

1. Retarded readers appear to retain unrelated letters and unrelated pictures of objects presented visually, better than they retain unrelated words presented orally.

2. Achieving readers appear to retain unrelated pictures of objects presented visually, better than they retain either unrelated words or sentences presented orally.

3. When related and unrelated items are compared:
   (a) Retarded readers appear to retain related sentences better than unrelated words when both are presented orally. However, they appear to retain unrelated directions better than related sentences when both are presented orally.
   (b) Achieving readers appear to retain unrelated pictures of objects better than related sentences, when the pictures were presented visually and the sentences orally.

4. When unrelated verbal and unrelated nonverbal items are compared:
   (a) Retarded readers appear to retain unrelated directions better than unrelated words, when both were presented orally.
   (b) Achieving readers appear to exhibit no differences in retention of verbal and nonverbal items whether presented orally or visually.

5. When digit span tests are compared:
   (a) Retarded readers appear to retain digits forward, visual and auditory, better than digits reversed auditory.
   (b) Achieving readers appear to retain digits forward, visual and auditory, better than digits reversed auditory.
   (c) They also appeared to retain visual digits forward better than auditory digits forward.

When the test and retest results of Brown's (1966) study were compared to the psychological test patterns of other retarded reader populations, specifically Stauffer and Johnson, the post-test results more closely approximated the reported results of other retarded reader populations than did the pre-test results.

In other words, test findings and patterns in the intellectual, memory-span and associative-learning areas appear to be more consistent with those cited in the literature when Brown re-administered tests in those areas, than were those from the initial diagnosis.

In summary, the literature cited attempts to provide a theoretically sound foundation supported by various authors concerning the placement of Phase I in the program as the initial phase and specific activities in the program for the teacher to implement in a learning-disabled or language-impaired classroom. It could also be utilized by a speech and language specialist in working therapeutically with SLD children and children with communication disorders.

REFERENCES

Banas, Norma, and Wills, I. H.: *Success Begins with Understanding.* San Rafael, Academic Therapy Publications, 1972.

Bannatyne, Alex: Reading: An auditory-vocal process. *Academic Therapy Quarterly, VIII:*429-431 (Summer, 1973).

Blumberg, Harris M.: An Investigation of the Associative Learning and Memory Span Abilities of 50 Brain Injured Youngsters with Normal Intellectual Potential. Unpublished Doctoral Dissertation, Philadelphia, Temple University, 1967, pp. 26-30.

Brown, C. G.: Longitudinal Study of the Psychological Test Results of a Severely Retarded Reader Population. Unpublished Doctoral Dissertation, Philadelphia, Temple University, 1966.

Chase, Richard A.; Cullen, John K., Jr.; Farge, Nancy, and Baker, Peggy: The development of auditory feedback monitoring: I. Delayed auditory feedback studies on infant cry. *Journal of Speech and Hearing Research, II:*85-93, 1968.

Chase, Richard A., Mobley, Richard L., and Yeni-Komshian, Grace.: The development of auditory feedback monitoring: Delayed auditory studies on the speech of children between two and three years of age. *Journal of Speech and Hearing Research, II:*307-315, 1968.

Clark, D., and Hutchinson, Barbara. Auditory and visual discrimination skills of normal and articulation-defective children. *Perceptual Motor Skills, 26:*259-265, 1968.

Flack, Velma: Auditory processing for the child with language disorders. *Exceptional Children, 39:*413-416, February, 1973.

Gardner, Riley W.: "Teaching the Hyperactive and Brain Injured Child." In Cruckshank, William M. (Ed.): *The Teacher of Brain-Injured Children: A Discussion of the Basis for Competence.* New York, Syracuse U. Press, pp. 139-146.

Gottesman, Ruth L.: Auditory discrimination ability in Negro dialect-speaking children. *Journal of Learning Disabilities,* 5:38-45, February, 1972.

Johnson, G. L.: Certain Psychological Characteristics of Retarded Readers and Achieving Readers. Dept. of Psychology, Teachers College, Philadelphia Temple University, 1956.

Meier, John H.: Prevalence and characteristics of learning disabilities found in second grade children. *Journal of Learning Disabilities,* 4:8-19, January, 1971.

Morgan, C., and Stella, E.: *Physiological Psychology,* 2nd ed. New York, McGraw-Hill, 1950.

Oakland, Thomas and Williams, Fern C.: Auditory perception: Diagnosis and development for language and reading abilities. Special Publications, Seattle, 1971.

Rabinovitch, M. Sam, and Trehub, Sandra E.: Auditory-linguistic sensitivity in early infancy. *Development Psychology,* 6:74-77, 1972.

Stainback, Susan B., and William C., and Hallahan, Daniel: Effect of Background Music on Learning, *Exceptional Children,* 39:109-110, October, 1973.

Stauffer, Russell C.: Certain psychological manifestations of retarded readers. *Journal of Educational Research,* XLI:410-417, February, 1948.

Tobin, H., and Lasky, E. M.: Linguistic and nonlinguistic competing message effects. *Journal of Learning Disabilities,* 6:46-53, April, 1973.

Development of Factual Recall Information Available for Ready Recall

The author, during the late sixties, proposed that as most brain-injured youngsters had learning disabilities and if similar patterns or measures of memory-span and associative-learning tasks could be shown to be statistically similar to non-brain-injured subjects where previous efforts had placed in study and research, then it would be worthwhile to attempt remedial procedures, i.e. word-learning, requiring associative-learning and memory-span abilities, such as the Fernald technique or its modification used at the Reading Clinic at Temple University.

Blumberg (1968), when investigating the associative-learning and memory-span abilities of brain-injured youngsters with normal intellectual potential, concluded:

Figure 2-2

Based on the results of the associative-learning test findings, the brain-injured population showed statistically significant differences in their ability to associate materials when a change was made in both type of modality utilized and type of material being associated. The following differences were predicted and found significant by the application of the "F" test:

* They had least difficulty when making associations between visual non-wordlike materials and spoken words.
* They had less difficulty making associations with visual materials involving wordlike forms and spoken words than with visual-visual materials involving wordlike forms.
* They had the greatest difficulty making meaningful associations between visual-visual materials involving wordlike forms.
* They had a significant degree of difficulty making meaningful

associations between visual-visual materials of a nonverbal nature.

It was apparent that the brain-injured population functioned similarly to the associative-learning population or remedial readers as discussed and cited in the literature. It was also apparent that the significant differences in the brain-injured population's ability to make associations of different types should be considered in any initial diagnostic testing.

It would seem that the non-brain-injured youngsters functioned similarly on measures of memory span and associative learning, as investigators of remedial readers cited in the literature, when these variables are considered. Although some were not significant statistically, all predictions about the better ability of the fifty nonorganic associative-learning-problem subjects on specific measures were confirmed.

When considering the differences between the brain-injured and non-brain-injured youngsters in tests of memory span and associative learning, the following characteristics were noted about the two populations:

There was no difference between the groups when their associative-learning test results were considered. The two groups functioned in a similar manner at the 1 percent level in all cases except on the measure of visual-visual wordlike material as compared with visual-auditory wordlike material.

When the memory-span results were inspected, there was only one statistically significant difference between the two groups. This was in their ability to handle a test of verbal opposites as compared with their mental age. On this measure, there was a statistically significant difference between the groups at the 1 percent level.

When the results for the two groups of subjects were considered collectively, and the memory-span test results were inspected, statistically significant similarities between the two groups' functioning were noted in their ability to handle visual tasks versus auditory tasks and their higher intellectual functioning as compared to their ability to handle a task of oral directions. The similarity between their functioning on tasks of recall of digits auditorially presented approached significance. On this measure, both groups functioned similarly, i.e. better on tasks of forward recall than reverse recall.

It was apparent that these two groups performed similarly on measures of memory span and associative learning. There is a statistically significant difference between their ability to handle memory-span items involving verbal opposites and oral directions.

Thus, it could be inferred that remedial procedures found effective in developing the associative learning and memory-span abilities requisite for learning, currently used with nondifferentiated remedial readers, could be implemented with brain-injured youngsters with word-learning difficulties.

Studies where brain-injury *per se* has not been a factor dealing with associative learning *per se* as it deals with factual information for ready recall have continued on in the late sixties and early seventies.

Estes and Huizinga (1974) explore modality learning with learning disabled children.

> The subjects were administered ten item paired associate learning task using late visual and auditory presentations. The visual presentation produced a greater number of correct responses than did the auditory. A shift from the visual to auditory presentation of the same material produced an initial interference effect which was not exhibited in a shift from auditory to visual presentation. . . .

The authors state that the "educational implications of these findings must await the action of studies utilizing a broader range of visual stimuli and systemically comparing different modes of presentation over different guide levels (both of which are in progress. . . .)"

Tauber (1966-67) studied thirty kindergarten children and found three tests significantly predictive of difficulty in mastering fundamental skills: (a) Knox Cube Test, (b) Verbal Language Development Scale, and (c) Auditory Discrimination Test (dissimilar word-pair items). The last two tests showed a combined multiple correlation of 0.92, and Tauber suggested that these two tests should be studied on a larger school population.

Sterritt and Rudnick (1966) studied the relationship of auditory and visual pattern recognition to reading on fourth-grade boys. Rudnick, Sterritt, and Flax (1967) researched third-grade boys. At the fourth-grade level, the only modality related to reading was the auditory; at the third-grade level, both auditory and visual modalities were found to be related to reading. This suggests, with increasing age, auditory functions in language become increasingly more important in reading.

The ability to associate symbols and experience is a basic requisite for successful academic progress. It has been shown that children with learning disabilities and/or communication disorders have significant difficulty making meaningful associations between visual wordlike materials. Much work has been done regarding the investigation of learning through single or multisensory motor modalities. The program and its specific activities is based on a multisensory approach to the development of associations available for ready recall.

REFERENCES

Blumberg, Harris M.: The associative-learning and memory-span abilities of brain-injured youngsters, *Academic Therapy Quarterly, III*, pp. 262-273, Summer, 1968.

Estes, Robert E., and Huizinga, Raleigh J.: A comparison of visual and auditory presentations of paired-associative learning task with learning disabled children. *Journal of Learning Disabilities, 7*:44-50, January, 1974.

Rudnick, Mark, Sterritt, Graham M., and Flax, Morton: Auditory and visual rhythm perception and reading ability. *Child Development, 38*:581-87, June, 1967; Review of Educational Research, Vol. XXXIX, No. 1.

Sterritt, Graham, and Rudnick, Mark: Auditory and visual rhythm perception in relation to reading ability in fourth grade boys. *Percept Mot Skills, 22*:859-64, June, 1966; Review of Educational Research, Vol. XXXIX, No. 1.

Tauber, Rosalyn: Identification of potential learning disabilities. *Academic Therapy Quarterly, 2*:116-19, 123, Winter, 1966-67; Review of Educational Research, Vol. XXXIX, No. 1.

Concept Development

There have been many articles, studies, and theories related to concept formation. Initially much of the work was done with

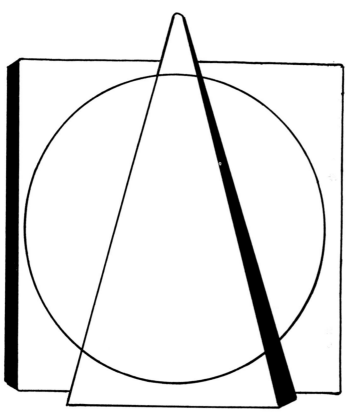

Figure 2-3

animals: cats, dogs, chimpanzees, and monkeys. Most of the research studies dealt with the animals being trained to differentiate one form from other forms. A study requiring generalization to a particular characteristic of objects varying in multiple ways are recognized as studies of concept formation. Ranking the mammals who have been heavily researched one could find from most superior to least superior, the rank as follows: two-year-old children, chimpanzees and monkeys, cats, dogs and rats (Stone, 1951).

Weinstein (1945) is one of the researchers best known for color categorization as an indication of subhuman concept formation. Harlow (1937, 1942, 1943, 1945, 1949, 1950, 1951), Kohler (1925), Maslow (1934), and Yerkes (1934) are some of the prominent names in early research in comparative psychology dealing with concept formation.

Research on concept formation separates itself into several categories. Those selected related to this program are studies on perceptual judgment and discrimination, conceptual style, organization, recall and memory.

Learning theory plays an intricate role when programming concept development.

> Learning theories fall into two major families: stimulus-response theories and cognitive theories, but not all theories belong to these two families. The stimulus-response theories include such diverse members as the theories of Thorndike, Guthrie, Skinner, and Hull. The cognitive theories include at least those of Tolman, the classical gestalt psychologists, and Lewin. Not completely and clearly classifiable in these terms are the theories of functionalism, psychodynamics, and the probabilistic theories of the model builders. (Hilgard, 1956)

Perception, Fine Motor Ability and Concept Development

The visual aspect of perception must be considered even though this program deals with auditory language in its initial

TABLE III

RELATIONSHIP BETWEEN BENDER TEST AND WISC SCORES
KOPPITZ (1965)

WISC	1st & 2nd Grade Chi-square	P	3rd & 4th Grade Chi-square	P	All 4 Grades Chi-square	P
Full Scale IQ	3.0	.10	4.4	.05	7.3	.01
Verbal IQ	5.9	.02	2.1	.10	7.4	.01
Performance IQ	5.3	.02	8.1	.01	11.9	.001
Subtests						
Information	not significant		not significant		not significant	
Comprehension	not significant		not significant		not significant	
Similarities	not significant		not significant		not significant	
Arithmetic	2.6	.10	8.3	.01	10.3	.01
Picture completion	4.9	.05	2.4	.10	6.8	.01
Picture arrangement	7.4	.01	2.4	.10	10.3	.01
Block design	2.6	.10	3.9	.05	7.3	.01
Object assembly	5.3	.02	6.6	.10	12.1	.001
Coding	not significant		2.8	.10	Not significant	

stages. There has been a great deal of work relating visual motor perception to language ability and other functions associated with intelligence in young children.

The above chart shows "that the Bender Test is closely related to general intelligence as measured on the WISC Full Scale IQ for children in the third and fourth grades and somewhat less so to the WISC Full Scale IQ of the first and second grades.

"The Verbal IQ on the WISC revealed a close relationship to the Bender performance of the younger group of subjects. This seems to support Bender's statement that the Bender Test is related to language ability in young children. As children grow older, tests of verbal intelligence demand not only factual information but also logical reasoning and social understanding. None of these bear a clear relationship to the copying of Gestalt figures. It is not surprising, therefore, that the chi-square comparing Verbal IQ and Bender performance of the third and fourth graders was not statistically significant." (Koppitz, 1965)

Basic to the development of concepts is the discrimination and recognition of form—size and color, perceptual skills of which numerous studies have been conducted.

The reader is referred to "The Perception of the Visual Word" for a further detailed treatise on the visual perception of space which they feel is the basic problem of all perceptions (Gibson, 1950).

Piaget and Concept Development

Study of developmental changes regarding general mental ability of which concept formation and development are an intricate part has been conducted throughout the past decades. Piaget (1947) has focused much of his research and study on the developmental changes and differences in perception and reasoning of younger and older children. As this author considers the theories of Piaget closely related to the remediation of language dysfunction, as defined in this book, a brief summary of Piaget's conclusions are presented.

> He reports that the changes are qualitative, that the older child thinks in quite a different way from the younger. The child must

first learn to make perceptual comparisons and to abstract from his sense impressions certain constructs or "schemata." His first schemata are merely the identifications of objects: for instance, the recognition of his mother as the same person no matter how her dress, posture, and other superficial appearances change. He gradually builds one schema upon another, thereby acquiring a repertoire of tools of thought. Once he realized that "an object" exists, he can think of it as continuing to exist even when hidden; this stage is necessary before he can be expected to find a hidden object. He later develops ideas of shape (constant even though the retinal image changes), size, identity, order, etc. For example, the preschool child may be able to compare the size of two blocks, selecting the larger. There is a certain age where he can judge each pair correctly, and yet cannot arrange a whole series in order. He focuses on one pair at a time, and cannot think of the overall order. A schema or idea such as "order" may first appear in a concrete form; i.e. the child can compare two bead chains only when they are laid out side by side. Then he learns to hold the abstract order in mind so that he can compare, for example, a straight chain with one twisted in a "figure eight." When the idea of order is completely abstracted, he can solve logical problems such as "Town A is north of B, and C is south of B; what can you say about A and C?" (Cronback, 1960).

To briefly reiterate, the work of Piaget has dealt with describing and establishing a sequence of the growth of intelligence and the child's organization and construction of the world which surrounds him. Piaget's major thesis is that the basis of intellectual ability, like the reality and world they create, result in an organization somewhat greater than the combination of hereditary and environmental experience. According to Piaget, all mental growth is initiated with the activity of the child; this activity results in ideas and facts irreducible to the combination of heredity and experience from which it was found.

Other Considerations

Odom (1972) determined that a developmental lag exists between the perception and production of facial expressions. He selected thirty-two kindergarten and thirty-two fifth-grade children. Each of the thirty-two kindergarten and thirty-two fifth-grade children participated in one of two types of discrimination task and one of two types of production task. The results indicated that both age groups correctly discriminated more of the eight assessed expressions than they produced. The older children made more correct discriminations and productions than the younger children, but contrary to expectations, the difference between discrimination and production increased with age.

The use of the Wechsler Intelligence Scales are good indicators of concept development. This author feels that spatial ability (Picture Completion, Block Design and Objective Assembly) compared with verbal conceptualization ability (Comprehension, Similarities and Vocabulary) are excellent indices of concept development. Bannatyne (1973) uses these as some of the indicators of highly gifted children with learning problems.

Another pioneer in child development, education and concept formation is Maria Montessori. A great educator, her revolutionary approach to teaching has had a significant influence on modern teaching. It is this author's opinion that the classical approach has great implications for the programming of learning disabled children. However, much of her work, although sensorial, is heavily weighted with visual, kinesthetic and tactile stimuli; the auditory area is treated lightly. Her basic principles of concept formation can be readily adjusted and included in any well planned program dealing with concept development. For a more detailed description of her philosophy, life and work, the reader is referred to Standing (1957).

To completely survey the literature on learning theory and concept formation would require many volumes. It is felt that the studies and authors cited are sufficient to warrant acceptance of the sequence of activities presented in the program in Chapter 3, phase or stage three, Concept Development.

REFERENCES

Bannatyne, Alex (ed.): Programs, materials and techniques. *Journal of Learning Disability, 6,* No. 6:12, June/July, 1973.

Biber, Barbara, *et al.: Problem-Solving Situations. Life and Ways of the Seven-Year-Old.* New York, Basic Books, 1932.

Cronbach, Lee J.: *Essentials of Psychological Testing,* 2d ed. New York, Harper & Row, 1960, p. 245.

Standing, E. M.: *Maria Montessori, Her Life and Work.* New York, Manter Book of Arrangement with Academy Guild Press, 1957.

Harlow, H. F.: Experimental analysis of the role of the original stimulus in conditioned responses in monkeys. *Psychol Rec, 1:*62-68, 1937.

Harlow, H. F.: Responses by Rhesus monkeys to stimuli having multiple-sign values. In McNemar, Q. and Merrill, M. A. (Eds.): *Studies in Personalities.* New York, McGraw-Hill, 1942, pp. 105-123.

Harlow, H. F.: Solution by Rhesus monkeys of a problem involving the Weigl Principle using the matching-from-sample method. *J Comp Psychol, 43:*217-227, 1943.

Harlow, H. F.: Studies in discrimination learning by monkeys: III. Factors influencing the facility of solution of discrimination problems by Rhesus monkeys. *J Gen Psychol, 63:*213-277, 1945.

Harlow, H. F.: Studies in discrimination learning in monkeys: V. Initial performance by experimentally naive monkeys on stimulus-object and pattern discriminations. *J Gen Psychol, 63:*3-10, 1945.

Harlow, H. F.: The formation of learning sets. *Psychol Rev, 56:*51-65, 1949.

Harlow, H. F.: Analysis of discrimination learning. *J Exp Psychol, 40:*26-30, 1950.

Harlow, H. F., Meyer, D. R., and Settlage, P. H.: Effect of large cortical lesions on the solution of oddity problems by monkeys. *J Comp Physiol Psychol,* 1951, p. 44.

Hilgard, Ernest R.: *Theories of Learning.* New York, Appleton-Century-Crofts, Inc., 1956, p. 8.

Kohler, W.: *The Mentality of Apes.* New York, Harcourt, Brace, 1925.

Koppitz, Elizabeth M.: *The Bender Gestalt Test for Young Children.* New York, Grune & Stratton, 1965, p. 48.

Maslow, A. H., and Groshung, E. P.: Influence of differential motivation on delayed reactions in monkeys. *J Comp Psychol, 18:*75-83, 1934.

Odom, Richard D., and Lemond, Carolyn M.: Developmental differences in the perception and production of facial expressions. *Child Dev, 43:*359-369, 1972.

Piaget, Jean: *The Psychology of Intelligence.* London, Kegan Pau, 1947.

Stone, Calvin P.: *Comparative Psychology,* 3d ed. Englewood Cliffs, New York, Prentice-Hall, 1951.

Wachs, F. F. *et al.: Merrill-Palmer Quarterly, 17:*283-317, 1971.

Weinstein, B.: Evolution of intelligence behavior in Rhesus monkeys. *Genet Psychol Monogr, 31:*3-48, 1945.

Wener, Leo C.: Activity Level and Motor Inhibition: Their Relationship to Intelligence Test Performance in Normal Children. *Child Dev, 42:*967-971, 1971.

Yerkes, R. M.: Modes of behavorial adaption in chimpanzee to multiple-choice problems. *Comp Psychol Monogr, 10:*108, 1934.

The Development of Accurate Verbal Discourse or Syntax

In reviewing and discussing the literature related to stages or phases one and two of this program, it had been observed that various authors investigating brain-injured and nonspecific reading disability populations on measures of memory span and associative learning also noted a significant difference on their ability to handle measures of oral language development such as the Verbal Opposites Tests from the Detroit Test of Learning Aptitude.

Meir (1971) in his investigation of the incidence and charac-

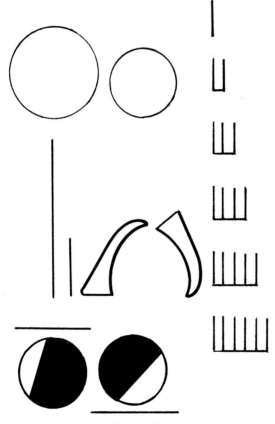

Figure 2-4

teristics of second-grade children with learning disability in eight Rocky Mountain States observed that the "ILD group performed considerably less well than controls on the Peabody Picture Vocabulary Test (Dunn, 1965) . . . far less well on all parts of the Picture Story Language Test (Mykelbust, 1965). . . . These specific language deficits were further corroborated and more clearly delineated by a new Test of Concept Utilization (Crager and Spriggs, 1970)."

Bannatyne (1971) reported that dyslexic readers received intermediate scores in the conceptual category requiring abilities more closely related to language functioning. Rugel (1974) reported that disabled readers achieved significantly lower than normal readers on the Vocabulary Sub-Test in four populates. He basically agreed with the same profile of abilities that Bannatyne found for genetic dyslexics.

Recently the language sample of children has been used both diagnostically and for remediation. Tyack (1973) showed how samples of a child's language can be used as part of a diagnostic evaluation, as a basis for remediation, and as a measure of his progress.

The Illinois Test of Psycholinguistic Abilities has been heavily researched as a diagnostic instrument as well as a basis for developing programs of academic and language remediation (Kirk and Kirk, 1971), (Kirk, McCarthy and Kirk, 1968), (Sievers, 1963), (McCarthy, 1963), (Olson, 1963), (Bateman, 1963), (Kass, 1963).

Investigations have considered other aspects of child development with regard to language which have been incorporated in this program. Ausubel (1968) in his author's summary states Piaget and his followers seriously denigrate the role of language in symbolic thought by denying that it plays a process (operative) role in the transformational and combinatorial aspects of thinking. It is shown that both the representational function of words in designating ideas and the refining function of verbalizing emergent products of thought are crucial operative aspects of thinking. The very emergence of complex logical operations ("interiorized actions," according to Piaget) would also be inconceivable in the absence of language. Thus preoperational (prelinguistic) thought is qualitatively discontinuous with operational (linguistic) thought.

Factors Affecting Language Development

Elardo (1971) in his abstract notes states the following: This study assessed the effectiveness of five hours of distributed training on three-year-old children's comprehension and production of the possessive, negative, passive and negative-passive syntactic structures. Ss in the experimental group made significant gains on tests of grammatical ability.

Snow (1972) states in his author's summary that the assumption that language acquisition is relatively independent of the amount and kind of language input must be assessed in light of information about the speech actually heard by young children. The speech of middle-class mothers to two-year-old children was found to be simpler and more redundant than their speech to ten-year-old children. The mothers modified their speech less when talking to children whose responses they could not observe, indicating that the children played some role in eliciting the speech modifications. Task difficulty did not contribute to the mothers' production of simplified, redundant speech. Experienced mothers were only slightly better than non-mothers in predicting the speech-style modifications required by young children. These findings indicate that children who are learning language have available a sample of speech which is simpler, more redundant, and less confusing than normal adult speech.

The Harris and Hassemer (1972) study indicates that the educational environment (model) has a greater effect on the complexity of children's sentences than actual language spoken. In their authors' summary they state the effects of the complexity of the sentences spoken by a model upon the length and complexity of sentences spoken by monolingual children hearing English sentences, bilingual children hearing Spanish, and bilingual children hearing English, were assessed. Second-and fourth-grade boys and girls served as Ss. A clear modeling effect was found, as well as an effect of grade level on sentence length. No significant effects of sex or language were found. The results suggest that modeling can indeed affect the complexity of children's sentences even in the absence of reinforcements or instructions to imitate.

In a small sample clinical study the application of morphology rules was investigated (Wiig, *et al.*, 1973).

The authors' summary states when the use of morphology was compared in high-risk and learning disabled children and normal controls of the same age, sex, intelligence, and socioeconomic background, the following emerged:

(1) Patterns of educationally significant discrepancies were noted in both high-risk and learning disabled children.

(2) High-risk and learning disabled children gave significantly fewer correct responses than their controls, indicating morphological deficits.

(3) Both high-risk and learning disabled children exhibited varying rather than overall delays in the acquisition of specific morphological rules.

(4) High-risk and learning disabled children shared the greatest relative reductions in the mean percentages of correct responses for third person singular of verbs, possessives, and adjectival inflections.

(5) The high-risk and learning disabled children showed less predictable patterns of difficulty than their controls and evidence of lack of transfer of phonological conditioning rules across morphological categories.

(6) A quantitative method for characterization of the morphological deficits was used which may serve as the basis for the development of appropriate strategies for prevention and remediation.

Bartel and Axelrod (1973) explained the relationship between the reading ability of the Negro inner city student and the degree and manner in which they used nonstandard English. They concluded in part, with the design limitations mentioned above, the present study adds weight to the view that the interference of non-standard Negro English is a factor related to the reading failure experienced by black, inner city, lower socioeconomic students. It would seem that further experimentation with beginning readers in nonstandard English, as well as systematic familiarization of nonstandard speaking children with standard English, is to be encouraged.

Rentel and Kennedy (1972) examined the effectiveness of pattern drill relative to (a) the reduction or phonological and grammatical variations from the standard South Midland dialect, and (b) the promotion of reading ability. The sample consisted of 120 rural Appalachian first-grade students enrolled in six intact classes. For a six-week period, three randomly assigned classes received pattern instruction, designed to modify subjects' rural Appalachian dialect. The remaining three classes served as controls. Post-test data consisted of frequency of phonological and grammatical variations from standard provided by a panel of judges and it was scored on the Word Reading subtest of the Stanford Achievement Test. Post-test data were analyzed initially by a 2 × 3 × 3 mixed model analysis of variance. Results indicated that subjects receiving pattern practice were better able to approximate the grammatical patterns of the standard Southern Midland dialect; however, significant changes in phonology and reading were not observed.

In this section the author has attempted to survey the literature regarding language development diagnostically, as well as from a factor-related perspective. The various activities outlined in Chapter 3 have their basis in research as well as pragmatic diagnostic evaluation of the effectiveness of various pedagogical approaches.

REFERENCES

Ausubel, David P.: Symbolization and symbolic thought: Response to Furth. *Child Dev*, 39:4, 1968.

Bannatyne, A.: *Language Reading and Learning Disabilities*. Springfield, Thomas, 1971.

Bateman, B.: Selected studies on the Illinois Test of Psycholinguistic Abilities. Urbana, University of Illinois Press, 1968.

Bartel, Netie R., and Axelrod, Judith: Nonstandard English usage and reading ability in black junior high students. *Except Child*, 39:653-655, May, 1973.

Elardo, Richard: The experimental facilitation of children's comprehension and production of four syntactic structures. *Child Dev*, 42:130, 1971.

Harris, Mary B., and Hassemer, Wendy G.: Some factors affecting the complexity of children's sentences: The effects of modeling, sex and bilingualism. *J Exp Child Psychol*, 155, 1972.

Kass, Carrine: Conference on Learning Disabilities. Lawrence, Kansas, Nov., 1966.

Kirk, S. A., and Kirk, W.: *Psycholinguistic Learning Disabilities: Diagnosis and Remediation*. Urbana, University of Illinois Press, 1971.

Kirk, S. A., McCarthy, J. J., and Kirk, W.: *The Illinois Test of Psycholinguistic Abilities*. Revised edition: Examiner's manual. Urbana, University of Illinois Press, 1968.

McCarthy, J. J.: Selected studies on the Illinois Test of Psycholinguistic Abilities. Urbana, University of Illinois Press, 1968.

Rentel, Victor M., and Kennedy, John J.: Effects of pattern drill on the phonology, syntax, and reading achievement of rural Appalachian children. *American Educational Research Journal*, IX:IV, Winter, 1972.

Rugel, R.: WISC subtest scores of disabled readers. A review with respect to Bannatyne's recategorization. *Journal of Learning Disabilities*, 7:60-65, January, 1974.

Sievers, Dorothy J. et al.: *Selected Studies on the Illinois Test of Psycholinguistic Abilities*. Urbana, University of Illinois Press, 1963.

Snow, Catherine E.: Mothers' speech to children learning language. *Child Dev*, 43:23, 1972.

Tyack, D.: The use of language samples in a clinical setting. *Journal of Learning Disabilities*, 6: April, 1973.

Wiig, Elisabeth H. et al.: The use of English morphology by high-risk and learning disabled children. *Journal of Learning Disability*, 6, No. 7:59-66, August/September, 1973.

Development of Imagination

Imagination is vital to a creative constructive learning process. In previous sections some of the research presented pertains to the perceptual basis of concept development and formation. Concepts must be developed before a child can apply his innate creativity.

Play is one of the more vital arenas for the development of imagination. The value of play as an activity was reaffirmed by Olson (1959). "Play creates many practical situations in which

Figure 2-5

the child discovers and observes, and reasons and solves problems."

Hartley, Frank and Goldenson (1952), who wrote the most complete analysis of children's play and its potentialities both for understanding young children and encouraging their development, emphasized the importance of:

> . . . creative activities and play opportunities within preschool and early school settings. . . . What is perhaps not so frequently em-

phasized is the great plasticity of the young during these years, their instant response to environmental impacts, their relative freedom from compartmentalization, and their consequent readiness to benefit from favorable experiences and to assimilate these into their growing concept of self.

They distinguished eight functions which dramatic play serves in ages three to five and one-half years:

1. To imitate adults.
2. To play out real life roles in an intense way.
3. To reflect relationships and experiences.
4. To express pressing needs.
5. To release unacceptable impulses.
6. To reverse roles usually taken.
7. To mirror growth.
8. To work out problems and experiment with solutions.

The importance of play to the child's cognitive development was emphasized by Lewis (1963):

> The importance of imaginative play in a child's cognitive development is that it readily expands into exploratory and constructive play which, as it presents him with successive problems, demands the exercise of reasoning. . . . For instance, in playing with water, he explores its physical properties and is confronted with problems which he may try to solve.
>
> In the growth of this exploratory and experimental play, language may play a part of ever-increasing importance. . . . He verbalizes his own acts, and so aids his perception, helps his recall of relevant past experience, helps his imaginative constructions, his anticipations and predictions and so fosters his conceptual and generalized thinking in the direction of reasoning. . . . The effects of language are immeasurably reinforced as the child comes to play with others— particularly if adults take interest in what he is doing. Language then helps to make play more imaginative, more constructive and a greater stimulus to reasoning.

Research on Creativity

In the Review of Educational Research (1969), an excellent summary of research done in the 1960's is presented. The following material was selected from that volume.

In a graphic description, "Creativity—A Blind Man's Report on the Elephant," Yamamoto (1965) reported the confusion among creativity researchers. He demonstrated that philosophical differences among research workers were responsible for failure to agree about creativity. Studies in the past three years have continued to reflect (a) different points of departure in the definition of creativity, (b) different assumptions and presuppositions about creativity and (c) different research strategies among researchers with different orientations. In addition, the criterion problem has influenced creativity research throughout the mid-1960's (White and Williams, 1965).

Researchers continued to investigate whether creativity is independent of the general intelligence factor. Clark, Veldman, and Thorpe (1965) reported a creativity-intelligence dichotomy consistent with the earlier work of Getzels and Jackson (1962), although Marsh (1964) had contradicted the Getzels-Jackson position with his analysis and had concluded that the conventional IQ remained the best single criterion for creative potential. The confusion remained as Cicirelli (1965) added that creativity did not interact with IQ to boost achievement, while the research by Schmadel, Merrifield, and Bonsall (1965) suggested that children of high IQ may be both gifted and creative.

The research of Wallach and Kogan (1965) highlighted the period as they differentiated modes of thinking in children and introduced a single dimension or characteristic of intelligence which could be considered a facet of creativity. These investigators defined individual difference in the ability to produce many unique cognitive associates as this characteristic. Ten measures of this ability proved to be highly intercorrelated while correlations between these measures and intelligence tests proved to be very low. Subsequently, the new dimension—ability to generate unique and plentiful associates—was used by Wallach and Kogan to investigate group differences in personality, self-concept, fantasy, and conceptual abilities among young children.

Wallach and Kogan specified the term creativity by defining it as the ability to generate unique and plentiful associates. However, this single ability may prove more popular with researchers than with educators. The multifactor creativity test battery developed by Torrance (1966) has been widely used for research and holds promise for changing classroom instruction on behalf of the creatively gifted.

The development of imagination is directly related to perception, cognitive ability, concept formation and creativity. Research has noted that play is one of the more vital arenas for the development of imagination. Although intelligence plays an important part in itself, it is not the only variable identified when defining creativity. It was shown that the ability to generate unique and plentiful associates is one of the basic requisites to creativity. The development of association has been considered in previous discussions relating to Section 1 and 2 of the program.

The development of imagination is one of the most interesting and challenging aspects of the instructional situation. Hopefully, the total scope and sequence presented in this book will reinforce its development.

REFERENCES

Cicirelli, Victor G.: Form of the relationship between creativity, IQ, and academic achievement. *J Educ Psychol*, 56:303-308, December, 1965.

Clark, Charles M., Veldman, Donald J., and Thorpe, Joseph S.: Convergent and divergent thinking abilities of talented adolescents. *J Educ Psychol*, 56:157-163, June, 1965.

Hartley, Ruth E., Frank, Lawrence K., and Goldenson, Robert M.: *Understanding Children's Play*. New York, Columbia University Press, 1952.

Frierson, Edward C.: The gifted. *Review of Educational Research, XXXIX:* 25-37, February, 1969.

Getzels, Jacob W., and Jackson, Phillip W.: *Creativity and Intelligence*. New York, John Wiley, 1962.

Gowan, John C.: *Annotated Bibliography on Creativity and Giftedness*. San Fernando Valley State College Foundation, 1965.

Joncich, Geraldine: A culture-bound concept of creativity. *Educational Theory:* 133-143, July, 1964.

Kneller, George F.: *The Art and Science of Creativity*. New York, Holt, Rinehart and Winston, 1966.

Lewis, M. M.: *Language, Thought and Personality*. New York, Basic Books, 1963, p. 126.

Marsh, R. W.: A statistical re-analysis of Getzel's and Jackson's data. *Br J Educ Psychol*, 55:91-93, February, 1964.

Mooney, Ross L., and Razik, Taher, A.: *Explorations in Creativity*. New York, Harper and Row, 1967.

Olson, Willard C.: *Child Development*, 2d ed. Boston, D. C. Heath, 1959, p. 49.

Schmadel, Elnora, Merrifield, Philip R., and Bonsall, Marcella R.: A comparison of performances of gifted and nongifted children on selected measures of creativity. *California Journal of Educational Research*, May, 1965.

Wallach, Michael A., and Kogan, Nathan: Cognitive originality, physiognomic sensitivity, and defensiveness in children. U. S. Department of Health, Education and Welfare, Office of Education, Cooperative Research Project No. 1316B, Durham, Duke University, 1965.

White, William F., and Williams, Robert E.: Identification of creativity and the criterion problem. *Journal of Secondary Education*, October, 1965.

Widmer, Emmy Louise: *The Critical Years: Early Childhood Education at the Crossroads*. Scranton, International Textbook, 1970.

Yamamoto, Kaoru: Creative thinking abilities and peer conformity in fifth-grade children. U. S. Dept. of Health, Education and Welfare, Office of Education, Cooperative Research Project No. 2021, Kent, Kent State University, 1965.

Yamamoto, Kaoru: Validation of tests of creative thinking: A review of some studies. *Except Child*, 31:281-290, February, 1965.

Development of Thinking and Comprehension Skills

The author's isolation of thinking and comprehension from the other phases is artificial. It can be pragmatically agreed that the area of thinking and comprehension is innate in all stages vital to adequate language development.

As stated in the introduction to the program in Chapter 3, the "present program is spiral in its development and cyclic in its reinforcement." All of the research cited in discussion of the previous phases or stages is relevant to the area of comprehension. The research related to phases 3 and 7, Concept Development and the Development of the Ability to Handle Visual Symbolic Language Related Material is particularly germane to this phase. This writer, however, has placed this phase in its present temporal position in the outlined sequence because of his theory of the reading process. This writer has pragmatic evidence from a teacher observation day-to-day data collection that if emphasis

Figure 2-6

is placed on understanding, drawing conclusions, selecting the main idea, separating relevant from irrelevant, recalling important factual detail, making inferences, following and recalling sequence of events and other vital comprehension skills on a listening or auditory-language level initially, then given instructional attention to the development of accurately decoding visual symbols, the development of the total reading process can be accomplished much more quickly, soundly and efficiently. Thus, this section was placed both theoretically and practically before the phase pertaining to visual symbols and after the phases dealing with Concept Development and the Development of Accurate Verbal Discourse or Syntax.

There have been programs, conferences and research studies that have focused specifically on thinking and comprehension. Several have been selected as examples for inclusion in this section to illustrate the need to be aware of the importance of this phase in all academic areas. Kress (1960) notes:

> The comprehension bases of thought and communication then could be said to lie in the richness of the life experience of the individual, in his ability to differentiate and categorize this experience to form concepts, and in his skill at using commonly understood symbols for the purpose of manipulating these concepts. Agreement among men about the realm and content of their concepts will enhance their ability to communicate more precisely with each other and understand, even when they do not agree.
>
> The major role of the educator seems to lie in his acceptance of the responsibility for bringing each individual who comes under his charge to the full realization of his potential for being able to communicate with his world. That world is made up of more than those who live about him. It encompasses all of those who ever lived and recorded a message for man of any age to interpret and understand. Experience—concepts—language: this is the eternal triangle that differentiates man from all other forms of life.

Rosenthal (1973) when discussing recent advances in the neurophysiology of some specific cognitive functions states:

> For some time now, cumulative neuropsychological evidence has indicated that, indeed, the left and right sides of the brain may well be differently specialized in function. Generally speaking, on the basis of information predominately from right-handed persons, it appears that the left hemisphere of the brain has to do with verbal language, and analytic capacities, while the functions of the right hemisphere related more to spatial, relational, synthetic, holistic, Gestalt-type abilities.

However, his article focuses on the development of associations between visual symbolic arithmetic and reading material as compared to the thinking of comprehension skill that is vital in these two academic areas.

Achievement tests of general and critical thinking convey important aspects of reading (Trela, 1967). Trela's work centered about an effort to discriminate the singularity of any of several reading tests in measuring critical reading-thinking. The important question of the study was: Are reading tests that profess to evaluate thinking or problem-solving in verbal form able to measure factors apart from those demanded by general reading ability? Or, said another way, are these selected tests purporting to assess critical reading measuring traits or variables distinctly different from those measured by tests of general ability? A comparison of achievement on tests of general ability with achievement on tests of critical reading ability was used as a basis of ascertaining the uniqueness of certain of the measures in evaluating critical reading.

Several analyses were made of how the high, middle and low achievers in general reading comprehension (Stanford test) differentiated upon measures of critical reading. Approximately two-thirds of the high achievers and two-thirds of the low achievers in general reading ability also achieved correspondingly on the three critical reading measures used in the study. There was a slightly greater tendency for the low achievers to maintain the same relative position on all these tests than there was among the high achievers. Between 88 and 94 percent of the thirty-three most average achievers on the Stanford test also scored within one standard deviation from the means on the ITED, STEP, and Watson-Glaser tests.

Moffitt (1968) labels the consideration of such general properties of thinking (such as recalling, comprehending, relating facts, making inferences, drawing conclusions, interpreting, and predicting outcomes) as being specifically factors of "reading," a "major misconception." He states, as an illustration of his premise, that "these are all mental operations that go on in the head of a nonliterate aborigine navigating his outrigger according to

cues from weather, sea life, currents, and the positions of heaven-
ly bodies." He claims, in other words, that reading comprehension is simply "comprehension," and believes that the child who
has difficulty in grasping an idea or relating facts of inferring or
drawing conclusions has a general cognitive problem—a thinking
problem, traceable to many possible sources. None of these
sources, in Moffitt's view, directly concerns printed words. He
believes that the solution to such thinking problems lie in many
activities besides reading—conversing, games of logic, dramatic
work, writing, and "simply getting more life experiences." In
brief, Moffitt questions the whole concept of "reading skills"
beyond the level of word recognition, and thus treats comprehension as a separate entity as equally important as handling visual
symbolic language related material, decoding, and recognition,
or any label given the ability to demonstrate that the association
of experience with printed symbols has taken place. Moffitt's
theory supports this writer's theoretical and pragmatic bias.

Anderson (1972) feels that vital to the area of comprehension
is an analysis of the processes involved in transferring ideas from
the printed page to abstract ideas. The analysis must be broad
enough to include learning from oral discourse. The workable
basis of this analysis must include the processes involved in
learning from written discourse. Parts of the text are first encoded
in terms of observable perceptual characteristics. As the relevant perceptual features of the test are orthographic, he labels
this phase "orthographic encoding." He defines the next state as
"phonological encoding" as it involves acoustic features such as
series of words rendered into implicit or explicit speech. The
last stage he labels "semantic encoding" because the individual
may bring to a level of awareness meaningful representation
based on the words he sees or hears himself subvocalizing.

He notes briefly that the ability to coordinate the surface information embodied in the orthographic and phonological codes
according to linguistic rules in order to arrive at a correct semantic encoding is vital to the total process. He states "it is not
necessary to know the precise form and the mental organization
of meanings in order to recognize the occurrence and nonoccur-

rence of comprehension. The trick will be to devise techniques for constructing questions that can be answered if a person has semantically encoded a communication but not answered if it has been encoded only perceptually or phonologically."

In summarizing this section, it can be stated that comprehension is defined as "the ability to extract meaning from a written selection especially the meaning and implication of the whole paragraph" (Money, 1967). This definition can be expanded to include verbal discourse and the ability to glean meaning from spoken language and the implication of an individual's statements.

The various authors included in this section have dealt with comprehension as it relates to both visual and auditory symbols. In Chapter 3 the program suggestions are auditory in nature, in the beginning, readiness or primary levels, but include visual symbols as the child develops a basic sight vocabulary.

If listening precedes speaking, reading and writing in the currently acceptable progression of the development of the communication processes, then placement of this phase where it is temporally in the program it is both theoretically and practically sound.

REFERENCES

Anderson, R.: How to construct achievement tests to assess comprehension. *Review of Educational Research, 42:*145-170, Spring, 1972.

Kress, R. A.: *That All May Learn to Read.* Syracuse, School of Education, Syracuse University, 1960, p. 39.

Moffitt, A.: *A Student-Centered Language Arts Curriculum.* Boston, Houghton, Mifflin, 1968.

Money, John: *The Disabled Reader. Education of the Dyslexic Child.* Baltimore, Johns Hopkins Press, 1967, p. 377.

Rappaport, D.: *Diagnostic Psychological Testing,* vol. I. Chicago, Yearbook Publishers, 1946.

Rosenthal, Joseph H.: Recent advances in the neurophysiology of some specific cognitive functions. *Academic Therapy, VIII:* Summer, 1973, p. 424.

Reusch, Jurgen, and Kees, Weldon: *Nonverbal Communication.* Berkeley, University of California Press, 1956.

Trela, Thaddeus M.: Comparing achievement on tests of general and critical reading. *Journal of the Reading Specialist, 6:*140-141, May, 1967.

Vinacke, W. E.: *The Psychology of Thinking.* New York, McGraw-Hill, 1952.

Developing the Ability to Handle Visual Symbolic Language Related Material

The Reading Process

A story is told of a man who received a letter in a foreign language that he spoke fluently but could not read. He had a friend

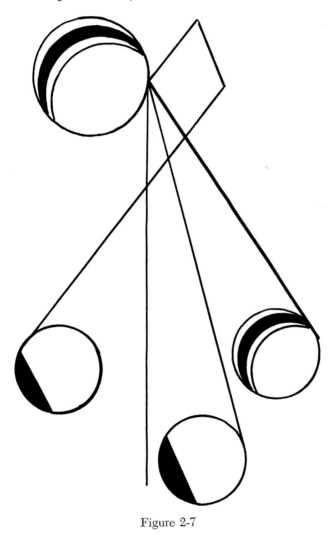

Figure 2-7

who could make the sounds indicated by the writing, but who understood not a word. (This, incidentally, is not strange to those who learned the ritual use of a second language.) The man who received the letter took it to his friend who said the words that gave joy to the recipient of the message. Which one was reading? (Frost, 1967).

The communication process is the ability to share ideas meaningfully. In many instances, reading constitutes the indispensable avenue of communication. Four stages in the communication process are listening, speaking, reading, and writing. The third step, reading, has been defined as the handling of visual symbolic material by reconstructing the facts behind the symbols. Tinker and Bond (1957) put it this way:

> Reading involves the recognition of printed or written symbols which serve as stimuli for the recall of meanings built up through the reader's past experience. New meanings are derived through manipulation of concepts already in his possession. The organization of these meanings is governed by the clearly defined purposes of the reader. In short, the reading process involves both the acquisition of the meanings intended by the writer and the reader's own contributions in the form of interpretation, evaluation, and reflection about these meanings.

William S. Gray (1960) presents four components of the reading process: "word perception, comprehension of the words represented by the ideas, reaction to these ideas, and assimilation or integration of the ideas with previous knowledge or experience."

George Spache (1969) presents five major concepts of the reading process: "reading as skill development, reading as a visual act, reading as a type of perception, reading as a reflection of cultural background, reading as an act involving the higher mental processes."

It is in regard to the last concept that the following statement is made:

> Reading is often likened to a communication process, a direct interpretation of the printed symbol into the reader's thought processes. In this sense, the act of reading is not a word recognition act

or a translation of words into complete thoughts, but a fluent almost instantaneous combining of words into complete thoughts.

This appears to emphasize the most basic function of reading which is the recognition of the ideas behind the printed symbols. Communication deals with ideas. For an author to truly communicate his ideas, they need to be understood by the reader of his book. A child could be taught to repeat sentences from some meaningful piece of prose and to decode additional sentences, but unless there is understanding and meaning involved, to me, there is no true communication.

Russell Stauffer (1969) reinforces this concept of reading. ". . . reading is a mental process requiring accurate word recognition, ability to call to mind particular meanings, and ability to shift or reassociate meanings until the constructs or concepts presented are clearly grasped, critically evaluated, accepted and applied, or rejected." The man quoted at the beginning of this paper had "accurate word recognition" but none of the other concepts listed by Stauffer. The man who heard the contents of the letter was able to "call to mind particular meanings," and to apparently fulfill the remaining requirements of Stauffer's definition except for the first. It might appear that neither man was truly reading.

Stauffer traces the appearance of his concept of reading in definitions of the reading process over the past 140 years. Reading was at first considered a synthesis of the letters into the spoken word standing for the idea, and it still is by some people today!

In 1938 Horace Mann spoke out against this method: "The result is that more than eleven-twelfths of all children in the reading classes in our schools do not understand the meaning of the words they read; that they do not master the sense of the reading lessons, and that the ideas and feelings intended by the author to be conveyed to, and excited in, the reader's mind, still rest in the author's intention, never having yet reached the place of their destination." (Stauffer, 1969)

In 1913 Edmund Burke Huey also condemned the purely decoding view of reading by stating: ". . . until the insidious thought of reading as word pronouncing is well worked out of our heads, it is well to place the emphasis strongly where it really belongs, on reading as *thought-getting*, independently of expression." (Stauffer, 1969)

In 1937 Ernest V. Horn discussed the symbolic character of language: "The author, moreover, does not really convey ideas to the reader; he merely stimulates him to construct them out of his own experience. If the concept is already in the reader's mind, the task is relatively easy, but if, as is usually the case in school, it is new to the reader, its construction more nearly approaches problem-solving than simple association." (Stauffer, 1969)

Arthur Gates in 1948 shared new insights from research on reading:

> Reading is not a simple mechanical skill; nor is it a narrow scholastic tool. Properly cultivated, it is essentially a thoughtful process. However, to say that reading is a 'thought-getting' process is to give it too restricted a description. It should be developed as a complex organization of patterns of higher mental processes. It can and should embrace all types of thinking, evaluating, judging, imagining, reasoning, and problem-solving. Indeed, it is believed that reading is one of the best media for cultivation of many techniques of thinking and imagining. (Stauffer, 1969)

Semanticists add an interesting insight to the reading process. Emmett A. Betts describes reading as "the reconstruction of the facts behind the symbols," an ideas he attributed to Count Alfred Korzybski. The meaning intended by the author is not always that found by the reader because the experiences of the reader may differ substantially from those of the writer.

Rynin states that the view that language cannot explain things ". . . must not be understood as meaning that there is nothing to learn about the causes and effects of sensible things, about the relations in which they stand. We learn by vision the nature of sounds, et cetera, but we learn by experience the relations in which sights, sounds, feels, et cetera, stand to one another." According to semanticists, reading is a mental process of reconstructing the experiences behind the language. (Stauffer, 1969)

Rynin's statement would indicate that the man who said the words could not be said to be reading. The man who heard the words could reconstruct the experiences behind the language and therefore could read them. But he needed the other fellow to decode the printed symbols to obtain the experiences.

In thinking of methods that would provide a reader with both vital facets of the reading process, A. Sterl Artley in J. L. Frost (Ed.) (1967) states:

> If . . . we should conclude that the reading process is multi-faceted, involving comprehension, reaction, and the translation of perceived ideas into behavior . . . then word perception falls into place as a means to an end—a stimulus to meaning. This is not to say that word perception is unimportant, for it is apparent that meaning cannot be created if the symbols that serve as triggers are inaccurately perceived. Moreover, it is far more than what is involved in phonics, for it includes all of the techniques that one uses to perceive words—analysis of word structure, context, phonics, and the use of the dictionary. But instruction in word perception must be geared into the on-going process of interpretation; it must be a part of it, not divorced from it.

In the introduction to a book on teaching art appreciation to young people there is a cartoon showing two small boys looking at a book. "See, Hanky," says one, "the words are for people who can't read the pictures." (Chase, 1951) To summarize the main point of this section, it may be stated that ideas are for people who can read the words! According to David Russell, reading is thinking. Chomsky (1957) also states that reading is a reconstruction of the facts behind the symbols.

If we accept the above definitions of reading, then a child who is at the decoding or word recognition level of reading is indeed not reading, for he is attaching no meaning to what he is reading.

In truth, the very purpose of this supposes that the child is deriving meaning from language for there can be no communication without meaning.

For many learning disabled the first step in reading—*decoding* or attaching a verbal name to the written symbol—is indeed a stumbling block. Robinson (1969) discusses the fact that this may be due in part to the fact that we present the child with lists of meaningless sight words and then present him with a basal reader which uses an artificial language pattern and expect him to learn to read.

Marion Monroe (1971) states that reading as a process of word calling without understanding or interpretation brings little or no satisfaction. Any ideas the reader gleans from the printed page are often not those the author intended to communicate. Reading becomes a fruitless chore if the child gets nothing of value from it. He becomes bored, resentful, discouraged, or apathetic.

Robinson (1969) further states that if reading instruction is begun with a language experience approach, it is not artificial to the learner because of the use this approach makes of the learner's own vocabulary and sentence structure.

Flavell and Wohlwill (1969) list five major concepts an individual needs in order to achieve an end in learning; in this case, reading:

1. Existence—knowing that what one individual perceives, thinks, or feels in a situation may be apprehended differently by another;
2. Need—knowledge that certain situations require an individual to understand and act on the fact that another's point of view may differ from one's own;
3. Prediction—the process of making guesses with some accuracy about what the pertinent points are in a situation;
4. Maintenance—the ability to establish and maintain one's own and another's point of view in dynamic equilibrium, and
5. Application—knowing how to apply what one knows about another's role attributes in a communication task.

The above seeks to point out that reading is an active process in which one is aware of another's viewpoint in relation to one's own and is seeking to equilibrate the two in order to derive meaning from what is being read.

Important Considerations

Weintraub (1967) says that there is a distinct relationship between reading and the first of the communication processes, listening. Sonenberg and Glass (1965) have concluded that the sounds which a subject has the most difficulty articulating accurately give the same subject difficulty in sound discrimination, a factor which is essential to a phonics program in reading.

That all of the communications skills, listening, speaking, reading, and writing, are interrelated and that the organization of such material so as to be relevant to children was pointed out by Levin and Rohwer (1968). They concluded that provision of an organizational pattern in which there is continuity of thought facilitates learning. If this organization is centered around the child's own experiences, it is much more meaningful to him and he learns more as a result. (Denley, 1969)

Anastasiow (1971), in referring to the relationship of oral behavior and reading behavior, states that the child must first develop a decoding system that is consistent with the code. That is, he must *learn* the relationship of the spoken word to the written symbol. Secondly, the child's previous ability to comprehend and decode speech auditorily is critical to decoding print. He further states that oral language is an insufficient and inaccurate predictor for many children in their capacity to learn to read. His feeling on this topic is that the important factor in learning how to read print is letter-sound relationships that transfer from word to word. The elements of the structure that he discovers are related but not completely dependent upon his total language development which may be reflected in his oral production.

One possible fallacy in our thinking about poverty children is that they possess poor language skills because they speak a variant of standard English. Anastasiow feels that when the speech of these children is measured by the maintenance of sentence meaning, the number of so-called language errors drops considerably. Given training in auditory skills to decode spoken language and to understand what is required of them, these children can and do learn how to read standard English.

Stewart (1969), in discussing the relationship of the Negro dialect and the ability to read, recommends the development of beginning reading materials that are written in Negro nonstandard English and then the use of systematically organized materials to lead the student to eventual reading of materials written in standard English. Stewart feels that at present the Negro youngster meets great interference between his own oral language patterns and the language of reading textbooks. Until the day that such material is developed and available, perhaps this is another argument in favor of the language experience approach to reading. In an interesting aside, Shuy (1969) has indicated that reading errors produced by nonstandard speakers show that the greater the difference between the standard and nonstandard features, the more likely it is that a child will learn to read the standard English version accurately. Conversely, the less basic the difference between the standard and nonstandard, the more likely it would be for the child to make transformations and read the standard phrase using nonstandard structure.

Monroe (1971), in an explanation of a child beginning to learn the value of printed material, states that sooner or later in the child's early life, he makes an important discovery. He finds that there is another system of language that is closely related to the one he hears and speaks. He discovers visual language, the printed and written symbols for oral language. When he sees another reading and writing and when he listens to stories read to him, he becomes curious about print and wants to learn to read and write by himself. He may not have discovered that print stands for language before coming to school, however, if his home is devoid of books and no one has ever read to him.

She further states that communication by language is a "four-lane bridge" between communicants over which ideas are interchanged; grammar is the road bed of all four; all are verbal skills and use about the same grammatical arrangements of words in sentences, although oral language is more abbreviated and informal than written language. When one shifts from one method of communication to another, the only things that change are the neurophysiological mechanisms. The sensory and motor pathways used by an individual depend upon his purpose and mode of communication.

The ability to handle visual symbolic language related material has been researched heavily. Early research began with Dejerine (1892), Hinshelwood (1917), and Orton (1937) in the 1800's and 1900's. With regard to reading, the term dyslexia is often used to denote the inability to associate experience with the printed symbol. There was a great deal of work done in this area in the sixties by Blumberg (1968), Harris (1961), Fries (1963), Bateman (1963), Luria (1966), Gray (1960), Chall (1967), Kirk (1962), Johnson and Myklebust (1967), Downing (1962), Gattegno and Hinman (1966), and Bannatyne (1966). It is the authors' opinion that during the sixties learning disabilities came to the foreground and stimulated interest once again in a process that has been investigated for decades.

Remediation techniques have been developed stressing multisensory approaches. Betts (1950), Hegge, Kirk and Kirk (1940), Gillingham and Stillman (1940), Fernald (1943), and Bannatyne (1966) are some of the investigators who have developed techniques to remediate problems in word learning.

From the foregoing discussion, it would appear conclusive that the oral language development of a child is imperative if he is to learn to read. It could also be said that the four communication processes are interwoven and dependent upon each other.

REFERENCES

Anastasiow, Nicholas: Oral language and learning to read. *Language, Reading, and the Communication Process.* Newark, International Reading Association, 1971.

Artley, A. Sterl: Significant issues in the teaching of reading. An unpublished paper quoted in Frost, J. L.: *Issues and Innovations in the Teaching of Reading,* Chicago, Scott, Foresman, 1967, p. 193.

Bannatyne, A. D.: The color phonics system. In Money, J. (Ed.): *The Disabled Reader.* Baltimore, Johns Hopkins Press, 1966.

Bateman, B.: Reading and psycholinguistic processes of partially seeing children. *CEC Research Monographs,* Series A., No. 5, 1963.

Betts, E. A.: *Foundations of Reading Instructions.* New York, American Book Co., 1950.

Blumberg, Harris: Dyslexic problems and behavioral consequences. *Am Orthopt J, 18:* , 1968.

Bond, Gay L., and Tinker, Miles: *Reading Difficulties. Their Diagnosis and Correction.* New York, Appleton-Century-Crofts, 1957, p. 3.

Chall, J.: *Learning to Read: The Great Debate.* New York, McGraw-Hill, 1967.

Chase, Alice E.: *Famous Paintings. An Introduction to Art for Young People.* New York, Platt & Munk Co., 1951, p. 5.

Chomsky, Noam: *Syntactic Structures.* Mounton, The Hague, 1957.

Dejerine, J.: Contribution a l'etude anatome-pathologique et clinque des differentes varietes de cecite verbale. *Mem Soc Biol,* 4:61-90, 1892.

Denley, Robert: NCTE/ERIC Report of Research in Listening and Listening Skills, Elementary English, 46, April, 1959.

Downing, J. A.: Experiments with an augmented alphabet for beginning readers in British schools. Paper presented in New York at the meeting of the Educational Records Bureau Conference, November, 1962.

Flavell, John H., and Wohlwill, Joachim F.: *Studies in Cognitive Development.* New York, Oxford University Press, 1969.

Fries, C. C.: *Linguistics and Reading.* New York, Holt, Rinehart and Winston, 1963.

Frost, J. L.: *Issues and Innovations in the Teaching of Reading.* Chicago, Scott, Foresman, 1967, pp. 316-317.

Gattegno, C., and Hinman, D.: Words in Color: I. The morphologico-algebraic approach to teaching reading. In Money, J. (Ed.): *The Disabled Reader.* Baltimore, Johns Hopkins Press, 1966a.

Gattegno, C., and Hinman, D.: Words in Color: II. The current status of words in color in the United States. In Money, J. (Ed.): *The Disabled Reader.* Baltimore, Johns Hopkins Press, 1966b.

Gillingham, A., and Stillman, B.: *Remedial Training for Children with Specific Disability in Reading, Spelling and Penmanship.* New York, Sackett & Wilhelms, 1940.

Gray, W. S.: *On Their Own in Reading,* 2d ed. Chicago, Scott, Foresman, 1960, p. 10.

Gray, W. S.: *Gray Oral Reading Tests. Manual of Directions.* New York, Bobbs-Merrill, 1963.

Harris, A. J.: *How to Increase Reading Ability,* 4th ed. New York, David McKay, 1961.

Hegge, T. G., Kirk, S. A., and Kirk, W. D.: *Remedial Reading Drills.* Ann Arbor, George Wahr, 1940.

Hinshelwood, J.: *Congenital Word-blindness.* London, Lewis, 1917.

Holt, John: *How Children Fail.* New York, Pitman, 1964.

Holt, John: *How Children Learn.* New York, Pitman, 1969.

Johnson, D. J., and Myklebust, H. R.: *Learning Disabilities: Educational Principles and Practices.* New York, Grune and Stratton, 1967.

Kirk, S. A.: *Educating Exceptional Children.* Boston, Houghton Mifflin, 1962.

Levin, Joel R., and Rowher, William D. Jr.: Verbal organization and the facilitation of serial learning. *J Educ Psychol, 59*:186-190, June, 1968.

Luria, A. R.: *Higher Cortical Functions in Man.* New York, Basic Books, 1966.

Monroe, Marion: *The Child and His Language Comes to School: Language, Reading and the Communication Process.* Newark, International Reading Association, 1971.

Orton, S. T.: *Reading, Writing and Speech Problems in Children.* New York, W. W. Norton, 1937.

Robinson, H. Alan: *Toward Significant Living.* 34th Educational Conference of the Educational Records Bureau, October, 1969.

Russell, D. H.: *Children Learn to Read,* 2d ed. New York, Ginn & Co., 1961.

Shy, Roger W.: A linguistic background for developing beginning reading materials for black children. In Baratz, Joan C. and Shuy, Roger W. (Eds.): *Teaching Black Children to Read.* Washington, D. C., Center for Applied Linguistics, 1969, pp. 117-137.

Singer and Ruddell: *Theoretical Models and Processes of Reading.* Newark, International Reading Association, 1970.

Sonenberg, Charlotte, and Glass, Gerald G.: Reading and speech: An incidence and treatment study. *Reading Teacher, 19*:197-201, December, 1965.

Spache, Evelyn, and Spache, George: *Reading in the Elementary School.* Rockleigh, Allyn and Bacon, 1969, pp. 34-37.

Stauffer, Russell G.: *Directing Reading Maturity as a Cognitive Process.* New York, Harper & Row, 1969.

Stewart, William A.: On the use of Negro dialect in the teaching of reading. In Baratz, Joan C. and Shy, Roger W. (Eds.): *Teaching Black Children to Read.* Washington, D. C., Center for Applied Linguistics, pp. 156-219.

Strickland, Ruth G.: *Language Arts in the Elementary School.* Indianapolis, D. C. Heath, 1951.

Weintraub, Samuel: What research says to the reading teacher. *Reading Teacher, 20*:639-647, April, 1967.

Writing

Writing, or the integration of the visual-motor system using paper and pencil, is one of the three methods the child has to express himself—speech and body language being the other al-

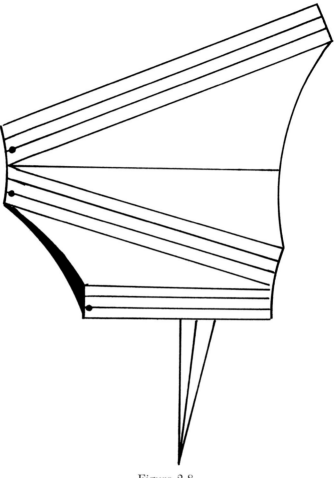

Figure 2-8

ternatives. The use of paper and pencil is a requisite to positive reinforcement of visual symbolization.

According to Cruickshank (1961):

> Writing is one of the most crucial learning activities. The difficulties in motor coordination which are such a basic part of the child's problem are more evident (though not necessarily present to a greater degree) here than in any other academic subject. The developmental kinesthetic approach to learning is here available as an indispensable aid to reading; the senses of touch and motion

are used to help fix in the child's mind the look and sound of letters. The physical activity of writing channels his restless energy and gives him the rare experience of using that energy in a way which calls forth praise. It is perhaps for this reason that the child most often begins to take great pleasure in writing. Certainly this is an activity that often provides the experience of success which he needs to overcome his initial feelings of fear and failure; and in the process his bizarre or frustrated behavior is lessened. Indeed, a restless, unruly child often becomes a model of industrious virtue when he is presented with a specific and suitably simple writing assignment.

Writing is also an invaluable tool in helping the child to see letters and words as wholes (Gestalts) instead of as the disconnected parts in which they usually appear to him.

It has been established that adequate development of hand coordination is the basis of writing, either cursive or manuscript.

Kephart and Roach (1966), Ayres (1964), Frostig *et al.* (1961), and Beery (1967) are some of the authors of tests to evaluate the various aspects of visual perception, perceptual fine motor ability, or visual-motor integration. Beery (1967) when discussing the assessment and remediation of visual-motor difficulties specifically emphasizes the need to "Test Down and Teach Up."

The following outline shows the assessment and teaching strategy for visual-motor skills (Beery, 1966).

Test	Level V	: Visual-Motor Integration	
Down	Level IV	: Visual Perception	
	Level III	: Tracing	
	Level II	: Tactual-Kinesthetic Sense	Teach
	Level I	: Motor Proficiency	Up

Assessment (testing) begins with the complex tasks and proceeds downward toward the simple tasks. Teaching begins with the simple tasks and proceeds upward toward the complex tasks.

Kephart and Roach (1966) note:

> The Perceptual-Motor Survey was designed primarily to detect errors in perceptual-motor development. To date it is a qualitative scale which designates areas for remediation. The survey was not designed for diagnosis, *per se*, but to allow the clinician to observe perceptual-motor behavior in a series of behavioral performances.

The specifications for the inclusion of an item in the survey were that it must: (1) tap some perceptual motor area; (2) be easy to administer and require a minimum of special equipment; (3) be representative of behavior familiar to all children; (4) have scoring criteria simple enough and clear enough that a minimum amount of training would be necessary for administration; and (5) not be over-structured so that it elicits a specific learned response.

This fifth specification is very important and needs to be explained in more detail. Most individuals with clinical experience have often heard the comment from the referring teacher that "Johnny," the non-achiever, does much better when he receives individual attention. Thus, a tutor is often recommended to bridge the achievement gap between Johnny and his peers. Quite often this treatment procedure is palliative rather than curative, since Johnny's real problem may be in structuring social and learning situations.

In this area as all others, praise and primary reinforcement combined with instructional procedures, can substantially increase the rate of verbal recall of letters and improve printing skills (Fauke *et al.* 1973).

It is not the intent to survey all the literature dealing with the visual perceptual motor area or the processing of the haptic system. Several more commonly known and respected authors have been briefly discussed in an attempt to reinforce the importance of the visual-perceptual motor-system, not as an isolated skill but as a necessary requisite to writing one of the three avenues the child has open to him for expression of self and concept development.

Carter and Synolds (1974) state "that brain-injured children who have poor handwriting are in fact trying too hard to write and using too much energy in the process. An audio-taped relaxation program was devised and presented to thirty-two boys who were in special classes for minimally brain-injured children. An equal number of randomly selected age mates were chosen as controls. Relaxation training was administered to the experimental group three days a week for four weeks. Results indicated that: (1) the program was effective in enhancing the quality of handwriting; (2) there was transfer effect to nonexperimental situations; (3) the changes were stable over time; and (4) there was very high interjudge reliability of handwriting quality."

It had been previously noted in the discussion of research related to the Development of Adequate Auditory Perception, Discrimination, programs for perceptual motor and visual perceptual handicaps. The Vanguard School Program, the Frostig Program, the materials developed by Keith E. Beery and discussed in his Administration and Scoring Manual have all proved effective in dealing with specific problems in the visual perceptual fine motor area.

There have been a few programs developed, specifically related to writing for the Learning Disabled Child. However, none of them were part of the scope and sequence relating writing to language and the development of effective communication process.

Hopefully, this program will correlate and intertwine writing, a formal application of processing kinesthesis with paper and pencil material, to produce an effective mode of expression of concepts, language and social and emotional development.

REFERENCES

Ayres, Jean: *Sensory Integration and Learning Disorders.* Los Angeles, Western Psychol. Services, 1972, p. 292.

Ayres, Jean: Types of perceptual motor deficits in children with learning difficulties. Lecture presented to the Los Angeles County Elementary Guidance Assoc., April 27, 1964 and quoted by Dorne, W., and Cherry, C.: *Readings in Education of Exceptional Children.* New York, Selected Academic Readings, 1968.

Berry, K. E. and Buktenica, N.: Developmental Test of Visual Motor Integration. Chicago, Follette, 1967, p. 14.

Carter, John L., and Synolds, Donald M.: Effects of relaxation training upon handwriting quality. *Journal of Learning Disabilities,* 7:53, April, 1974.

Cruickshank, W.: *A Teaching Method for Brain-Injured and Hyperactive Children.* Syracuse, Syracuse University Press, 1961, p. 191.

Fauke, Joyce, *et al.:* Improving of handwriting and letter recognition skills. A behavior modification procedure. *Journal of Learning Disabilities,* 6:296-301, May, 1973.

Frostig, Marianne E., *et al.:* Perceptual and Motor Skills, Vol. 12, 1961.

Readings in Education of Exceptional Children, edited by W. Dorne & C. Cherry, Selected Academic Readings, New York, N. Y., 1968.

Grotberg, Edith: Review of Educational Research, Vol. 35, No. 5, 1965, Pages 413-425. *Readings in Education of Exceptional Children,* edited by W. Dorne and C. Cherry. Selected Academic Readings, New York, New York, 1968.

Kephart, Newell C., and Roach, Eugene G.: *The Purdue Perceptual-Motor Survey.* Columbus, Charles E. Merrill, 1966, p. 53.

CHAPTER 3

SEQUENTIAL LANGUAGE DEVELOPMENT: A THEORETICAL AND PRACTICAL GUIDE FOR TEACHERS OF THE LEARNING DISABLED CHILD

INTRODUCTION

FROM THE TIME A CHILD is born, he is surrounded by language. From this cacaphony of sights and sounds, touching and moving, a child must pick out those sensations that have meaning for him. Thus, language first becomes a way of experiencing self-awareness and recording and retaining material that slowly builds this identity. However, the importance of language goes far beyond that. Language becomes a way of interpreting, organizing, and transforming experiences into meaningful behavior. It provides the child with a way to manipulate his environment for purposes of self-expression and, later on, self-preservation.

This aspect of language, represented by concept formation and critical thinking, forms the necessary base of cognitive development for every child. The child's ability to think, of course, is developed from the concepts he has readily available for use. These concepts are learned; they are not innate. Concepts can only be learned by having many different language experiences and accurately cataloging these experiences with similar previously learned impressions.

Of the many programs around regarding language acquisition, most of them fall short of giving the teacher a sequential picture of what she is striving toward, limit the teacher's creativity and do not take into consideration the differences amongst students which exist in each classroom. Today, most prominent researchers agree that language capability and the development of logical thinking go hand-in-hand. According to Ausubel (1963) "Parallel analysis of the development and thought . . . suggest that growth and local thinking is in large measure, tied to growth and language capability." It is important, therefore, to teach our children to compare, analyze, deduce and imagine beyond the given information. This is, in essence, what this program purports to do.

The present program has been developed to assist the classroom teacher and language specialist dealing with the learning disabled or language impaired child by providing specific activities to develop, strengthen, or reinforce eight specific stages in a sequence of language development which are spiral in their development and cyclical in their reinforcement. The need for such a program is based on the following:

1. Much of the current research and theory regarding the acquisition of a first language by children
2. How central processing dysfunction affects such acquisition
3. The language deficits common amongst learning disabled children

These points are discussed in Chapters 1 and 2 along with research supporting the program in general and its specific phases. The main objectives of the program are as follows: (1) Increase the awareness of the relationship between language and achievement; (2) Increase awareness of the logical sequential order of language, and (3) Provide a general scope and sequence with regard to development of what is considered the eight aspects of language development and provide some specific activities from which the teaching staff can further develop their own activities, taking into consideration the format of the group and each individual youngster's strengths and weaknesses with regard to their language area.

The eight basic aspects or stages of language development as reported by this program are:

I. Development of auditory awareness and accuracy in auditory skills.

II. Development of concrete factual information available for ready recall.

III. Concept development.

IV. Development of accurate verbal discourse and syntax.

V. Development of imagination skills.

VI. Development of thinking and comprehension skills.

VII. Development of the ability to handle language related visual symbolic material.

VIII. Development of writing skills.

In any instruction situation the steps of a Structured Learning Activity should be used as guidelines.

Structured Learning Activity

The student's instruction should always include the steps of a Structured Learning Activity.

(a) His background of experience should be tapped and evaluated.

(b) He should be motivated to become involved in any type of material he is presented.

(c) If the materials are of a reading nature, silent reading should precede oral reading.

(d) Comprehension and understanding of material and the concepts inherent in it should be carefully assessed, whether it be a perceptual, gross-motor, arithmetic or reading-learning activity.

(e) Follow-up activity should be utilized to reinforce those skills developed in any Structured Learning Activity.

(f) Accurate auditory and visual perception should be utilized as aims throughout all aspects of his program.

(g) He should be encouraged to utilize the skills he has developed in the instructional situation as independently as possible in all aspects of his environmental interaction.

THE PROGRAM

I. Development of Accurate Auditory Perception, Discrimination, and Memory

A. Identification of Sound

Figure 3-1. Developing auditory skills using commercial materials.

1. Children are to be directed in their awareness of sound, the absence of sound and too much sound.
   a. What is *quiet?*
   b. What is *noise?*
      (1) sources of noise
      (2) effect of noise on our ears and on the communication process
2. Point to the direction of sound(s).
   a. How do we determine the direction of a sound source?
      (1) It seems louder in one ear than in the other.
      (2) Our eyes see something and later we hear from that direction.

      b. Why is it difficult to tell where sound comes from at certain times?

        (1) The source of the sound may be equidistant from both ears.

        (2) The sound may *echo* and confuse us as to where it came from.

B. Development of gross sound discrimination of environmental sounds, animals and musical instruments

  1. Determine if certain sounds are the same (alike) or different.

  2. Have them match the sound with their own voice, if possible, or with a mechanical device. Have the child bark like a dog or use his desk top like a drum.

  3. Have them name the sounds they hear (environmental sounds only). This is beginning work in perception. (This is also a good time to check on whether a child knows the concept of same and different.)

  4. Let the children play with objects or instruments that make distinctive sounds, as a rattle, bell, or musical toy.

C. Begin work on auditory association

  1. Use language activities such as the following:

    a. Name animals.

    b. Select pictures of animals.

    c. A duck says . . . . . . ; a cow says . . . .

    d. I see a barn. In a barn we have . . . .

    e. Have the children select concrete objects which produce the sound they hear.

    f. Have the children select pictures which produce the sound they hear.

    g. A police car sounds like this: . . . .

    h. Do you hear this sound inside or outside?

    i. Have children select pictures of body parts:

        We use our feet to . . . .

        We use our eyes to . . . .

        We use our mouth to . . . .

2. Have the children use rhythm instruments and create a rhythm that makes you feel like
   a. moving—fast or slow,
   b. going to sleep,
   c. running,
   d. skipping, or
   e. walking.

D. Begin work on auditory sequential memory
   1. Have the children copy a gross auditory pattern, i.e. bell ringing, drum sounds, buzzer board, or xylophone chiming.
      a. As the child's ability improves, increase the amount of sounds heard and the complexity of the pattern.
      b. As the child's ability improves, increase the time interval between the stimulus and response.
   2. Have child repeat back word at the sound of buzzer. As the student's ability improves, lengthen the time between stimulus word, buzzer, and word student is to repeat.
   3. Review the pictures of animals or household items and when all children can readily identify them, ask them to place the pictures on the blackboard in the order dictated by the teacher. Begin with two or three pictures and see how far you can extend the skill.
   4. Have the children repeat related syllables, i.e. "The big dog," or "My friend is happy." When the children have increased their ability to do the skill, the instructor can present auditorily the related syllables in a mixed order and see if the children can unscramble them, i.e. "dog the big" or "happy my is friend."
   5. Spend a great deal of time on sequential direction following. (This skill is vital to academic success.) Understanding and following verbal directions is a skill that should be emphasized, reviewed, and ex-

tended throughout the year. A weakness in auditory skills at any integrative level may confuse the student when the teacher is giving directions or when she is lecturing to the class.

   a. Let the children perform motor tasks while you give verbal directions.

   b. Dictate numbers, letters, or names of shapes to the class and increase the length of the series as their skill develops.

   c. Read short stories to the class and see who can answer your four or five questions about what you just read.

6. Next, the students can work to repeat unrelated and then related syllables, i.e. pig, tree, girl, or tā, sē, lū, or pō.

   a. Always begin on a low level and build up the number of syllables according to the child's ability.

   b. Begin with monosyllabic concrete words, i.e. boy, tree, car.

   c. When the children can repeat unrelated syllables and words, add comprehension to this activity, i.e. "My brother is five feet five inches tall and weighs 145 pounds." After the child repeats the sentence, ask him specific information contained in the sentence.

   d. Listen for the number of syllables heard in a word, i.e. present the word: dad-dy, bas-ket-ball. What is the word? How many syllables in the word?

   e. When the child can perform reasonably well at this task, begin work on sound blending. This is done the same way, only the words are broken, i.e. fa-ther, Pop-si-cle®.

E. Begin work on fine sound discrimination.

1. This includes hearing minimal differences between sounds that are in words

    a. whose phonetic characteristics are very different, i.e. big–little, man–baby, paper–paper. (Can the child accurately repeat the two words? Were the two words the *same* or *different?*);

    b. that have the same beginning sound or the same ending sound, i.e. big–brown, mitt–hot. Have the child repeat the two words and ask him to tell which sounds are the same in both words, and

    c. that are only slightly different, i.e. that have only one phoneme that distinguishes the two words, i.e. hot–hat, sit–set, man–ment. (Which word should I use to make this sentence correct?)

        The ice cream is very told.

        My dog has long fair.

2. Short vowels are often very difficult for a child with an auditory problem. The ability to rhyme can be used to overcome this difficulty if a concrete to abstract, simple to complex basis is followed.

    a. Long vowels should not be introduced until the concept of rhyming is established. Consonants should have one color and long vowels a second color. Sandpaper or wooden letter forms should be used. Ask the child the following:

        (1) Do two words rhyme which have similar sounds?

        (2) How do rhyming words help us? The child should understand that the skill will help him in reading and spelling.

        (3) Use auditory discrimination tapes with activities such as animal sounds, environmental sounds, and all sounds except those involving short vowels.

    b. Introduce short vowels by using color and tactile clues to distinguish from long vowels patterns. Keep color pattern constant.

        (1) Have child make up list of short vowel families by substituting initial consonant multisensory materials.

(2) After child has established short vowel concept with multisensory materials, proceed
to paper and pencil task activities such as
word families, substitution of initial consonant, selecting one of four rhyming words to
complete an (1) oral sentence, and (2) written sentence.

F. Auditory Closure

Auditory closure is the ability to identify a word, even
when part of the word is missing. This skill is often required to understand persons who speak with an accent
or when part of a conversation is missed because of
nearby noises. This skill can be taught by the following:

1. Leave out part of a word that is being presented,
   i.e. tele. ision, cow. oy, . otdog. (Later, as their
   skill develops, use sentences in the same manner.
   My . ar nee. .s . ashing. How o. . are you?)

2. Speak with an accent and have the students tell you
   what you have said.

3. Put a stick between your teeth and speak to the class.

G. Auditory Figure-Ground Drill

The child is given practice following verbal directions
in the presence of background noise. The teacher may
give directions regarding the drawing of certain shapes,
completing a diagram on a sheet of stenciled paper, or
building certain objects. All this is done with a record
player, radio, or television in the classroom. Adjust the
volume of the competing noise to a level that is just
slightly lower than the level of the teacher's voice.

1. Why is it easier to do our work when it is quiet in
   the room?

2. Now, let's do the same work without the radio playing and compare our results.

H. By this time, the students should be ready to tell you
distinctive speech sounds which are heard at the beginning, medial, and end positions of words.

A good activity for this would be a game called "Head

Tummy, Toes." Make sure students know the body parts. Tell the students they are listening for the snake (or any other sound). The teacher says a word. If the student hears the snake sound at the beginning of the word, he touches his head; in the middle, he touches his tummy, and at the end he touches his toes. (Remember to make sure that all students understand the concept of beginning, middle and end before this activity is attempted.

II. Development of factual information available for ready recall.

   A. Have the children orally tell their own stories. Developing the child's language begins with the child and his own personal world. His name and the names of his family, how they are related to him, where he lives, his phone number, his family car, the family pets, his weight, height, his age, his birthdate and any similar facts give the child a stronger self-awareness and equip him with enough facts to expand his fund of information.

   Next, expand his world to those with whom he comes in contact daily and let him compare his world with theirs.

   B. Have the children make and guess animal sounds. Example: Bear is one. Bears are two. What do they say when they talk to you? (Peabody Language Development Kit.)

   C. Show and Tell

   In the initial stages of this activity, emphasis should be placed upon the weight of the information related by the child and less emphasis upon the grammatical correctness of his stories. Encourage the student to describe the object, its uses by him, where it is found and why he chose it. Although speaking in complete sentences is the eventual goal, little mention should be made of this until the child is comfortable in speaking before a group of peers. On Monday morning, younger students enjoy reliving their weekend experiences by relating them to the group. Each student is expected to make some contribution, however limited or in what form it may be.

D. Always have a concrete experience to go along with all new concepts with young children and impaired older ones. In science, build a planetarium; in reading, act out a story.

E. Develop facts corresponding to achievement level. Give each child the opportunity to verbally express what he is doing with his hands. It is important to plan activities in large blocks of time to permit each child to express himself. Some students will require lengthy periods to find the words he wants to use and to use them appropriately.

F. For young children, present many language experiences to develop information such as:

1. Making butter in class
2. Role playing
3. Science experiments
4. Sense training experiences
5. Oral discussion of the child's art work

All phases of the above activities should be verbalized. Remember, the child is able to successfully integrate new information with previously learned concepts only when his language background is sufficient to permit his comprehension of the new material or activity. Who is the child and what level of language does he comprehend? (Many good activities can be found in *Language Motivating Experiences for Young Children* by Rose Engel.)

III. Concept Development

Since you will already have done some auditory perceptual training, begin concept development with some of the materials you used in auditory work. Classify the materials used and show how certain of them have similar characteristics.

A. Begin sense training.
   1. *Smell* different foods with and without blindfold.
   2. *Feel* objects placed inside a bag or with a blindfold.
   3. *See* objects.
B. Teach shapes.
   1. Teach and review all basic shapes.
   2. What objects have these shapes in them? Look around the room.
   3. Verbalize how a shape is made.
C. Size concepts. Example: A *ball* is smaller than a *house*.
   1. Give examples of large *vs* small, fat *vs* skinny, tall *vs* short.
   2. Compare the sizes of different animals used earlier in the program.
D. Spatial Concepts—before, after, next, early, and late should be used, incorporating concrete materials first.
   1. Let each child practice using the concepts in sentences he gives orally.
   2. Let each child find the word on the board and write a sentence for it. Example: "I was late."
E. Have students put a mannequin together while verbalizing the parts of the body. Remove pieces from the doll and ask what is wrong. What can you do with the different parts of the body, i.e. hand?
F. Work on broad classifications. Begin this with matching color, size and shape and discuss how things are similar and different according to the three above mentioned topics.
G. Verbally decode actions done with parts of the body. Example: I clap with my . . . . I swing a bat with my . . . .
H. Give the students practice in following directions using parts of the body. Example: Touch your nose.
I. Ask questions referring to parts of the body. Examples:

1. What do you do with your eyes?
2. What kinds of things can you do with your hands?
J. Reinforce occupations. Example: She helps us to learn; she is my . . . .
K. Describe the functions of things found in the home.
   1. My mother cleans the carpet with a . . . .
   2. She bakes cakes in the . . . .
   Present the picture to reinforce the concept.
L. Brainstorming. Examples:
   1. Name five animals.
   2. Name five types of flowers.
   3. Name five things that have engines.
M. More advanced classifications. Examples: Things that come in:
   1. a pair
   2. a jar
   3. a bunch
N. Begin work on relationships. Examples:
   1. Opposites
   2. At breakfast, I drink . . . .
   3. Snow is cold; fire is . . . .
   4. How are all shoes the same?
   5. A shovel and a spoon: How are they the same? How are they different?
IV. Development of Accurate Verbal Discourse or Syntax
Keep in mind that it is best to relate the discourse to the child's immediate environment and only later expand to the rest of the world. If at all possible, ask the children to give all answers in a complete sentence. Insist that the child address you and the rest of the class with sentences only.
A. Classroom learning responses
   1. Teach nouns, singular and plural. Example: Here is a dog. Here are two dogs. Here are six dogs.
   If student is ready, introduce irregular plurals:
   Here is one *foot*. Here are two *feet*.
   Here is a mouse. Here are three *mice*.
   2. Teach pronouns, singular and plural.

Figure 3-2. Mr. Donald E. Roth working in speech and language development.

3. Teach regular verbs; add irregulars if student is ready. Example: I run fast. I ran fast yesterday.
4. Teach the children orally how to make a negative response using the whole sentence. Example: No, I do not have a pencil.
5. Teach adjectives. Begin with size, shape and color. (At this time, we can reinforce how things are similar and different, according to their size, shape and color.)
6. Work on prepositions. Discuss parts of the body, relating them to other parts of the body by the use of prepositions. Example: My mouth is under my nose.
7. Teach adverbs. Finally, say a sentence to the class: "I am going now." Ask the students what questions this statement answers. How? When? Where? Who? What?
8. Stress pronouns.
B. Social Responses
1. Work on conversational speech. Examples:
a. Every Monday morning is a good time to let each student review the happenings of his weekend. With young children, accept whatever they say. Later, try and shape their verbal responses into proper form. It is often necessary to repeat the

child's ideas immediately after he says them, using proper syntactic structure.

   b. You need to borrow a pencil; what would you say?

   c. For older students: A boy asks you on a date and your mother would not let you go. How do you tell him?

   d. You wanted to borrow your dad's car. How do you ask for it?

2. Developing labels for feeling words or labeling emotions.

   a. Discuss the meaning or label for facial expressions or body gestures.

     (1) Have child select pictures of faces of animals that are happy, sad, or crying.

     (2) Have child find pictures of entire animal that shows the same feeling.

   b. Discuss things that are pleasant to you and things that are unpleasant.

   c. Stress that each person views these things differently from their background of information.

   d. Use oral and written sentences the child commonly hears that denote emotion.

3. Work on introductions: How do you introduce a friend to mother?

4. Work on general conversational ability. Example: What would you discuss at dinner? Have the children get into a group and role play a dinner conversation.

5. Begin work on how to make more interesting and more descriptive sentences. Example: The child says "I saw a dog." The teacher then asks how he could make the sentence interesting and give more information about the dog. The child says "I saw a big, brown, furry dog."

V. Development of Imagination

  A. Teach the concept of "Let's pretend." Use cartoons and children's programs to reinforce concept.

   B. Begin pantomime:
      1. Act out how different animals move.
      2. Read a simple poem and have students act it out.
      3. Work on sequential pantomime. Example: What do you do from the time you get up until you go to school?
   C. Play charades. (Another example of body language)
   D. Present a picture card of animals and/or people, and have them make up a short story.
   E. Using closure to develop imagination
      1. Name the parts of various animals and ask questions such as: Do all animals have tails? Which animals have four legs?
      2. Show a picture of part of an animal and have child describe as much of the rest of the animal as possible.
      3. Show one card of a two card sequence and have child tell the end of the sequence. Proceed up to as many as a five or six card sequence.
      4. Show child middle and end of sequence and ask child how it began.
      5. Show the child beginning and end of story and ask student to fill in the middle of the story.
   F. Use role playing activities starting with animals and proceeding to human roles.
 VI. Development of Comprehension
    Comprehension depends upon needs of the individual and total development of the language program in which reading is now introduced, if it has not already been.
    • Children must move from concrete to abstract using familiar objective situations.
    • The oral language background of the child is used to develop word learning and recognition.
    • Experiences associated with each concept are planned so that they occur in situations where the child can deal with concrete materials.

- When one skill is dependent on another, the basic skill should be introduced and continually reinforced.

These steps should be initiated and continue throughout a successful language development and reading program. Many of these specific activities have been introduced in previous phases.

A. Level One

Comprehension at the *primary level* depends upon the child's personal experiences.

1. Follow one-step directions.
2. Give opposite of an idea.
3. Identify the speaker in a conversation.
4. Visualize what he hears.
5. Judge which one of two sentences or paragraphs goes with a picture and which one does not, of those that he hears.
6. Draw conclusions of one, two, or three statements of related ideas.
    a. Judge which picture fits a set of clues.
    b. Solve a riddle when given two or more clues.
7. Development of character.
    a. Identify various characters from auditorily presented stories.
    b. Appreciate and differentiate moods (determined) from auditorily presented stories (happy, sad, glad, angry, scared).
    c. Follow changes in location (movement from part to home from auditorily presented stories).
    d. Use picture clues to aid comprehension of story being told.
8. Language clues to comprehension.
    Develop the ability to:
    a. Recognize multiple meanings of words.
    b. Identify definite and indefinite words and phrases. (Maybe it was a girl like Peggy.)
    c. Identify the first sounds.

    d. Identify the rhyming patterns (in, out).

    e. Recognize the possessive nouns (grandma's pen).

    f. Draw and support inferences (sun shines—caused by sunlight).

9. Interpretation and inference from language usage.

    a. Interpret intonation clue signaled by inflection in voice.

    b. Follow a phrase where *you* is understood: "Want to play a game?"

    c. Follow the meaning of *it* when used as a subject and as a direct object (someone lost *it. It* is mine.)

    d. Understand the idea of ownership indicated by personal pronouns (her room).

10. Comparison and contrast.

    a. Establish cause-effect relationship (colors mixed to create another).

    b. Anticipate predicted outcome (what the third color will be like).

    c. Follow directions given through imperative form. (*You* must go home.)

    d. Recall details.

    e. Determine realism or imagination, fact or fantasy.

11. Sequential order of ideas of stories told by teacher and aided by pictures.

    a. Follow sequence determined by characters.

    b. Organize ideas to draw conclusion.

    c. Appreciate the development of plot.

    d. Follow sequence determined by actions.

    e. Understand chronology.

    f. Follow events.

    g. Use qualifying words (little, black).

12. Recognition of style.

    a. Follow and appreciate the formal conversation exchange.

    b. Infer emotions from speaking style and descriptive words.

13. Appreciation of contrasting ideas.

    a. Recognize main idea of story auditorily presented.

    b. Evaluate importance of main ideas.

    c. Understand importance of figurative language (city of water).

    d. Classify (according to size, etc.).

    e. Evaluate importance of ideas.

14. Recognition of problems.

    a. Identify cause and effect relationships.

    b. Recognize sequence.

    c. Recognize feelings and emotions.

    d. Find solutions to problems.

15. Appreciate a tale of fantasy.

    a. Identify characters.

    b. Infer feelings of mood.

    c. Appreciate the part that location and circumstances beyond their control play in the story.

    d. Identify cause-effect relationships (many smaller ones that lead up to major direct result).

    e. Use picture clues that infer moods and actions.

16. Evaluating ideas.

    a. Identify problems. (What causes the weather change?)

    b. Formulate hypotheses. (What reasons might ac-account for this change?)

    c. See relationships among details.

17. Play format.

    a. Recognize speaker.

    b. Follow the action.

    c. Recognize the setting.

    d. Combine ideas from separate sources.

18. Organization of ideas.

    a. Recognize main ideas.

    b. Recognize supporting details. Understand cause-effect relationships.

    c. Evaluate relevancy of ideas.

    d. Evaluate need for sequence (logical).

   e. Summarize using main idea.
   f. Recall facts.
  19. Solution of practical and social problems.
   a. Recognize problem situation (clock lost, shoe lost).
   b. Appreciate characterization.
   c. Follow sequence of events.
   d. Appreciate humor.
   e. Recognize emotions from actions.
   f. Anticipate outcome.
  20. Using contrasts as aids to comprehension.
   a. Recognize similarities and differences.
   b. Make contrasts.
   c. Recognize identifying characteristics.
   d. Classify.
   e. Understand time concepts.
   f. Recognize sense of humor.
B. Level Two

By second grade we are assuming the child can recognize words and meaning. Thus, reading material is used in addition to auditory material.

Children at any level have an amazing grasp of language. We, as teachers, with the correct reading program, can help the child with his comprehension ability if we use the child's previous accomplishments, experiences, and language background.

1. Sequence and Scope of Comprehension Abilities
  a. Each ability, when it is essential to the understanding of a particular selection, should be handled initially in familiar, objective situations rather than at the purely symbolic level. Children must move from the concrete to the abstract.
  b. The child's oral language background should be used as a basis for word learning and meaning.
  c. The first experiences with each ability should be planned so that they occur in situations where the

child can deal with relatively simple concrete materials, perhaps even discrete elements, rather than with very complex and abstract sets of ideas.

d. When one skill is obviously dependent on another, the basic skill has been introduced and reinforced before the child is expected to apply it as part of a larger general ability. The more inclusive a particular ability is of others, the more steps have been taken to reach readiness for learning it. This is taking the child from the known to the unknown, such as the skill of drawing conclusions which depend on specific skills such as the ability to handle understanding a main idea, details, and sequence of events.

e. Language experiences and comprehension development: some or all could be applied to certain stories that the child reads or has had read to him. The teacher would select the goals that they wanted the child to accomplish from each story. Example:

1) Appreciation of mood and sequence
2) Appreciation of sequential order of ideas and events.
3) Following and interpreting a plot at two levels
4) Evaluative and critical thinking
5) Inference and generalization
6) Development of the plot
7) Development of characters
8) Development of creative thinking
9) Recognizing main ideas and supporting facts
10) Appreciation of humor
11) Appreciation of sensory images
12) Interpreting facts and drawing conclusions
13) Language clues to word recognition and comprehension
14) Interpretation and inference from language usage

C. Level Three

Some or all could be applied to certain stories that the

child reads or hears. The teacher would select the goals that they wanted the child to accomplish from each story. Example:

1. Problem analysis and solution
2. Sequential order of ideas and events
3. Understanding of author's style and approach
4. Appreciation of plot development through problem evolution and solution
5. Appreciation of organization of ideas and events
6. Recognizing rhyming sounds
7. Understanding development of a character
8. Recognizing problem and sequence of events leading to the solution
9. Organization of ideas
10. Development of the plot
11. Interpreting reaction and feelings
12. Organization of materials
13. Reactions and feeling of characters
14. Recognizing relevancy, roles and relationship
15. Reactions to an unpleasant situation
16. Organization of information
17. Relationships between generalized and specific information
18. Author's intent and purpose
19. Evaluating a fairy tale in play form
20. Comparison and contrast
21. Language clues to word recognition and comprehension
22. Interpretation and inference for language usage

D. The scope and sequence is determined by:

1. Each skill must move from the concrete to the abstract by using concrete situations rather than symbolic (using the child's actual experiences).
2. Written symbolization would be based upon the child's oral language background.
3. Situation should occur so that the student can deal

with experiences related to simple concrete materials.

4. The more inclusive a particular skill or ability is of others, the more steps have been taken to reach readiness for learning it. The basic foundations of the skill have to be established in a logical, sequential manner.

E. Level Four

A suggested program of comprehension development which should prove appropriate would include in the reading manuals situations displaying:

1. Character development
2. Language clues to a word recognition and comprehension
3. Interpretation and inference from language usage
4. Literary style
5. Recognizing main ideas and supporting details
6. Rhymes in poetry
7. Sequence
8. Specialized word meanings
9. "Built in" aids to comprehension
10. Special language, i.e. figure of speech
11. Informal speech
12. Inference, i.e. to follow as rapid sequence of events without transition statements or signal words
13. Play format (character scene, narrator, understanding and recognition)
14. Organizing information and following directions

F. Level Five

1. Development and motivation of character
2. Language clues to word recognition and comprehension
3. Interpretation and inference from language usage
4. Appreciation of the steps in a well-developed plot
5. Appreciation in humor
6. Understanding the nature and function of a myth

7. Appreciating use of figurative language to achieve effect
8. Understanding characterization, mood and plot
9. Understanding the form of a play, its style and plot development
10. Sequential order of ideas and events
11. Understanding types of information in an essay
12. Appreciating fantasy as a literary form
13. Appreciating mood in an autobiographical sketch
14. Developing them and understanding how

VII. Development of the Ability to Handle Language Related Visual Symbolic Material

Always use *age*-appropriate materials to insure motivation and interest, i.e. experience stories with older children (9-12) and experience charts with primary ages (5-8).

A. Tradition Approach
  1. Sight
    a. Phase I
      (1) Words on chalkboard
      (2) Labeling
      (3) Picture words
      (4) Copying words
      (5) Matching pictures to words
      (6) Outlining words
      (7) Flannel boards
      (8) Pantomiming
      (9) Flashcards
    b. Phase II
      (1) Helper charts
      (2) Presenting new word before reading a selection
      (3) Studying new words after a selection has been read
      (4) Distinguishing between words of similar length and shape
      (5) Distinguishing between words in pairs
      (6) Homonyms

(7) Using new words in sentences
  c. Phase III
    (1) Reading new words orally from board
    (2) Following directions given on a chart
    (3) Saying words child has written on slip of paper because he doesn't know them
2. Context Clues
  a. Phase I
    (1) Using pictures in connection with presentation of a word
    (2) Introducing new words in advance, or reading with the aid of pictures
    (3) Using picture-word cards
    (4) Using picture clues on the bulletin board
    (5) Anticipating meaning through examination of pictures in a series
    (6) Selecting words that are already in the child's vocabulary
    (7) Using questions to help pupils learn words
    (8) Anticipating words when listening
    (9) Taking advantage of typographical aids
  b. Phase II
    (1) Anticipating meaning through completion exercises
    (2) Discussing with the class appropriate techniques of identifying words through context
    (3) Becoming acquainted with words related to the theme of the selection
    (4) Having pupils find the word in a group of words which means the opposite or almost the opposite of the first word in the row
    (5) Writing on the chalkboard a sentence with a "new word" that a pupil has given orally
    (6) Giving riddles, in written form, for the pupil to solve
    (7) Providing pupils with pictures to complete so that they fit sentences that accompany them

(8) Giving the pupils duplicated pictures on which various words that they are learning are illustrated

(9) Using transparencies with an overhead projector

c. Phase III

(1) Becoming acquainted with words related to the theme of the selection

(2) Learning to recognize synonyms and antonyms

(3) Using a word in a sentence to summarize the thought of a preceding sentence or group of sentences

(4) Taking advantage of typographical aids

(5) Making effective use of context to aid in pronunciation

B. Phonetic Approach

1. Phase I

a. Teach single consonant sounds in initial position that are consistent in their sounds.

b. Teach short vowel sounds.

c. Combine consonant and short vowel sounds.

d. Final consonant sounds

2. Phase II

a. Blends

b. Consonant digraphs

c. Long vowel sounds and silent *e*

3. Phase III

a. *r, l,* and *w* controlled vowels

b. vowel digraphs and dipthongs

c. diacritical markings

C. Structural Analysis

1. Phase I

a. compound words

b. regular verbs and endings such as *s, ed, ing*

c. nouns and regular plurals

      d. contractions

2. Phase II

      a. nouns and variants

      b. prefixes and suffixes

      c. nouns and irregular plurals

      d. syllabication

3. Phase III

      a. ability to locate a word quickly

      b. ability to learn the pronunciation of a word

      c. ability to find the spelling of a word and related abilities

         (1) spelling

         (2) syllabication

         (3) hyphenation

         (4) abbreviations

         (5) capitalization

      d. ability to learn the meaning of a word

Figure 3-3. Chalkboard work is vital in developing writing skills.

D. Linguistics
   1. Phase I
      Two and three letter patterns using short vowels
   2. Phase II
      Regular spellings with double consonants and other digraphs in consistent uses
   3. Phase III
      Words with semi-irregular spellings
   4. Phase IV
      Words with irregular spellings
VIII. Development of Writing Skills Using Cursive or Script Letters Forms—General Instructions for the Teacher
   A. Teach meaning of terminology
      1. Base Line
         a. This is the line all lower case cursive letters are started.
         b. The line is located above the bottom line.
      2. Bottom Line
      3. Middle Line
         a. This line is located above the base line.
      4. Top Line
      5. Space
         a. That area between lines
      6. Up and Down
      7. Right and Left
      8. Stroke Lines
   B. Teaching Tools
      1. Posted Cursive alphabet
      2. Chalkboard and chalk
      3. Newsprint paper
         a. Large 18 x 12 inch unlined paper
      4. Lined writing paper
      5. Writing tools
         a. Crayons
         b. Pencils
         c. Grease pencil

    d. Fingerpaints

    e. Stylus (for use with clay)

C. Procedure for introduction of a letter at the chalkboard

  1. Name the letter out loud. (This is for writing and will not conflict with reading.)

  2. Find the letter in the posted alphabet.

  3. Instructor writes large letter on the blackboard.

    a. Use an arrow to indicate where letter starts.

  4. Instructor writes letter again giving oral detailed description on letter form.

  5. Instructor points out trouble spots.

  6. Student airwrites letter.

    a. Student is in a standing position.

    b. Student uses preferred writing arm in a firm or still extended position beginning at a 45 degree angle to the floor.

    c. The arm moves as one unit with no wrist or finger movement.

    d. The eyes and hand follow the large pattern on the chalkboard.

    e. The name of the letter is said aloud by the student as he airwrites.

    f. The letter is written a minimum of five times in the air.

    g. Instructor must observe the student's movement from a position behind the student and correct errors in movement.

  7. Student traces large pattern of letter on the chalkboard a minimum of five times.

  8. With pattern on the chalkboard, student writes the letter five times always naming the letter.

    a. The letter should be of same size as the traced letter.

  9. Student writes letter five times without a pattern to observe.

  10. Student writes the letter with eyes closed.

11. Touching the finger to the blackboard in tracing may be indicated before the use of chalk.
12. Variations of the chalkboard introduction to increase tactile knowledge of the letter.
    a. Finger write
       (1) in sand
       (2) in mud
       (3) on rough carpet
       (4) on textured fabric (velvet, suede cloth, flannel)
       (5) on sandpaper
13. The instructor must always name the letter as she writes it to encourage the student in the procedure which gives oral and auditory reinforcement.
14. Correct body position and manner of holding chalk in the hand must be taught every student before he works at the chalkboard.
    a. Writing is started at student's nose level. Have him touch his nose to the board. This haptic sensation lasts as an orientation to a proper place to start writing.
    b. Chalk is held in the hand by the butt and rests lightly in the palm.
    c. No part of the hand touches the chalkboard when using chalk.
    d. Student stands eighteen inches away from the board.
D. Writing on Paper
   1. Proper body position is taught
   2. Paper placement on the desk
      a. Right-handed person has paper placed at 33 degree angle following natural line of arm.
      b. Left-handed person has paper placed at same degree but in opposite rotation following natural slant of arm.
   3. Pencil position is that the pencil is held lightly be-

tween the forefinger and thumb with movement coming from the shoulder.

E.

    1. Newsprint 12 x 18

      a. The use of newsprint follows instruction of the letter at the chalkboard.

      b. It is folded in half giving a 9 x 12 surface.

      c. With the fold on the right a pattern is written.

      d. Student traces pattern five times.

      e. With paper open letter is written on the next side.

      f. Paper is turned over and student writes letter form (without a pattern to observe) on the left side of paper.

      g. On the right side of paper, student writes letter with eyes closed.

      h. Every time the letter is written student names the letter out loud.

    2. Special lined paper

      a. Size of spaces varies, going from large to small as the student becomes proficient.

        (1) Recommended that space between lines start at 1½ inches.

        (2) The smallest space will be one-half of the space in normal lined notebook paper.

      b. There are four basic lines: upper, middle, base line (which may be colored) and the bottom line.

      c. Consequently, there are three spaces.

      d. The unit of four lines should be separated from succeeding units by a sizeable space.

    3. The base line must be indicated by color or by an arrow.

    4. Regular notebook paper

      a. Use each space as one full space for writing.

      b. Indicate base line by arrow.

F. Sequence of letter introduction

    1. Selection

    a. Letters are introduced as a *family* depending on the approach stroke.

      (1) The first family is composed of *i, t, u, w, j, p* and *r*.

      (2) The second family is *a, d, g, q, o* and *c*.

      (3) The third family is *l, b, h, k, f, e* and *s*.

      (4) The fourth family is *n, m, v, y, x* and *z*.

    b. The letters *i* and *t* must be introduced in sequence as they will lead into the connecting of letters to form a word.

    c. The *i* is the measuring letter as it fills one space.

    d. The letters *t* and *d* are called *teenage* letters, as they are not quite grown up and do not reach the top line.

G. Connecting letters

  1. The first connection of letters will be the *i* and *t* to make the word *it*.

    a. This step occurs first at the chalkboard with the previous procedure for letter introduction followed.

    b. The paper work on the word follows the prescribed steps for single letter introduction.

    c. At this time, the basic writing lines must be used on the chalkboard and all other patterns.

    d. Alignment of letters is now introduced.

      (1) Alignment is keeping the connecting stroke on the base line.

      (2) The writing tool is not lifted from the surface until the last letter in a word is formed.

      (3) The *i* is dotted first and then the *t* is crossed in *it*.

      (4) The procedure is to start from the left and follow through to the right.

H. Adaptation of the procedure to manuscript or print

  If the manuscript or print letters must be used, the pro-

Figure 3-4. Mrs. Burlington and student.

cedure for the cursive letters may be used with modification. The most important area to be concerned with is that the student make the letter without lifting the writing tool before the letter is completed, which will eliminate the sticks and circle approach to making the letter.

TABLE IV

PEABODY *RELATIONSHIP* ACTIVITIES SEQUENTIALLY

Peabody I	Peabody II	Peabody III
27-3	8-3	4-3
34-3	9-2	9-2
43-2	11-2	14-2
51-2	13-1	19-2
53-2	20-2	24-2
56-1	24-2	29-2
58-1	29-2	34-2
66-2	34-2	39-2
67-1	43-2	44-2
70-2	44-1	49-2
73-1	49-2	54-2
76-2	54-3	59-2
83-2	59-2	64-2
91-2	64-2	69-2
94-2	69-2	74-2
98-2	74-1	79-2
106-2	79-1	84-2
108-3	94-2	89-2
119-3	99-2	94-2
132-1	109-1	99-2
135-1	119-3	104-2
137-2	132-2	109-2
142-1	149-2	114-2
143-2	154-2	119-2
150-2	159-1	124-2
154-2	165-2	129-2
159-1	169-2	132-3
161-2	174-2	139-3
175-2	179-1	144-2
179-1		154-2
		159-2
		169-2
		179-2

TABLE V

PEABODY *CRITICAL THINKING* ACTIVITIES

Peabody Primary	*Peabody I*
12-2	7-2
26-2	21-2
33-2	27-1
42-2	40-2
47-1	78-3
59-3	97-2
85-3	108-1
87-2	111-2
94-1	113-2
96-1	117-1, 2
97-2	119-2
98-3	123-1
114-1	127-2
122-3	129-2
133-1	131-2
134-1	133-1
136-2	136-2
144-1	145-1
143-2	146-1
146-3	149-2
153-3	153-2
155-1	162-2
156-2	170-1
157-1, 4	172-1
159-2	
160-3	
161-2	
162-1, 3	
168-1	
169-4	
171-3	
175-3	
179-3	

Sequential Language Development

TABLE VI

PEABODY *REASONING* ACTIVITIES

Peabody Primary	Peabody II	Peabody III
102-1	2-2	2-2
105-1	7-2	7-2
	18-2	12-2
	25-2	17-2
	31-2	22-1
	32-2	27-2
	37-2	32-2
	43-1	37.2
	47-2	42-3
	52-1, 2	47-3
	57-2	52-2
	62-2	57-2
	67-2	62-2
	78-2	67-2
	82-2	72-2
	87-2	77-2
	92-2	82-2
	97-2	85-3
	102-2	87-2
	107-2	92-2
	117-2	102-2
	119-2	112-2
	122-2	117-2
	126-2	119.3
	127-2	122-2
	130-2	126-3
	132-2	127-2
	139-3	129-3
	142-2	132-2
	147-3	137-2
	148-2	147-2
	152-2	159-1
	157-2	167-2
	160-2	
	166-1	
	167-2	
	173-2	
	177-2	
	179-2	

TABLE VII

PEABODY *CLASSIFICATION* ACTIVITIES

Peabody Primary	Peabody I	Peabody II	Peabody III
7-2	15-3	6-3	1-2
14-3	30-2	16-2	5-2
23-3	36-1	22-2	11-2
28-3	50-2	40-2	15-2
34-3	52-2	41-2	25-2
52-1	62-1	46-2	31-2
54-2	69-2	51-2	35-2
65-1	75-1	61-2	41-2
83-3	84-2	65-2	45-2
110-1	98-1	71-2	51-2
116-1	101-1	85-2	55-2
122-1	108-2	91-2	61-2
123-2	128-2	95-3	62-3
129-1	170-2	105-2	71-2
151-3		111-2	75-2
155-2		115-2	81-2
172-3		121-2	85-2
176-1		125-2	95-2
177-3		131-2	105-2
		141-3	111-2
		143-1	121-2
		151-2	131-2
		161-2	141-2
			142-2
			145-2
			165-2

AUTHOR INDEX

SUBJECT INDEX